How Fathers Help their Children Develop

Fathers influence their children's development in many ways, including financially and emotionally, but the literature revealing how and why is limited. This book brings together theoretical orientations and different disciplinary lenses to the study of how and why fathers matter for children's development. It challenges the commonly held view that fathers are only economic providers and points to the complex interplay between the love fathers have for their children and the money they have (or not) to support them. By integrating developmental science with economics, and drawing on real-life examples from qualitative research, the authors argue that fatherhood is a tale of two stories: love and money.

NATASHA J. CABRERA is Professor of Human Development and Quantitative Methodology at the University of Maryland, USA. She received the National Council on Family Relations award for Best Research Article regarding men in families in 2009. She is the coeditor of the *Handbook of Father Involvement: Multidisciplinary Perspectives* (2013), coauthor of *Parenting Matters* (2016), and co-principal investigator of the National Center for Research on Hispanic Families and Children.

RONALD B. MINCY is the Maurice V. Russell Professor of Social Policy and Social Work Practice at Columbia University, USA. He was the recipient of the Social Policy Researcher Award from the Society for Social Work and Research in 2021, the Frank R. Breul Memorial Prize for the Best Research Article in 2013, and the *Journal of Policy Analysis and Management*'s Raymond Vernon Memorial Prize for the Best Research Article in 2009.

How Fathers Help their Children Develop
Money and Love

NATASHA J. CABRERA
University of Maryland

RONALD B. MINCY
Columbia University

Shaftesbury Road, Cambridge CB2 8EA, United Kingdom

One Liberty Plaza, 20th Floor, New York, NY 10006, USA

477 Williamstown Road, Port Melbourne, VIC 3207, Australia

314–321, 3rd Floor, Plot 3, Splendor Forum, Jasola District Centre, New Delhi – 110025, India

103 Penang Road, #05–06/07, Visioncrest Commercial, Singapore 238467

Cambridge University Press is part of Cambridge University Press & Assessment, a department of the University of Cambridge.

We share the University's mission to contribute to society through the pursuit of education, learning and research at the highest international levels of excellence.

www.cambridge.org
Information on this title: www.cambridge.org/9781009209496

DOI: 10.1017/9781009209519

© Natasha J. Cabrera and Ronald B. Mincy 2026

This publication is in copyright. Subject to statutory exception and to the provisions of relevant collective licensing agreements, no reproduction of any part may take place without the written permission of Cambridge University Press & Assessment.

When citing this work, please include a reference to the DOI 10.1017/9781009209519

First published 2026

Cover image: Tetiana Garkusha/iStock via Getty Images

A catalogue record for this publication is available from the British Library

A Cataloging-in-Publication data record for this book is available from the Library of Congress

ISBN 978-1-009-20949-6 Hardback
ISBN 978-1-009-20946-5 Paperback

Cambridge University Press & Assessment has no responsibility for the persistence or accuracy of URLs for external or third-party internet websites referred to in this publication and does not guarantee that any content on such websites is, or will remain, accurate or appropriate.

For EU product safety concerns, contact us at Calle de José Abascal, 56, 1°, 28003 Madrid, Spain, or email eugpsr@cambridge.org

Contents

List of Figures	*page* viii
List of Tables	ix
Foreword	xi
Preface	xvii

1 Contemporary Fathers and Their Children in the US — 1
  1.1 Fathers in Resident Families — 3
  1.2 Fathers in Nonresident Families — 5
  1.3 How Do Fathers Matter for Children? Money versus Love — 5
  1.4 Caveats: What This Book Does Not Cover — 15
  1.5 Conclusion: Both Money and Love Matter — 16

2 The Role of Fathers in Child Development: Theoretical Perspective — 19
  2.1 Theories of Father Involvement — 20
  2.2 Theoretical Perspectives: How and Why Does Money Matter? — 24
  2.3 Theoretical Perspectives: How and Why Does Love Matter? — 28
  2.4 Limitations of Parenting Research — 32
  2.5 Integrating Theoretical Frameworks to Understand How Money Matters for Children — 34
  2.6 Conclusion — 35

3 The Money Story: Fathers' Financial Contributions and Children's Development — 36
  3.1 The Money Story for Resident Fathers — 36

	3.2	The Money Story for Nonresident Fathers	44
	3.3	Conclusion	52
4	The Love Story: Fathers' Emotional Contributions and Children's Development		54
	4.1	The Love Story for Resident Fathers	55
	4.2	The Love Story for Nonresident Fathers	67
5	Why Does Money Matter for Children's Development?: New Analysis Addressing the Gaps		73
	5.1	How Does Resident Fathers' Money Matter for Children?	73
	5.2	How Does Nonresident Fathers' Money Matter for Children?	83
	5.3	Conclusion	91
6	How Does Parental Money and Love and Children's Own Contributions Matter for Children's Development?		94
	6.1	Trends in Children's Well-Being in Families with Resident and Nonresident Fathers	98
	6.2	How Do Money, Parenting, and Children's Skills Matter for Children?	100
	6.3	Conclusion	108
7	Policies and Programs Implicated by Our Findings		111
	7.1	Social Policies that Support Fathers	111
	7.2	Conclusion	128
8	Implications for Policy and Program Change		130
	8.1	Transfer Payments	130
	8.2	Healthy Marriage Initiative	131
	8.3	Responsible Fatherhood Programs	132
	8.4	Child Support	136

8.5	Increase Fathers' Participation in Parenting Programs: Early Head Start Programs	145
8.6	Conclusion	145

Appendix A: Chapter 5 Resident Fathers	150
Appendix B: Chapter 5 Nonresident Fathers	163
Appendix C: Chapter 6	172
References	188
Index	221

Figures

5.1	Mothers' spanking by educational attainment by children's age/year (N = 1,281).	*page* 78
5.2	Mothers' reading to children by educational attainment by children's age/year (N = 1,281).	78
5.3	Fathers' spanking by educational attainment by children's age/year (N = 1,281).	79
5.4	Fathers' reading to children by educational attainment by children's age/year (N = 1,281).	79
5.5	Receptive vocabulary (PPVT) by educational attainment by children's age/year (N = 1,281).	80
6.1	Children's aggressive scores by fathers' residential status and children's age.	99
6.2	Children's receptive vocabulary scores by fathers' residential status and children's age.	100
A.1	Conceptual model.	155
A.2	Path analysis for age five model.	156
A.3	Path analysis for age nine model.	157
B.1	New theoretical model.	171
C.1	Latent difference score model of children's aggressive behaviors.	175
C.2	Regression analysis model with covariates[a].	175
C.3	Latent difference score model of children's PPVT scores.	176
C.4	Regression analysis model with covariates[a].	177

Tables

A.1	Unstandardized descriptive statistics, N = 1,281.	*page* 158
A.2	Summary of indices for the investment and new models at ages 5 and 9 based on household income and father's earnings.	161
B.1	Unstandardized descriptive statistics.	165
B.2	Financial support payments by analytical sample nonresident.	168
B.3a	Summary of indirect effects (continuous father's financial support).	168
B.3b	Summary of indirect effects (categorical father's financial support).	169
B.4a	Moderated mediation of indirect effect (continuous father's financial support at age nine).	170
B.4b	Moderated mediation of indirect effect (categorical father's financial support at age nine).	170
C.1	Means and variances of latent factors of children's aggressive behaviors.	178
C.2	Coefficients from the structural model of aggression, by resident versus nonresident fathers.	179
C.3	Means and variances of latent factors of children's PPVT scores.	183
C.4	Coefficients from the structural model of receptive vocabulary scores, by resident versus nonresident father	184

Foreword

Jay Fagan, Ph.D.

Natasha Cabrera and Ron Mincy's book, *How Fathers Help their Children Develop: Money and Love*, is an important addition to the research, theory, and policy literatures on fathers and families. I have been involved in fathering research and practice for more than thirty years. I was drawn to this area of scholarship for several reasons. One of the main reasons was that fathering research was new and promised to avoid the trap of falling into traditional research silos – or at least, so I believed. Research silos occur when scholars do not exchange ideas with researchers in disciplines other than their own. I believed in the notion of cross-disciplinary research. I am a PhD social worker, and social work does not claim to own a particular area of knowledge of human behavior. It draws from multiple bodies of knowledge that are relevant to helping persons in need. It is therefore considered to be a profession that values cross-disciplinary views of human behavior.

I was excited about studying fathers because I thought this new field of research would be different from other fields that relied on discipline-specific ways of understanding behavior. Psychology, sociology, economics, political science, and biology are all relevant to fathers, just as they are relevant to mothers. My efforts to work across disciplines involved working with researchers in different disciplines. I collaborated with scholars including developmental psychologists Natasha Cabrera and Rob Palkovitz, family sciences researcher Alan Hawkins, parent-education practitioner Glen Palm, speech and language researcher Aquiles Iglesias, and sociologist Jessica Pearson. I learned a great deal from these individuals, and I believe that I was able to integrate a wide range of disciplines into my own research.

I also became involved with the National Center for Fathers and Families (NCOFF), led by Dr. Vivian Gadsden at the University of

Pennsylvania. The center brought together researchers and scholars from various disciplines, but, most importantly, it brought together researchers and practitioners to share knowledge about fathers. The mission of NCOFF was to improve the life chances and well-being of children and the efficacy of families by facilitating the positive involvement of fathers. At the heart of NCOFF's agenda for research, practice, and policy was the development of seven core learnings and a framework for the field. Although the core learnings addressed important cross-disciplinary issues faced by many fathers, such as joblessness and role transitions, it did not advance a cross-disciplinary theoretical framework for studying fathers.

Over the years, I observed that the field of fathering was anything but cross-disciplinary. Developmental psychologists, sociologists, and economists all conducted research examining child outcomes. Sometimes the approaches used by researchers in the various disciplines were indistinguishable from one another. At other times, researchers applied theories and methods that were unique to their discipline. I also observed that researchers in each discipline were not always aware of the research being conducted in other disciplines. Lack of attention to research in disciplines other than one's own can stymie the development of knowledge. Researchers have not completely ignored the importance of love when they conduct studies focused on money influences on children. Likewise, they have not ignored money when the focus was on love. For example, developmental psychologists are cognizant of the impact of money. However, for the most part they have controlled for income or socioeconomic class, rather than examining money as having equal importance with love.

Despite the efforts of some researchers to conduct cross-disciplinary research, studies of fathers lacked ways of truly integrating knowledge across disciplines. Natasha and Ron say it succinctly in their new book: "one of the challenges of interdisciplinary research is that fundamentally each discipline has a different way to conceptualize the world, measure it, and consequently intervene to change it." *How Fathers Help their Children Develop* challenges "the one-dimensional view of fathers that the economic and developmental psychology literatures have adopted that fathers are mostly providers but not nurturers or vice versa." The authors provide a comprehensive and exhaustive review of the literature on the influences of money and love on children's development, and they present their own innovative research on the effects of money and love on children in this book. By problematizing both money and love, the end result is a deep exploration of the ways in which money and love impact child outcomes.

Another important contribution of this book is the application of different theories to examine parent effects on child outcomes. The authors apply the parent investment model (a theoretical perspective from economics) in one study presented in the book. In Chapter 7, they apply the ecological model to examine the contributions of parenting and household income to the development of aggression and cognitive skills in children aged three to nine. The application of theories from different disciplines demonstrates the authors' cross-disciplinary study of child development.

In addition, the book makes the case for a better research approach to understanding why fathers matter by focusing on the contributions that fathers, mothers, and children make to child outcomes. In Chapter 6 of the book, Natasha and Ron examine how increases in money (household income or child support) and love (parental involvement) are associated with children's language and social behavior skills over the course of early childhood. This analysis is conducted with children who live with their fathers in two-parent families as well as with children who live in single-parent households where their fathers are nonresident. The authors find that residential context is important for understanding the influences of love and money. Natasha and Ron conclude that it is not surprising that the development of children in coresident and nonresident families differs. These findings are important and have the potential to guide future research.

The authors are also successful in showing how science supports policy and program investments in both the love and money dimensions of fatherhood. Policymakers and program administrators will find this book essential for developing programs that address both the love and money aspects of fathering; for example, the child support system in the US would benefit greatly from adopting policies based on the concepts of love and money. The child support program serves a quarter of all children in the US. Most noncustodial parents are fathers. Federal regulations require each state to establish a formula for determining the amount of child support that a nonresident parent must pay. These guidelines must consider parental income and the costs of raising children in determining the required support orders. States frequently establish orders that are difficult for low-income fathers to pay (i.e., that are higher than the percentages of income required of moderate and high-income fathers; see Pearson & Wildfeuer, 2023). As a result, only 46 percent of custodial parents received full child support payments in 2013 (Center for Law and Social Policy, 2017). Most of the arrears were owed by low-income fathers. The child support program has the potential to promote and discourage economic and emotional involvement of fathers with their children (Pearson & Wildfeuer, 2023). The program could improve the collection of support with the adoption of policies such as giving states discretion to decide how child support orders are set and modified. It could also support fathers by establishing realistic child support orders which include avoiding interest charges that result in the generation of unpayable debt. Researchers and policymakers have also suggested that expanding the purposes of the child support program to include promoting child well-being (i.e., love) would be an important improvement to the system. The child support system is ultimately charged with improving the lives of children.

I cannot think of another book or article that has brought together the expertise of researchers in two disciplines to achieve a common goal: understanding how children develop. It is my hope that this book will be a model for future researchers to study children and families. Nevertheless, there are challenges for researchers adopting this model for studying children's development. For example, how does this model account for the influences of father–mother coparenting relationships on children? A growing body of research has shown that coparenting relationships are important influences on children. *How Fathers Help their Children Develop* is a must-read for policymakers, program administrators and staff, and family scholars.

REFERENCES

Center for Law and Social Policy (2017). Low-income fathers struggle to pay child support [blog post]. www.clasp.org/blog/low-income-fathers-struggle-pay-child support/.

Pearson, J., & Wildfeuer, R. (2023). *Policies and programs affecting fathers: A state by state report.* https://centerforpolicyresearch.org/wp-content/uploads/FRPN_State-By-State-Policy-Full-Report_0-4.pdf.

Preface

Writing this book has been a labor of love, to use a perfectly overused cliché. After many years of close collaboration, discussion, disagreements, and compromise, we are proud to have completed this important and provocative book. A key lesson is that researchers have made a lot of progress in developing the empirical rationales and evidence to support fathers' role in their children's well-being. Nevertheless, this work has been done mostly in academic silos, with not enough communication among them. This book is an attempt to connect those silos; to join two different scholarly perspectives – the view of economists and the view of developmental scientists – to get a better sense of *how* and *why* fathers' parenting is paramount for children's well-being. We believe that bringing these two most important strands of scholarship together can ultimately help us to design more targeted policies and programs for children and their families.

Although, fathers, like mothers, play multiple roles in their children's lives, in this book we focus specifically on the dual roles of fathers in contributing both financially (the "money story") *and* emotionally (the "love story") to their children's development. This duality of roles and responsibilities sets the tone for the themes discussed in the book. This duality also has implications for the way we illustrate hybrid theoretical models (i.e., borrowing from both disciplines) that come together to address the gaps in the literature to better understand the roles of fathers in the lives of their children and to better inform policy decisions. Ultimately, the aim of the book is to serve a new generation of scholars who will, hopefully, dismantle these silos and engage in interdisciplinary scientific collaborations that advance science and policymaking.

The focus on the duality of roles – which we call the "money story" and the "love story" – is intentional and rooted in rigorous and thoughtful empirical evidence that fathers' financial contribution to children's well-being is directly related to fathers' ability to financially support them. Although the evidence for the "money story" is mostly correlational and the effects sizes are not very large, this is an important finding because it has been linked to a host of outcomes along an individual's lifespan. Children who are financially supported by their fathers tend to graduate from high school, have strong academic skills, go to college, get a job, and stay in the labor force. Admittedly, lots of factors condition these findings. The amount of money fathers provide matters; the consistency of the financial support is important; and, for fathers who do not live with their children, the modality of the support is significant. All in all, these findings have been the basis for the development and implementation of policies directed at men, especially those who do not live with their children. These policies also resonate very well with our cultural and social expectations that men are "good fathers" when they provide financial support for their children.

The evidence for the "love story" is equally patchy, inconsistent, correlational, and not very extensive compared to evidence for the contributions that mothers' parenting makes to their children's development. In fact, the parenting literature has historically not included fathers. This has changed in the last few decades, with more researchers, policymakers, and practitioners – as well as fathers themselves – keen to make the case that fathers' emotional support should be as important as their financial support. The evidence is unequivocal. Children who are loved by their mothers and fathers (as well as other caregivers), and who are emotionally supported throughout their lives, learn to trust and have positive relationships with others. They also learn to play and engage in learning activities that help them succeed in school, in work, and in life. These findings are important but do not typically inform public policies. For example, compared to policies that enforce child support for nonresident fathers, there isn't a lot of effort directed toward facilitating visitation/custody or supporting men to emotionally nurture their children. These policies also reflect the other side of social and cultural expectations about mothers and fathers: Fathers' support is instrumental support and mothers' support is emotional. As we argue in the book, this dichotomy does not hold up to the realities of contemporary families. Mothers have been working outside the home for decades and fathers have been providing emotional support since forever. Mothers contribute to the financial health and fathers contribute to the emotional well-being of their families. Studies have shown that fathers' parenting gives them joy, meaning, and positive mental health. Fathers who love their children and express this love in everyday interactions are also happier and healthier. Thus, we need a new scholarship that acknowledges these truths.

We believe that it is important, from the outset, to address the emotional depth of fatherhood. While financial contributions are essential, the love, guidance, and emotional availability of fathers are equally crucial in shaping the emotional well-being and development of their children. We explore how fathers nurture their children's self-esteem, provide a model of emotional resilience, and offer unique perspectives that help their children navigate the world. By framing fatherhood as a source of emotional sustenance as much as financial stability, we hope to set the stage for readers to appreciate the holistic impact fathers have on their children's development.

This is the context for why it is essential to acknowledge the multifaceted nature of fatherhood. In this book, the exploration of fathers as both financial providers and emotional nurturers invites readers to reflect on the often overlooked complexities of fatherly love and fathers' parenting behaviors, which unfold in a social and cultural context that often does not support them in the role of nurturers. Fatherhood, like motherhood, is not one dimensional; instead, fathers shape their children's lives in profound ways, both through the tangible resources they provide and through the intangible love, support, and guidance they offer.

The purpose of this book is to bring to light the significance of fathers' financial *and* emotional contributions to children's development – a topic that may sometimes be overshadowed by unidimensional discussions about paternal and maternal roles. Often, the focus in parenting narratives leans heavily on mothers, but this book challenges that paradigm by giving equal weight to fathers' emotional support of and influence on their children's lives. It serves as a reminder that fathers are central to raising well-rounded, confident, and emotionally resilient children. The book presents this message through various anecdotes, empirical studies, and new and illustrative analyses, providing readers with a deeper understanding of the many ways fathers impact their children's growth and development.

In writing this preface, it is important to highlight the evolving nature of fatherhood in contemporary society. Traditional views of fatherhood as solely providing financial support have shifted, with contemporary fathers taking on a more hands-on, emotionally engaged role than ever before. We need to acknowledge the challenges that fathers face in balancing career, personal life, and parenting. These challenges are significant and constitute an urgent plea for researchers and others to include fathers – those who live with their children and those who do not – in parenting research as well as in programs and interventions designed for parents. We hope that by acknowledging these shifting dynamics, we can help our readers understand that the book is not just about fatherhood in the past but about how the role of fathers is continuously evolving and expanding in today's world.

Although empirical evidence is important and significant, we also include some anecdotes from men themselves. These personal stories and testimonies are best able to tell men's stories. These stories humanize the concepts we discuss and provide real-life examples of how fathers contribute both love and money in their children's lives, and how they struggle to do so. For example, we've encountered fathers who feel abused by policies and practices that influence their interactions with their children. One young father described how, after two years of taking care of his infant daughter, being mostly in charge of all her basic needs, including feeding, playing, and entertaining her, his partner decided to separate and moved away to another state. Despite the challenge of distance, the judge only gave him two hours of visitation time every other week. The man was devasted. He wanted to know if there were empirical studies that he could send to the judge to change his mind about the inadequate visitation he was given. A couple of years ago, after a talk at Duke University about fathers, a young graduate student approached one of the coauthors, excited that his fiancé was pregnant and he was going to be a dad. Unfortunately, he was not allowed to be in the hospital with his partner. He felt the maternity unit was not welcoming him, especially because the couple wasn't married. These narratives are reflected in the book's themes, and they can be the stories of our partners, husbands, sons, or friends.

In closing, we hope that this book gives you, the reader, pause for thought and encourages you to reconsider societal assumptions about fatherhood. We invite you to shift your perspective and think beyond dichotomies or stereotypical portrayals of fathers as merely breadwinners or authority figures. We invite readers to embrace a more comprehensive and multidimensional view of fatherhood: one that places men in a network of relationships in families, and that celebrates fathers as sources of both financial support and emotional strength. In doing so, we aim to redefine and celebrate the critical role fathers play in nurturing, guiding, and shaping the next generation.

I Contemporary Fathers and Their Children in the US

On June 2022, as the world was trying to recover from the isolation imposed by the COVID-19 pandemic, a video of rapper and producer Jay-Z kissing his ten-year-old daughter on the cheek during a game went viral on Twitter. Although most of his public appearances attract a lot of publicity, this loving gesture toward his daughter received even more attention than usual. It showed a contrasting side of the music icon: as a nurturing and caring father. Positive images of men, especially of men of color, as loving parents are rarely, if ever, seen in the media. The reality is different: ethnically and economically diverse fathers are loving and affectionate toward their children and want the best for them.

The public narrative of fathers in the US is better understood in the broader sociocultural and demographic context. At the turn of the twentieth century, the family in the US underwent tremendous transformation due to several major social changes: Women's increased labor force participation, increased number of nonresidential fathers and out of wedlock births, increased involvement of fathers in two-parent families, increased "family complexity," and increased cultural diversity in the US (Brown et al., 2015; Cabrera et al., 2000; Diniz et al., 2023). Higher rates of divorce, cohabitation, nonmarital childbearing, repartnering, and remarriage have changed family life in the last fifty years or so and have resulted in increased family complexity (Brown et al., 2015; Kreider & Ellis, 2011; Gates, 2015). More than two decades later, we see the emergence of the "modern family" (Golombok, 2015); this term refers to new family forms that include lesbian mother families, gay father families, families headed by single mothers by choice, and families created by assisted reproductive technologies such as in vitro fertilization, egg donation, sperm donation, embryo donation, and surrogacy (Golombok, 2015; Brown, 2017). Collectively, these social trends have broadened the definition of what it means to be a family and have fundamentally changed the roles of mothers and fathers in these families.

Our focus in this book is threefold. First, we focus on two-parent, heterosexual, and biological families with fathers who are either resident or nonresident with children during early childhood. Despite the steady decline in the number of two-parent families, most children in the US live in two-parent families (US Census Bureau, 2020), and consequently most of the research, programs, and policies have been motivated by these families and their children. Second, we discuss resident and nonresident fathers separately because the ways "money and love" from fathers play out in children's lives depends on the type of families in which they are reared. Different types of families make different types of investments for their children (Hofferth, 2006). Children growing up with two-parent biological and heterosexual families often receive a greater share of parental resources and caregiving time compared to children living in single-parent families (Hofferth, 2006). Changes in family structure are inherently tied to family resources, therefore including money and time spent with children in the discussion help us understand how children fare in different types of families. Moreover, resident fathers' earnings constitute most of the household income in many two-parent households, while nonresident fathers contribute much less to household income in single-parent households, especially when nonresident fathers provide such support informally (Sariscsany et al., 2019). As a result, resident fathers exercise much more influence over child-related expenditures than do nonresident fathers. Because nonresident fathers do not reside with their children all the time, they have more difficulty than resident fathers engaging in a variety of activities that constitute everyday parenting (e.g., bathing, dressing, reading, and sharing meals). Nonetheless, their involvement should matter as well as the money they provide for their children. Importantly, our focus on these types of families does not in any way suggest that other types of families are not important or worthy of study. On the contrary: There is an urgent need to acknowledge in scholarship the diversity of families in which children are being reared in our modern society.

Third, although parents, including fathers, have a profound impact on their children's lives from cradle to grave, in this book we focus on the early years (birth to age nine), for a couple of reasons. First, children's development during the early years is foundational for outcomes along the life span (National Academies of Sciences, 2016). Early experiences are critical for brain development and so investments of time and money during the early years are most likely to have a profound and enduring effect on children. Second, most of the research on father–child relationships has been conducted with young children.

1.1 FATHERS IN RESIDENT FAMILIES

Who are resident fathers in the US? When we examine the demographic profile of fathers from the living arrangement of children we find this: In 2020, 67% of children aged 0–17 lived with two married parents, and 4% lived with two unmarried but cohabiting parents; 21% lived with their mothers only; 5% lived with their fathers only; and 4% lived with no parent (Federal Interagency Forum on Child and Family Statistics, 2022, Family Structure and Children's Living Arrangements section). Most children who lived with neither of their parents were living with grandparents or other relatives. Among children living with two parents, national data from 2020 show that the majority (91%) lived with both of their biological or adoptive who were married (only 5% were cohabiting), and only 9% lived with a stepparent (Federal Interagency Forum on Child and Family Statistics, 2022, Family Structure and Children's Living Arrangements section). In the same year, most children living with one parent lived with their mothers, some of whom had cohabiting partners who were not the biological fathers of their children. Older children were less likely to live with two parents: 67% of children aged 15–17, compared with 69% of children aged 6–14 and 75% of those aged 0–5. In terms of diversity, in 2020 the majority (76%) of White non-Hispanic and Hispanic (62%) children lived with two married parents, compared with less than half (38%) of Black children.

When we look at the demographic profile using a father's lens, we find that in 2020, more than 28,000 fathers in the US lived with children under eighteen, and the majority (86.5%) of those fathers also lived with a married spouse (US Census Bureau, 2020, table A3). Only 5.2% of those fathers cohabited with the mothers of their children; 3% cohabited with a partner with whom they do not share a child and 6% lived with their children as single fathers. Among all fathers living with children under eighteen, more than half (59%) were non-Hispanic Whites (hereafter, White), 10% were Black, and less than a quarter (21%) were Hispanic. A notable finding is the similarities among and differences between racial and ethnic groups.

Among White fathers living with children under eighteen, the majority (88%) also lived with a married spouse. Only 4% of those fathers cohabited with the mother of the child; 3% cohabited with a partner with whom they did not share a child and 6% lived with their children as single fathers. Among Black fathers who lived with their children under eighteen, the majority (74%) also lived with a married spouse. Only 10% cohabited with the mother of the child; 5% cohabited with a partner with whom they did not share a child and 12% lived with their children as single fathers. Similarly, among Hispanic fathers who lived with children under eighteen, the majority (80%) also lived with a married spouse. Only 10% of those fathers cohabited with the mother of the child; 3% cohabited with a partner with whom they did not share a child and 6% lived with their children as single fathers. Among all fathers who lived with children under eighteen, less than half had one or two biological children (42% and 38%, respectively); 14% had three biological children; and only 5% had four or more children. There are some interesting insights from these statistics. Among resident fathers, there are few differences by race and ethnicity: Most fathers reside with their children and are married, and only a small percentage are cohabitors. A noteworthy difference among ethnic and racial groups is that the number of fathers who are single fathers is double for Black families as compared to White and Hispanic families.

1.2 FATHERS IN NONRESIDENT FAMILIES

In contrast, nearly one in four (27%) of American men aged between fifteen and forty-four are nonresident fathers of children aged less than eighteen (Jones & Mosher, 2013). According to the Congressional Research Service (Landers, 2021), more than 9.7 million parents do not live with their children, 75% of which are fathers. The majority (81%) of nonresident fathers are men of color, and the majority (72%) have at most a high school diploma or GED. Just over two-thirds are younger than thirty-four years old (Arsenault & Stykes, 2019). That is, most nonresident fathers are economically disadvantaged. One recent simulation using modern child support guidelines found that most nonresident fathers would be unable to meet their taxes and basic expenses for food, clothing, housing, and transportation if they paid their formal child support obligations in full (Mincy & Um, 2019). Despite these difficult circumstances, Black and Hispanic nonresident fathers are more likely to see their children than White nonresident fathers, suggesting that residency may not be a requirement for paternal engagement for ethnic minority men (Cabrera et al., 2008; Ellerbe et al., 2018; Tach et al., 2010). However, the limited human capital of nonresident fathers and the fact that they may be supporting several children from different households make it challenging for these men to invest money and time equally for all their children.

1.3 HOW DO FATHERS MATTER FOR CHILDREN? MONEY VERSUS LOVE

Being a father in contemporary US society is a story best told in two parts. The first part of the story is based on cultural and social expectations that men must support their children financially. This is what we call the "money story" of being a father, wherein fathers have mostly economic value. From this perspective, being a "good dad" is rooted in a man's ability to support his children financially. Researchers have extensively focused on the type and consequences of men's financial contribution for their children's well-being. Not surprisingly, this view is prominent in the US and in most of Western Europe, and it is at the center of most of our policies and programs directed toward men.

The second part of the story is about fathers' emotional support for their children, or what we call the "love story" of being a father. Through this lens, the social value of fathers lies in their ability to nurture and support their children emotionally through building strong and healthy relationships that last a lifetime. In the USA, this view is almost completely underplayed in the public narrative of what makes a "good father," especially for fathers of color. This perspective, which minimizes men's emotional support for their children, is striking and is not supported by the empirical evidence. A large body of research has shown that fathers who have loving and supportive relationships with their children have children who are socially competent, have friends, perform well academically, and have productive lives. Also, not surprisingly, the emotional contributions that fathers make to their children is not the focus of policies and programs directed at them.

It is the disconnect between the research on the "love story" and that on the "money story" of being a father, and the policies and programs designed for fathers, that we wish to highlight in this book. The traditional view that fathers are the providers and mothers the nurturers is outdated (Golombok, 2015). A more updated version of the story of what it means to be a "good" father is that modern fathers provide for their children financially *and* emotionally, just like mothers. Fathers are important for their children's well-being in multiple ways, and their financial contributions *and* their love and emotional support are essential to the development of healthy and socially well-adjusted children (Cabrera et al., 2014).

1.3.1 *The Money Story: The Economic Perspective*

Economists study the effects of families on child well-being using approaches closely related to the core questions with which they are concerned: How do societies use their scarce resources to produce, consume, and distribute the goods and services that their members want or need? (Krugman & Wells, 2021). One of society's most important resources is the labor of its members, many of whom are parents. Economic theory suggests that parents use their earnings and other sources of income to consume goods and services and invest in the human capital of their children (Becker & Tomes, 1986). Doing so enables children to be more productive (and better paid) when they become workers and parents. In the economic literature there is no distinction between mothers and fathers; instead, economists assume that mothers and fathers want the same things for their children.

Of course, parents can use their own time to produce their children's human capital. For every hour they do so, they sacrifice wages, which they could use to buy goods and services from others (e.g., tutors and childcare providers). Whether mothers or fathers are more productive in child rearing, and whether the wages they earn exceed the cost of paying others to care for and educate their children, determine how much time mothers and fathers spend engaged in caregiving activities at home. According to the standard economic theory of the division of labor within households, biology and socialization make women more productive than men in child-rearing activities, beginning with breastfeeding and recognizing the cues infants provide about their needs. Gender socialization also extended this comparative advantage to the activities required to care for children of all ages (Becker, 1991). In parallel, developmental psychologists assumed that, during the early years, children formed stronger attachments to their mothers than to their fathers. Because of their comparative disadvantage in household production, men spend less time than women in household production and more of their time in work outside the home. This specialization increases their wages relative to women in external work. In turn, men's higher pay for outside the home encourages men to invest heavily in human capital, which tends to increase their productivity.

Changes in the productivity of mothers and fathers in market work and changes in conditions that affect their productivity – and, therefore, their wages – have important policy implications for child-related policies and practices. For example, such changes influence policies that affect the amount of time (e.g., parental leave) fathers and mothers spend engaged in child-rearing activities; who should get physical custody of children following a divorce or separation and who should pay child support; and who should be the focus of efforts designed to improve parents' effectiveness in child-rearing activities (home-visiting programs, Head Start, and Early Head Start).

In this book, we use "money story" as an overarching umbrella term to refer to fathers' ability to support their children financially. Fathers' financial responsibility is typically assessed as household income or socioeconomic status (SES), including proxy indicators of SES such as level of education, income, and occupation. At the core of the "money story" is the timeless question of what it means to be a "good", which has preoccupied scholarly inquiry since the nineteenth century (Pleck, 1983). From an economic perspective, the concept that a "good father" supports their children financially is straightforward. Money is essential for children's well-being and critical for their survival because it underwrites the material and educational opportunities needed to succeed in school and in life (Becker & Tomes, 1986). Money can be used to pay for necessities such as food and shelter, as well as to buy learning materials such as toys, books, and enriching activities that promote children's development. Therefore, focusing on money is justified because children depend entirely on household income for their development. This is most evident in how we consider resident fathers' earnings when determining benefits designed to reduce poverty (Eissa & Hoynes, 2004; for example, the Earned Income Tax Credit), and in our efforts to design and implement child support policies that require nonresident fathers to pay child support (Hodges & Vogel, 2021). It is not surprising, then, that a voluminous empirical body of research has consistently shown that money matters for children's well-being (Duncan et al., 2011; Duncan et al., 2019; Wimer & Wolf, 2020). What is less clear from this literature is *how* or *why* money matters. Research on this question is comparatively less extensive, has reached inconsistent conclusions, and has been less concerned with other important determinants of children's well-being, such as fathers' emotional support and children's own characteristics.

1.3.2 *The Love Story: The Developmental Science Perspective*

The bond between parents and children is the foundation of development, and so it is the most important thing parents can provide for their children. Attachment, or developing a strong bond with parents that is characterized by love, trust, and security, is based on strong and healthy relationships between parents and children. Even if parents spend time with their children on learning activities (e.g., reading versus watching TV) that have large impacts on their well-being, this time spent together will matter most when the relationship between them is strong, healthy, and reciprocal. The amount of money parents provide is, at best, a third-order concern for children's relationships with their fathers.

In contrast to the economic perspective, the developmental science literature has answered the question of who is a "good parent" by focusing mostly on the "love story," largely rooted in attachment theory (Bowlby, 1969). Children's developmental needs are embedded in basic needs for safety, love, support, and opportunities for learning. The emotional bond between parents and children and the reciprocal, responsive, and supportive care that parents provide are essential for child well-being in both the short- and the long-term. To assess the bond between parents and children as well as the quality of the relationship between them, scholars use a variety of research designs (e.g., cross-sectional, longitudinal), methods (e.g., surveys and observational studies), and data (including nationally representative datasets with large samples and small-scale observational studies with small samples of convenience; Cabrera et al., 2014; Volling & Cabrera, 2019). An extensive and diverse literature has shown that caregivers, who are mostly biological parents, are most influential because they are most proximal to the child, especially in the early years. This proximity ensures that parents develop meaningful, enduring, and loving relationships with their children that promote their well-being. Competent, sensitive, and supportive interactions between parents and their children are essential for relationship building, which, in turn, supports children's development across the lifespan (Teti et al., 2017).

But the "love story" of how fathers' relationships with their children enhance their growth and development is not easy to tell because the empirical evidence is limited, especially on certain groups of families. Research on the "love story" includes normative parenting practices, such as engaging in literacy activities (reading, telling stories), and meeting children's basic needs, such as food and shelter. What is considered optimal parenting for children's well-being has been mostly conducted with White middle-class, two-parent (mostly married), heterosexual families. That is, to date, most parenting studies have focused on White middle-class families (more specifically, WEIRD families: Western, Educated, Industrialized, Rich, and Democratic), thus there is little representation in the literature of the child-rearing practices, values, and norms of non-White families and how these result in happy and well-adjusted children (Volling & Palkovitz, 2021). The information we have on non-White families – who, because of structural inequalities in the USA, are more likely to be poor – comes from studies that compare their parenting behaviors to those of White parents – who, because of White privilege, are more likely to be middle class. These studies essentially tell us how parents of color measure up to White families. This deficit approach is not only scientifically flawed, but also yields a very skewed understanding of what is optimal parenting, for whom, and under what conditions. Researchers need to do a better job at chronicling "good" parenting in non-White middle-class communities to access a full spectrum of the multiple ways in which fathers under different social and economic circumstances rear happy and well-adjusted children.

Another difficulty in telling fathers' "love story" is that parenting research has taken an almost exclusive focus on mothers. Consequently, there is not as much information on fathers as there is on mothers. Until recently, studies of parent–child relationships did not include fathers. The near exclusive focus on mothers derived from the outdated belief that fathers are instrumental (i.e., should pay), and that mothers are nurturant (e.g., emotionally supportive) and the "spokespersons" for the family. It has been assumed that in two-parent families, fathers and mothers converged on their parenting practices and behaviors; accordingly, there was no need to include fathers in the research. This approach led to the general conclusion that mothers' parenting was paramount for children's development whereas fathers' was optional, or at least not essential. Excluding fathers from parenting research created a gap in our knowledge about what exactly it is that fathers do for their children, or what they should do for them (in terms of emotional support) to help them grow and develop. As families become more diverse, and as fathers' residency is not a prerequisite for parenting, the need to understand the independent or complementary contributions of fathers *and* mothers to their children's well-being has become more critical. There is hope that as evidence of the unique value that fathers have for their children's development increases, we will begin to fill in our knowledge gap about how and why fathers' love for their children is important for their development.

In recent years, the research community has tried to correct course by conducting more studies on normative patterns of parenting among families of color that take a strength-base perspective and include fathers (Cabrera et al., 2014; Schoppe-Sullivan & Fagan, 2020). Despite this progress, as a field we are still not at the point where we have enough empirical evidence on the "love story" for non-White families with resident or nonresident fathers to extract important insights about the types of fathering behaviors that are to be encouraged and promoted because they support positive child development. As is evident from a quick glance at several past issues of the *Journal of Child Development* (the flagship journal for developmental science researchers), most parenting studies today still do not include both parents, nor do they consistently identify the ethnicity, race, and SES of the samples. There is much work to be done, and we urge readers of this book to continue this work.

1.3.3 Bringing Together Economist and Developmental Science Perspectives

In an episode of the podcast *Freakonomics* (June 18, 2021; http://bit.ly/40yPC7q), psychologist Angela Duckworth lamented to the cohost, Steven Levitt, that one of the problems in research is that there are no collaborations between psychologists and economists. This comment cannot be further from the truth. We (the authors of this book) are living proof of this, and just one example of the fact that economists and psychologists who care about children's and family issues collaborate in research, although probably not as much as we should. In the tradition of the collaboration between Greg Duncan, a prominent economist, and Jeanne Brooks-Gunn, an eminent psychologist (authors of the 1997 ground-breaking book *Consequences of Growing Up Poor*), we write this book to bring our expertise on children, family, and policies designed to support them to bear on the question of how fathers best support their children's development. Our respective disciplines can further the cause of fathers and children by integrating our insights into a cohesive message.

As with most collaborations, this one was not easy and it took many years to get to this point. We each come from disciplinary traditions that espouse different theories, methodologies, and statistical methods. We have not overcome these differences; instead, we present information on fathers from each discipline and try to show that both perspectives are to some extent correct, but that neither one is correct on its own. We hope to motivate future researchers to collaborate across disciplines and produce research that is ecologically valid and that reflects families with all their complexities.

Despite our different disciplines, we agree on three things. First, society should find the best way to improve child well-being. Second, finding the best approach to promote and support children's well-being involves considering all resources that could make substantial contributions. Third, fathers' time spent on child-rearing activities and father–child relationships are among the most important neglected resources for children's well-being. Though economists often consider how productive inputs achieve a given outcome, they have thought less about how the time fathers spend with their children affects the child's well-being. Said differently, economists have thought little about the productivity of fathers' time in the child's well-being production function. Further, the absence of markets for fathers' time spent in child-rearing activities makes it difficult to apply the strategies economists normally use to proxy the productivity of inputs that are difficult to measure. Fortunately, developmental psychologists spend most of their time developing theories and methods to assess the productivity of the time parents spend in various child-rearing activities. In recent years, much of this thinking has focused on fathers' time. If we draw upon these theories and methods, we can provide guidance to policymakers and practitioners tasked with improving the well-being of America's children. However, to do this well requires attention not just on fathers' financial contributions, but also on the quality of relationships between fathers and their children.

The collective interest among researchers to focus on both money and love was aided by a significant development in the late 1990s that changed the field of fatherhood research. In 1997, the National Fatherhood Research Network Initiative, a collaboration between private and private sectors, called attention to the lack of national data on fathers and urged researchers and the private sector to acknowledge fathers' emotional contribution to their children's development and to include them into research, policies, and programs (Cabrera et al., 2002). The Fatherhood Initiative, as it was called, resulted in the inclusion of fathers in national datasets that collected data directly from fathers: not just about their financial responsibilities to their children (income and child support), but also about their parenting behaviors (aka the love story). These national datasets (e.g., The Early Childhood Longitudinal Study-Birth Cohort; Early Head Start Evaluation; the Future of Families and Child Wellbeing Study) were huge accomplishments because they provided researchers with unprecedented national father-reported data on fathers' parenting behaviors about *becoming a dad* and *being a dad* (Cabrera et al., 2002). These datasets changed the field of fatherhood research because, perhaps for the first time, they made available information about fathering behaviors obtained directly from the men themselves rather than from their partners, as had been the practice up to that point.

These large national datasets are not without limitations, however. They don't have in-depth measures of fathering behaviors or collect observational data on father–child interactions that give us the "love story." They collect information about the frequency of behavior, but not about quality of behaviors. Nevertheless, these datasets are widely used today and underpin much of the research that policymakers use to guide their programs and policies, as they enable researchers to generalize findings to the population level.

The limitation of these datasets was somewhat offset by the proliferation of small-scale studies that collected in-depth observational data – the gold standard in this type of developmental research – about father–child relationships (Cabrera et al., 2002). Although findings from small-scale studies are difficult to generalize to broader populations, they can facilitate the telling of the "love story" more comprehensively when used in the context of national data. Some new insights include the findings that that some fathers' parenting behaviors are the same as mothers', others are different from mothers', and still others are complementary to mothers' (Cabrera et al., 2014). The most insightful revelation is that fathers matter in different ways, and perhaps for different outcomes, at different points along children's developmental journeys. Importantly, there is now some evidence that the relationship between fathers and children is important and may be protective against risk and adversity in children's lives (Cabrera & Tamis-LeMonda, 2014; Lamb, 2010).

1.4 CAVEATS: WHAT THIS BOOK DOES NOT COVER

There are several caveats that should be kept in mind when reading this book. First, the reader will notice a lack of balance in the coverage of certain topics. This imbalance reflects the availability of research rather than the importance of the topic. In this way, it mirrors the biases, beliefs, and norms of the research community. For instance, in terms of children's outcomes there is more research conducted on social adaptation in younger children than older, especially when considering the role of the fathers. In comparison, there is little information about the relationship between fathers and adolescents or fathers and emerging adults.

Second, we take for granted that fathering and fatherhood unfold in a network of relationships with significant others, which are embedded in dynamic ecological systems that have reciprocal influence on fathers and children (Bronfenbrenner, 1979; Cabrera et al., 2014). From this perspective, fathers' behaviors, including parenting practices, are conditioned on their own past histories, biology, and current social and economic circumstances that include multiple contexts such as work, neighborhood, and community. In other words, everything matters to some degree. It would be impossible to do justice to all these forces to understand how fathers matter for children. Some of the studies on how money and love matter for children that we include in this book control for these contextual factors to isolate the effects of love and money, net of additional factors, but others do not. We have pointed this out whenever possible. Our focus on "love and money" should not be taken to mean that nothing else matters. Instead, the focus on these two aspects of parenting reflects the public policies and social preoccupations that dichotomize fathers' influences into these two domains.

Third, we also acknowledge that the parent–child relationship and how parents and children influence each other involve more than attachment bonds. Parenting is dynamic and complex: it involves major decisions (e.g., what college to attend), minor ones (e.g., what to have for dinner), and everything in between. The parent–child relationship is made up of the day-to-day parenting behaviors, feelings, and decisions and is determined by multiple factors, ranging from biological to cultural, social, and economic, that vary and interact with each other along the life span. Moreover, these aspects of parenting have been investigated using a variety of theories, including self-determination and social learning theory. These topics are not covered here because they are not commonly investigated in fatherhood research.

1.5 CONCLUSION: BOTH MONEY AND LOVE MATTER

In this book, we bring the economic and developmental perspectives to answer one critical question: Why do fathers matter for children? Fathers, like all parents, are emotionally *and* financially invested in their children's well-being and development. Most fathers view fatherhood as requiring not just financial support, but also emotional and long-lasting commitment to their children. Thus, treating fathers primarily as financial providers (and mothers primarily as nurturers) does not align with the realities of children and their caregivers. Moreover, research on fathers has shown that fathers' emotional contribution to children's development is unique and independent from mothers' contributions (Cabrera et al., 2007). That is, mothers and fathers are not the same, and mothers are not substitute for fathers.

We have three overarching goals for this book. First, we challenge the one-dimensional view of fathers that the economic and developmental psychology literatures have adopted: namely, that fathers are mostly providers but not nurturers, and vice versa. We also challenge the relative silence in the developmental science literature regarding the influence of having resources on fathering and child well-being and the view that children are more attached to their mothers than to their fathers. And we challenge the exclusion of parenting and developmental processes in the economic models that address the important question of how fathers (their love for their children or their money) matter for children's development. We need theoretical perspectives that can be adopted into economic/policy research that acknowledge that children thrive when they receive financial *and* other kinds of support from their fathers.

Second, and relatedly, we argue that we must pay attention to how fathers' money *and* love for their children are implicated in children's welfare. Children develop optimally when they have access to financial resources from their families and spend quality time with their fathers and mothers in a variety of enjoyable and enriching activities. Consequently, policies that promote and support either the "money story" or the "love story" miss the mark as they are not optimizing resources to benefit children. We make the case that to optimize development we must support and encourage both stories.

In Chapter 1, we present a discussion of who are fathers in the US and how the money versus love story has been told about them and their impact on children's development. In Chapter 2, we discuss the dominant theoretical perspectives drawn from economics (family investment model, family stress model) and developmental psychology (the developmental cascade model) about why money and love matter for children's development. In Chapter 3, we review the existing literature that tests theoretical models about why money matters for children's development, and in Chapter 4 we do the same thing for why love matters for children. Because most of the existing literature does not allow for associations between money and children's outcomes through father's interactions with them (love), in Chapter 5 we provide our own preliminary tests of these associations, using empirical models that integrate the three theoretical perspectives and allow for indirect effects of money on children's outcomes through father's and mother's engagement with children's learning activities. We test these models separately for resident and stably nonresident families using samples drawn from The Future of Families and Child One Well-Being Survey. In Chapter 6, we present new analysis that tests the idea that both money and love are important and that children are also active participants in their own development. These analyses were conducted specifically to address this shortcoming in the field and are meant to be preliminary and illustrative of the type of research that we need to do to really understand how fathers' contributions of love and money help their children thrive. These tests have limitations, especially regarding the absence of measures of the quality of parental engagement with children in learning activities. Nevertheless, we hope that they can provide researchers with some guidance regarding how they might develop a more balanced view of fathers' roles in children's development. We also hope our test results will inform policymakers about the policies and programs that can improve children's well-being not only by increasing the amount of money fathers provide, but also by engaging them more effectively in children's early development.

In our concluding chapters we review the status of policies that affect the financial and emotional support resident and nonresident fathers provide for their children (Chapter 7) and make recommendations for changes based upon our findings about the effects of money and love on young children's well-being (Chapter 8).

2 The Role of Fathers in Child Development
Theoretical Perspectives

Historically, the role that fathers play in the family has been mostly confined to that of provider (Cabrera et al., 2000; Volling & Cabrera, 2019; Pleck, 1983). Rooted in economic theories, a prominent view in the USA and in most of Western Europe is that a "good" father supports his children financially. How fathers' time spent with children affects children's well-being is not fundamental to the interests of economics. Economists want to know whether children would be better off by having fathers work more, work harder, or make more money so that they could purchase the goods and services, including childcare or experiences (e.g., extracurricular activities), that benefit children's well-being. The economic perspective motivates several lines of inquiry. First, spending time with children is a "consumption" activity that brings fathers pleasure, rather than an activity that increases children's well-being. Second, fathers' time spent with children (and other "home production" activities) affects women's labor force participation and earnings because when fathers spend time with their children, mothers are free to explore roles outside of the home sphere. Third, from the vantage point of equity in public policy, fathers spending more time with their children is a consumption good and as such it would increase nonresident fathers' utility. Thus, nonresident fathers might be willing to pay more financial support for their children, thereby increasing child well-being.

Despite the intuitive understanding that fathers provide more than just money, the ability to support their family financially is the central focus of most policies directed at men today (Pearson, 2018). Economists and other social scientists have conducted extensive research to demonstrate that fathers' financial contributions are directly related to children's development, and therefore this should be encouraged and promoted as the most important role of fathers (Duncan et al., 2011). A robust body of empirical evidence has shown that children who grow up without their fathers' financial support are more likely to drop out of school and be poor than children who do grow up with their fathers' financial support (McLanahan et al., 2013). Poor fathers who have limited education and income are likely to rear children who do not fare well in life. Children who grow up poor face several challenges that have long-term consequences for their development.

Living in poverty puts children at risk for a host of negative and challenging outcomes. Yes, depending on the timing, chronicity, and intensity of experienced poverty, some children can succeed – and even thrive. But there is little information about the factors or influences within these environments that might promote development. One possible explanation might be that children who thrive despite challenging economic conditions might have parents – fathers – who are able to provide other types of care, such as emotional support or strong relationships (which are typically ignored in the economic literature) that scaffold their development. Certainly, developmental science research shows that even low-income fathers can make strong contributions to their children's well-being and academic achievement through the bonds and relationships they have with them (Cabrera et al., 2020; Ferreira et al., 2016; Miller et al., 2020; Ward & Lee, 2020).

2.1 THEORIES OF FATHER INVOLVEMENT

Lamb, Pleck, Charnov, and Levine (1985) were the first scholars to suggest a tripartite model of "father involvement." (As an aside, there is no comparative construct of "mother involvement" in the literature.) Lamb and colleagues' model – referred to as "the tripartite model of father involvement" – suggests that father "involvement" with children falls into three domains: engagement with their children (i.e., direct interaction); accessibility (i.e., availability to the child); and the extent of responsibility toward their children (i.e., managing their child's life). The tripartite model has not been extensively tested in its entirety, with some domains having been more tested than others. The father engagement dimension of the model assesses the *frequency of father involvement*, typically measured by the amount of time fathers spend with their children. In addition, two of the model's domains – responsibility and availability – are inconsistently operationalized in the literature. For example, researchers have measured responsibility in various ways (e.g., financial contributions, management of daily care such as making doctors' appointments), making it difficult to synthesize this information across studies. As other conceptual models of being an engaged father developed, researchers began to acknowledge the need for incorporating additional components of fathering, such as emotional support or the quality of father–child relationships, into their empirical studies and theoretical models.

Building on Lamb and his colleagues' work, Palkovitz (1997) proposed a model of fathering that is rooted in the idea of nurturance or caring and includes three simultaneously functioning domains: cognitive, affective, and behavioral. Fathers may be involved with their child in multiple ways (e.g., communication, teaching, shared activities and interests) that go beyond providing financial support. There is not a lot of empirical research that has formally tested Palkovitz's model. Neither the Lamb et al. nor the Palkovitz model explicitly consider the dynamic and reciprocal nature of fathering. As ecological theories postulate, parents' interaction and communications with children depend on context, including characteristics such as children's age, temperament, and health, and other family and community characteristics. The omission in research on how children influence their own parenting through their health status and temperament is a notable limit of these theories.

In 2010, Pleck published a revised model of Lamb and colleagues' (1985) tripartite model, arguing that the early definitions of fathers' involvement did not fully encompass the multiple ways fathers might be involved with their children. Pleck placed greater emphasis on the quality of father–child relationships in representing paternal involvement. Specifically, he included five components: (a) positive engagement activities, (b) warmth and responsiveness, (c) control, (d) social and material indirect care (i.e., purchasing goods and services for the child), and (e) process responsibility (i.e., father's monitoring that children's needs were met). This model of paternal involvement provided a more comprehensive view of fathering that more accurately represented the ways in which research on this topic was expanding (and included the love and money stories), but still neglected to acknowledge other ecological and contextual variables and consider the dynamic interaction between children and parents that are important to consider in studies of families and parenting.

Other theoretical perspectives of fathering propose that fathers are fundamentally different from mothers in both function and form. A theory that has received some attention is Paquette and colleagues' (2003) Activation Relationship Theory (ART), which is rooted in attachment theory (Ainsworth & Bell, 1970; Bowlby, 1969). Activation Relationship Theory suggests that fathers typically play with their children in a way that increases children's state of arousal or excitement. In contrast, mothers tend to favor quieter, more nurturing styles of play. This "activation" is more likely to occur in securely attached father–child dyads, whereby children are free to learn and explore, knowing that they can trust their fathers. Some studies find that this activation is associated with children's regulatory skills – that is, children's ability to modulate how they feel (Islamiah et al., 2023; Paquette et al., 2003). The father–child activation relationship enables the child to become stimulated, overcome limits, and take chances in contexts where they feel confident and safe due to the presence of a secure base (i.e., the father). Within the context of this father–child activation relationship, children can develop the confidence to face the outside world, which is a key element of socializing children into being persons who can act and behave according to social norms and values. In parallel, Mirjana Majdandžić and colleagues proposed another way to conceptualize the uniqueness of father–child and mother–child relationships: children's problem behavior (CPB; Majdandžić et al., 2018). Essentially, CPB refers to parents' behaviors that include teasing, encouraging children to take risks in play, and encouraging them to get out of their comfort zones. The empirical evidence is limited, and is mostly based on European samples and some American studies. So, the validity of this construct is still emerging (Deneault et al., 2022). Theoretically, it is expected that fathers would engage in more CPB than mothers.

In 2014, Cabrera and colleagues published an expanded version of their ecological model of father–child relationships (Cabrera et al., 2014). Drawing from ecological theory (Bronfenbrenner & Morris, 2006) and the process of parenting model (Belsky, 1984), Cabrera and colleagues' model emphasized the ways in which contextual factors, including environmental and psychological contexts, shape children's development. This model theorizes the reciprocal and dynamic influences between fathers and their children that other parenting models often neglect. By placing fathering within an ecological and dynamic context, research can continue to expand by situating fathers in a network of interdependent relationships across multiple levels (family, neighborhood, community) that are embedded in the political, cultural, and social contexts that shape daily life. This heuristic model has been applied in some instances, but it is not widely used.

The evolution of fathering research and theories of fathering has been catalogued in several influential books and handbooks. Lamb's *The Role of the Father in Child Development* (2010) was highly influential because it provided cutting-edge scholarship on the impact of fathers on children's development, and it raised awareness of the neglect of fathers in research on parenting, policy, and practice. Building on this work and a confluence of political, economic, and cultural shifts, the scholarship on fathers' parenting behaviors has been growing at a steady pace (Cabrera et al., 2000; Schoppe-Sullivan & Fagan, 2020). Extant systematic reviews have examined the links between fathering and specific domains of children's development, such as literacy (Varghese & Wachen, 2015) and cognitive development (Rollè et al., 2019), and substantive reviews have described the evolution of fathering research in recent years (Cabrera et al., 2002; Schoppe-Sullivan & Fagan, 2020).

Another influential publication is the *Handbook of Father Involvement: Multidisciplinary Perspectives* 2nd edition (Cabrera & Tamis-LeMonda, 2014). This handbook was instrumental in collating scholarship from an array of disciplines, including economics and sociology. By bringing together sociologists, economists, psychologists, anthropologists, legal scholars, and others in the same volume, readers could become aware of the different lenses used to understand fathers, discover overlaps and differences, and foment opportunities for collaboration. *The Handbook of Father Involvement* has been an invaluable resource for scholars and practitioners interested in a more holistic view of understanding how fathers matter for children.

2.2 THEORETICAL PERSPECTIVES: HOW AND WHY DOES MONEY MATTER?

Regardless of theories about what fathers do for their children and how it benefits them, the most important aspect for policymakers is fathers' role as providers. An ample literature has shown that household income is significantly related to child well-being (see Cooper & Stewart, 2021, for a review). There is copious correlational evidence that children growing up in low-income households perform less well than their peers on a range of developmental outcomes and academic skills. However, the degree to which money itself matters and whether associations between money and developmental outcomes merely reflect other unobserved differences between families with low incomes and their wealthier counterparts is still uncertain (Cooper & Stewart, 2021). Cooper and Stewart conducted a systematic review of studies that used randomized controlled trials and quasi-experiments using statistical methods that enable them to make causal statements. The results showed that household income has a positive causal effect on children's outcomes, including their cognitive and social-behavioral development and their health. Cooper and Stewart's (2021) review finds a wide range of effect sizes from quasi-experimental and RCT studies. A change in annual income of $1000.00 affects cognitive outcomes by 5–37%, social and behavioral outcomes by 3–22%, children's health by 1–24%, and maternal depression by 4–15%. These results suggest that income is not the entire story. Investigations of the impact of money on the development of children are framed within two commonly used theoretical perspectives: the family investment model (FIM) and the family stress model (FSM).

2.2.1 Family Investment Model

Much of the knowledge we have today about the impact of money on children's development comes from the ground-breaking work of sociologists and economists who highlighted that parents' resources (such as income and education) are important for the development of children because they enable parents to make investments of time and money to promote their children's human capital (Becker & Tomes, 1986; Haveman & Wolfe, 1994; Mayer & Salovey, 1997). In their seminal book *Succeeding Generations: On the Effects of Investments in Children*, Robert Haveman and Barbara Wolfe (1994) follow a representative group of American children from their early years through to young adulthood. They examine multiple demographic background factors, such as childbearing age and employment status of children when they become young adults, that are influential in determining the human capital. In *Succeeding Generations*, Haveman and Wolfe (1994) show that fractured families, poverty, neighborhood quality, and a difficult economy place children's future at risk. They emphasize the importance of parents' education and, despite the apparent loss of time spent with children, the generally positive influence of maternal employment on children's later success.

The FIM, rooted in economic theory, predicts that parents with greater resources (e.g., income, education) are more able to purchase stimulating and enriching goods (e.g., books) and services (e.g., childcare, after school activities), and to invest time in learning activities (e.g., reading), than parents with fewer resources (Haveman & Wolfe, 1994; Cunha & Heckman, 2007; Kalil & Ryan, 2020). These purchases and investments help children learn and develop the skills they need to succeed in school and in life. Essentially, more (money) is always better, although there is not a clear threshold for how much money is enough and for what outcomes. Empirical studies that have tested this model have shown that parental investment in their children can take many forms (Cooper & Stewart, 2021). Having plenty of resources means that parents can meet children's needs, including health care and the quality of the home and neighborhood, which promote children's well-being. Additionally, parents can purchase cognitively stimulating materials (such as toys or books), enrichment activities (such as swimming lessons), and high-quality childcare (while they work). Parental investments may also take the form of time. While purchasing books or toys is important, the time parents spend reading and interacting in learning activities with their children may be even more important. Both types of investment are significant because they help children build human capital and economic success (Becker & Tomes, 1986). Children in resident families are more likely than children in nonresident families to have access to a variety of stimulating experiences and types of parental investments (Fagan & Lee, 2012).

In nonresident families, where money may be scarce, parents might make different types of investments. In these households, mothers might use money provided by nonresident fathers to purchase necessities such as food or to move to a home in a better neighborhood or a better school district, rather than purchasing educational materials such as books. The research confirms this view. On average, children in families with lower incomes tend to fare worse because they have limited access to educational learning materials that promote their development. Although many families with few resources are also able to spend time engaged in learning activities with their children, these activities might be more infrequent, of lower quality, and not as varied as the experiences of children who have access to more resources.

For parental investments to make a difference in children's development, they must be made in a timely manner (Duncan & Brooks-Gunn, 1997). It is not enough to have access to learning experiences. Because income affects the timing and kinds of child-related expenditures families can make, research has much to say about how different kinds of investments affect children's well-being at different points in development (Grant et al., 2023; Mistry et al., 2010). Investments during infancy are most effective because this is a unique period wherein parental investments can strengthen the foundations of children's healthy development. In this period of rapid brain development, the quantity and quality of early experiences is powerfully associated with children's development (Fox et al., 2010; Hodel, 2018). That is, the circumstances of children's childhood create favorable or unfavorable conditions for children's learning and development. The timing and duration of exposure to specific social and economic circumstances in childhood can result in unequal opportunities and learning inequities.

2.2.2 *Family Stress Model*

Another perspective commonly used in research to understand how and why money matters for children's development is the family stress model (FSM). The FSM was formulated in 1949, after World War II, by sociologist Reuben Hill, who explored the consequences of stressful and traumatic events on the family dynamic, in particular relationships among family members (Hill, 1949). The FSM is a hybrid model, combining economics and developmental science, and suggests that money is important for the development of children because it can reduce parental stress and thereby improve parenting (Masarik & Conger, 2017). The FSM hypothesizes that lack of money – measured as parent's perceived economic stress – harms children's development because it increases parenting stress and consequently reduces the quality of their parenting (Conger & Donnellan, 2007;

Conger et al., 1994; Puff & Renk, 2014). The quality of parenting refers to how responsive parents are to children's needs and whether they discipline them in a positive and developmentally appropriate way (Conger et al., 2002). A responsive parent does not use harsh punishment and engages with children in loving and responsive ways. Having a low level of income means that families must cut back on nonessentials (e.g., books), get help, or change their living arrangements, all of which can increase parental emotional distress and, in turn, cause an increase in harsh parenting. Harsh parenting behaviors can increase the probability that children will act out, exhibit more problem behaviors, and do less well academically. In contrast, the model hypothesizes that having more money reduces stress related to not having enough resources, which improves the quality of parenting and, subsequently, child outcomes (Thompson, 2014). There is an abundance of empirical evidence (albeit not very consistent) showing that parents who report low levels of household income also report high levels of stress and high use of harsh punishment to discipline their children, and are observed to be less warm and responsive to their children's needs (Kalil & Ryan, 2020; Masarik & Conger, 2017).

2.3 THEORETICAL PERSPECTIVES: HOW AND WHY DOES LOVE MATTER?

In contrast to economic theories, developmental theories hypothesize a strong connection between biology, timing of environmental inputs, and children's skill development. Children's developmental outcomes are the product of their cognitive ability plus parental investments made during the early childhood period. A theory that is widely used to study how the environment influences development is Bronfenbrenner's (1979) ecological theory of human development. According to this theory, child development is the result of interactions between the child and their environment that are embedded in a network of interdependent systems. The most influential interactions are with children's most proximal caregivers: in most cases, their parents. According to the ecological model, a child's environment is divided into five different systems: the microsystem (i.e., home and school), the mesosystem (i.e., the interaction between home and school), the exosystem (e.g., parents' jobs, teachers training, mass media), the macrosystem (e.g., legal system, welfare policies), and the chronosystem (e.g., technology, wars). The microsystem – which is the most immediate environmental setting and includes child, family, and school – is the most influential level of the theory. The microsystem includes fathers. Development is then the result of the influence of this complex system of relationships affected by multiple levels of the surrounding environment, from immediate family and school settings to broad cultural values, laws, and customs. To understand how children turn out, we need to consider the child and their immediate environment, as well as their interaction with the wider environment.

Because ecological theory does not really specify how interactions between children and their caregivers unfold in the microsystem, other theories have filled in the gap. If FIM is about resources (the more resources the better), developmental theory is about timing: the earlier the better. The quality of the early home environment (the microsystem) is typically assessed as the availability of educational toys, learning experiences such as reading, and other learning materials for children, which have concurrent and long-term association with later developmental skills, such as language or social skills (Bergen, 2021; Sénéchal & Lefevre, 2002). Although empirical evidence supporting the enduring effects of early experiences on children's development past middle childhood is limited, there is some evidence suggesting that the effect of children's early experiences on their level of achievement does not diminish over time. The evidence is particularly strong for language skills. Children whose parents read with them when they were of kindergarten age had significantly higher reading and mathematics scores in third grade than children whose parents read with them less often (Davis-Kean & Sexton, 2009; Davis-Kean et al., 2019). Similarly, the amount of speech parents direct to their children before the age of three accounts for more than half of the variance in children's cognitive performance and vocabulary at three and nine years of age (Hart & Risley, 1995). These findings make a strong case that early investment in children's lives pays dividends, and that not doing so not only places children at risk and incurs developmental delays that could have been prevented, but also makes it more difficult to reverse course.

An overwhelming number of studies have demonstrated that highly supportive, loving, nurturing, and consistent parenting is the most important driver of child development. *Parenting Matters: Supporting Parents of Children Ages 0–8* (2016), a report from the National Academies of Sciences, Engineering, and Medicine, reviewed research on parenting knowledge, attitudes, and practices (KAPS) and identified effective parenting practices that support children's development. The evidence-based parenting practices that the committee found to be associated with positive child outcomes include: loving and contingent responsiveness to a child's behavior (also known as serve-and-return interactions); established routines and reduced household chaos; shared book reading and talking to children; health-based practices, such as receipt of prenatal care, breastfeeding, vaccination, and ensuring children's adequate nutrition and physical activity; safety-promoting practices such as monitoring children's activities or behaviors, and household/vehicle safety; and the use of appropriate discipline. Theoretically, fathers' impacts on children are important because when they engage in warm and reciprocal parenting, children can succeed and thrive.

2.3.1 *Transactional Developmental Theory*

For multiple theoretical and methodological considerations, most parenting research – and certainly that which is disseminated to the media and the public in general – is based on studies of parenting that only account for the parental response to the child's behavior, not the child's response to the parent; thus, parenting is interpreted to be unidirectional: that is, from parent to the child. This could not be further from the truth. Parents' and children's influence is bidirectional: that is, from parent to child *and* from child to parent. Parents and children influence one another reciprocally through positive and sensitive interactions (Sameroff, 2009). Arnold J. Sameroff is an American developmental psychologist who is best known for his work on developmental theory and the protective and risk factors that contribute to children's mental health and psychopathology. With his collaborator, Michael Chandler, Sameroff developed the transactional model of development, which was first proposed in 1975, to explain how children and contexts (including parents) shape each other.

Any person engaged in an interaction or relationship with another person knows that transactional processes are an everyday occurrence (Bornstein, 2012). The transactional model is key to understanding the back-and-forth between biology (nature) and environment (nurture) in elucidating the development of children's positive and negative outcomes. At its core, the transactional model conceptualizes development as the continuous and bidirectional (reciprocal) influences between the child and their environment, including parents. The transactional model emphasizes the processes through which individual differences are preserved in the transactions between the child and their environment (Sameroff & Chandler, 1975). The most significant part of this model is its focus on the child's effects on parenting practices and behaviors. Children's reading experiences with their parents, for example, can lead to positive attitudes toward reading and, consequently, to increased interactions with parents, which helps in developing language skills (Crosnoe & Cooper, 2010; Farver et al., 2006).

Despite the fact that the article by Sameroff and Chandler (1975) has been referenced extensively in the developmental science literature and was selected as one of the top twenty studies that revolutionized development psychology (Dixon, 2002), it has not been extensively empirically tested. There is little empirical evidence about the reciprocal effects between children and parents (in particular, fathers), which might explain why this theoretical framework has not informed economics-rooted models of why money matters.

2.3.2 Developmental Cascades

Building on transactional theories of development, Masten and Cicchetti (2010) advanced the notion that developmental cascades denote the cumulative (or progressive) effects on children's development of the multiple transactions between children and their environment across numerous developmental systems. These cumulative outcomes spread across levels, domains, and different systems to have significant implications for adaptive behavior (Masten & Cicchetti, 2010; Masten et al., 2010). Children's skills development is, then, the result of snowballing interactions between the environment and genetically inherited differences across time. Environmental inputs, including the early learning environment, influence children's early skills, which then impact skills later in development and across domains. In other words, foundational skills (such as language skills) that are mastered early in development have cascading effects on other developmental domains (such as social competence), which then impact academic achievement at a later point in development. The take-away message is that success in early developmental tasks fosters competence in later tasks (Masten et al., 2005; Okano et al., 2020).

From the point of view of children growing and changing over time, "cascades" may be either negative or positive and may be influenced further by parents' investments and parents' stress, among other factors. Positive cascades may affect children's behavior and, in turn, later school achievement in positive ways. Some indicators of childhood success, such as school achievement, predict later success. In contrast, negative cascades have been used to understand the effect of childhood problems on difficulties in adulthood.

2.4 LIMITATIONS OF PARENTING RESEARCH

At the time of this writing, the parenting literature still focuses almost exclusively on White mothers in two-parent, middle-class families, and mostly excludes fathers, non-White, and low-income families (Cabrera et al., 2018; Lamb, 1975). Such exclusions from parenting research have had a significant impact on the scope of the information we have on parenting behaviors across an array of family structures and living arrangements. This omission is critically consequential because research on White families is used to design public policies and programs for all other types of families, without concern for ecological validity.

Excluding fathers from parenting research is problematic on several fronts. First, fathers' effects on children are unique or independent from that of their mothers, suggesting that fathers and mothers matter for child development in significantly different ways (see Jeynes, 2016, for a meta-analysis and review). Second, studies that do not include fathers are likely overestimating the effects of mothers on children's development – that is, the degree to which mothers' behaviors matter for children may be inflated. Third, the limited information on fathers makes it difficult to understand how fathers matter for children's development and how to support and optimize positive fathering behaviors. Fourth, without meaningful information on what fathers do and how, when, and under what conditions they matter, we will continue to design and implement interventions targeted to only one parent. Interventions that target one agent of change (i.e., the mother) when we know that there are at least two agents of change (i.e., mothers and fathers) may prove to be ineffective at best, and a waste of resources at worst. The dearth of information on fathers' impact on children in child-development studies also poses a challenge to researchers who design interventions aimed at preventing maladaptive development in young children, as fathers may be an underutilized resource to engage in these interventions. Lastly, unlike the research on mothers' parenting, which is almost exclusively rooted in attachment theory, there is no unified theoretical framework guiding research on fathers' parenting. Consequently, what we know about fathers is less theoretically coherent and more variable.

2.5 INTEGRATING THEORETICAL FRAMEWORKS TO UNDERSTAND HOW MONEY MATTERS FOR CHILDREN

As discussed above, one of the challenges of interdisciplinary research is that, fundamentally, each discipline has a different way of conceptualizing the world, of measuring it, and, consequently, of intervening to change it. In terms of measurement, developmental theories as well as the FIM and the FSM have mostly included maternal parenting, so the ways in which economic stress or poverty impacts fathering behaviors, other than providing financial support, is relatively unknown. The FIM and the FSM are not dynamic and do not consider developmental changes in both parents and children.

However, there are also opportunities that can bring the two perspectives together to shed light on how both money *and* love matter for children's development. For instance, researchers can take a developmental cascades perspective and integrate it with the FIM to study *how* money matters for children. From this integrated theoretical perspective, we can hypothesize that the impact of parental resources (education and household income) on children's development can also operate via other aspects of children's early development. Early determinants of development (such as income) can initiate spreading effects across a domain (such as language skills at age one, for example) that result in distal outcomes at age three (e.g., reading; Shrout & Bolger, 2002). Understanding how parental resources and investments affect developmental cascades (both positive and negative) may lead to targeted interventions in childhood that can interrupt a negative cascade or reinforce a positive one use an ecologically valid model.

Another way to bring these frameworks together is to test the FIM and the FSM including father-level variables. For example, the FIM could be tested not just through maternal investments of time and money but also through paternal investments of time. The FSM could be tested to examine whether economic stress affects children's development also through paternal stress and depression and negative fathering behaviors.

2.6 CONCLUSION

This chapter reviews the existing literature on the dominant theoretical perspectives drawn from economics (FIM, FSM) and developmental psychology (the developmental cascade model) about associations between money and children's well-being. Most of the existing literature does not allow for associations between money and children's outcomes through father's interactions with children (love). Thus, we provide our own by integrating the three theoretical perspectives and allowing for indirect effects of money on children's outcomes through both fathers' and mothers' engagement with children's learning activities.

In the forthcoming chapters, we test a model derived from integrating these theories separately for resident and stably nonresident families using samples drawn from The Future of Families and Child One Well-Being Survey. Our measure of money for resident families is total household income during the child's preschool years, most of which comes from father's earnings. Our measure of money for stably resident family tests is the amount of formal and informal financial support nonresident fathers provide during the same years; however, we also control for total household income, most of which comes from mother's earnings and public benefits. These tests have limitations, especially regarding the absence of measures of the quality of parental engagement with children in learning activities. Nevertheless, we hope that they can provide researchers with some guidance for how they might develop a more balanced view of father's roles in children's development.

3 The Money Story
Fathers' Financial Contributions and Children's Development

Loving and protective parents rear children who have the cognitive, social, emotional, and physical skills they need to thrive and succeed (Bornstein & Cote, 2004). An empirically based view in parenting research is that the psychological well-being of parents, the quality of their parenting, and the learning experiences and social environments in which they rear their children interact in dynamic ways to either promote or hinder children's development (NAS report, 2016). Because parents are most influential in children's lives, especially in the early years, a question of persistent interest to researchers is: What are the dimensions of parenting that fundamentally matter for children's development and well-being? Across disciplinary research, two dimensions of parenting stand out as key for children's development: Parents' ability to support their children financially (what we call in this book "the money story"), and parents' ability to support them emotionally through supportive and attentive caregiving ("the love story").

3.1 THE MONEY STORY FOR RESIDENT FATHERS

The last few decades have witnessed a seismic change in attitudes toward the role that mothers *and* fathers play in their children's development. Twenty years ago, it was almost impossible to find diaper-changing facilities in men's public bathrooms – changing diapers was seen mostly as a mother's task. It was routine to see long queues for women's public bathrooms, with mothers and their children patiently (or not) lined up. But a causal observation of public spaces today reveals that things have changed for the better. Now, diaper-changing tables in men's public bathrooms are commonplace (although the queue to the women's public bathrooms is still longer than the queue for the men's). No one blinks when they see a father in a public space such as a park – once the sole domain of mothers – playing with his children. Social media such as Instagram and TikTok are replete with content featuring "cool" dads, who let their daughters paint their nails pink and are not afraid to show love and affection to their children in public spaces. Many men's groups organize annual conferences (such as DAD 2.0 and their "DAD 2.0 Summit") focused on fathers, with the aim of challenging "traditional ideas of masculinity" and promoting a "new type of dad" whose masculinity is enhanced rather than challenged by being= involved with and nurturing to their children (https://time.com/3717511/dad-summit-manhood, accessed January 2023). This modern view of fathers, and the acceptance that fathers are parents just like mothers, defy "father myths" as only playmates and the "bumbling father" stereotypes.

Despite these welcome social changes, there is still a deeply held belief that fundamental to being a good dad is their ability to pay (not play) that is, to support their children financially. The central focus of inquiry for sociologists, economists, and public policy wonks over recent decades has been the question of how fathers' money matters for children's development. At the core of this research is the idea that money is essential because it enables parents to invest both time and finance in their children (Duncan et al., 2011).

A very large scholarship that has focused on the question of how paternal investments matter for children by using an influential study of the consequences of unmarried single-motherhood for children is the Future Families (formally, Fragile Families) and Child Well-Being Study (FFCWS) (https://ffcws.princeton.edu/news/ffcws-changes-name-future-families-and-child-wellbeing). The FFCWS is a longitudinal investigation of approximately 5,000 children born between 1998 and 2000 in the USA. The study recruited participants in medium to large cities and included an over-sample of births to single and cohabiting unmarried mothers (Reichman et al., 2001). Detailed data have been obtained on children's cognitive development and behavior problems from birth to the present. Among other things, findings from analyses of this dataset have advanced researchers' understanding of the impact of household income on child development and have shaped the public discourse on this topic. In general, researchers have found that family income has a positive effect on children's cognitive and behavioral assessments, but the effect is small relative to other family background variables (Aughinbaugh & Gittleman, 2003; Berger & McLanahan, 2015).

It is also notable that the effects of money on child outcomes are not observed on all child development outcomes with the same magnitude or are not explicable through the same mechanism (Cooper & Stewart, 2021). Yeung and colleagues (2002) found that for academic achievement scores at ages 3–5, the family's ability to invest in a stimulating learning environment was the most important mediating pathway. For behavioral problems, in contrast, maternal distress and parenting practices were most important, so increases in household income changed mothers' use of harsh parenting sufficiently to affect children's behavioral problems. These findings are significant on at least two levels. At the child level, they suggest that parents who can support their children financially but still experience a lot of stress might have children who, despite academic achievement gains, are not very well adjusted socially. Children who are not well adjusted tend to experience psychological difficulties that can interfere in other domains, such as work and school. Money does not seem to be enough to have well-adjusted children. At the policy level, these findings suggest that even if money reduces parental distress, there are other sources of stress that can jeopardize parenting and, subsequently, child well-being. So, again, just focusing on money as a source of stress misses the bigger picture.

A question of interest to fatherhood scholars is how much money is needed to observe income effects on children's development. One study found that raising permanent income by $13,000 per year would improve children's cognitive scores by 15 percent of a standard deviation (SD) and reduce behavior problems by 20 percent of a SD at age three (Taylor et al., 2004). Similarly, using the FFCWS dataset, Berger and colleagues (2009) reported that raising permanent income by $9,000 per year per family yielded one-fifth of a SD increase in Peabody Picture Vocabulary Test (PPVT) scores for three-year-olds and an 11–23 percent of a SD decrease in behavioral problems. These results are small judging by the effect sizes found in experimental studies of publicly funded transfer programs, such as Head Start (Cowan & Cowan, 2019; Duncan et al., 2009). Effect size is an important indicator of the practical significance of the result because it measures the magnitude of the effect of an independent variable on a dependent variable in an experiment or a quasi-experiment. Put simply, effect size measures the strength of the association between two variables: small effect sizes suggest a small effect that may or may not be cost effective. Nevertheless, these small effects are practically significant because children growing up poor are at heightened risk for a host of academic and social challenges, as compared to other children.

Most recently, a randomly controlled experimental study of the effects of money on children's development, Baby's First Years (BFY), has contributed much-needed causal information on this topic (Yoo et al., 2022). The BFY study recruited 1,000 diverse, low-income, mother–infant dyads. Shortly after giving birth, mothers were randomized to receive either a large or nominal monthly unconditional cash gift. Infant brain activity was assessed at approximately one year of age in the child's home, using resting electroencephalography (EEG). The BFY study did not recruit couples, so there's little information from the fathers about their own behaviors; nor is there information on whether the father's contribution in the form of earnings of resident fathers or (formal/informal) child support from nonresident fathers was spent in consultation with the father. Mothers' expenditures (e.g., buying toys, books, and other educational experiences or purchasing basic necessities) might also be different. Not including fathers is an important omission because fathers' behaviors might potentially determine (directly or indirectly) how money matters.

In a study using data drawn from the BFY, researchers found that infants in the high-cash-gift group showed more power in high-frequency bands than infants in the nominal group (Troller-Renfree et al., 2022). Although changes in the high-frequency band reflect neuroplasticity that has been associated with the development of subsequent cognitive skills, the development of cognitive skills depends on several factors, including sensitive parenting, temperament, and other environmental factors, not just brain activity (Troller-Renfree et al., 2022). It is an empirical question as to whether the initial gains in brain activity will materialize as cognitive gains.

3.1.1 Why Does Money Matter?

Despite the voluminous scholarship suggesting that higher levels of income are associated with better outcomes for children, there is less consensus on *why* money matters – that is, what are the mechanisms or the pathways through which money is channeled to children? This is a critical question because mechanisms point to potential points of intervention. To date, there is little information on the "why" question, but this is a question that no doubt will be answered in the years to come. These findings are highly awaited because findings from experimental studies to date have shown that small increases in income-supplement programs have not boosted parental warmth, monitoring, or provision of learning activities, nor have they reduced parental stress and harsh discipline as hypothesized (Duncan et al., 2009).

A study using the National Longitudinal Survey of Youth (NLSY) found that the strongest factor mediating the association between income and children's cognitive development is maternal cognitive stimulation (e.g., reading; Guo & Harris, 2000). Also, Yeung and colleagues (2002), using the Panel Study of Income Dynamics (PSID) and its 1997 Child Development Supplement, found that maternal engagement in learning activities is the most important mediating mechanism that explains the importance of money for children's academic achievement. However, Berger and colleagues (2009) used the FFCWS and found that mothers' level of responsiveness to their children – an indicator of the quality of mother–child relationships – explained the association between increases in income and increases in children's cognitive and behavioral problems. The inconsistency in these findings suggests that money might operate through multiple aspects of parenting, as well as through other mechanisms, including paternal investments of time in learning activities, that have not yet been theoretically specified and tested. None of these studies examined whether increased income also increased fathers' engagement in children's activities or increased his sensitivity towards his children. Moreover, these studies report small effect sizes. A small effect size in this case means that money might not be the only or the strongest influence on development – or, at least, not in the way it has been assessed in the literature.

The other way in which money is hypothesized to matter for children's development is through the effects that it has on parental stress based on the FSM model. Some studies have found that although parents with low household income perceived greater distress compared to parents with higher household incomes, only high-SES families' distress was associated with children's problematic behaviors (Scrimin et al., 2022). In addition to the inconsistencies, most of the studies testing the FSM have done so with mothers and have not included fathers. In other words, we do not empirically know whether low levels of income also increase fathers' parenting distress. So, a few questions remain: Does economic stress also cause fathers to be emotionally distressed? And, consequently, does this cause more negative interactions with their children?

3.1.2 Limitations

There has been some controversy over the years about the empirical evidence to support the FIM and the FSM models. The evidence is sparse, mixed, and doesn't tell a coherent story. There are several potential reasons for these mixed findings. First, studies of whether money matters include both resident (cohabiting and married) and nonresident families. This approach, although statistically valid, may produce inaccurate estimates because it assumes that parents across family types invest their time and money in their children in similar ways (Hofferth, 2006; Kalil et al., 2014). Even if studies statistically control for family structure, the findings may obscure significant differences between investments made by resident families versus investments made by nonresident families. Second, studies of why money matters have mostly tested pathways through maternal investments of time or have used maternal reports of the home learning environment. As a result, these studies do not test the possibility that increased resources are also channeled through paternal investments of time. Plenty of evidence suggests that fathers' time spent with children has increased over the last few decades. Contemporary fathers are spending more time engaged in learning activities with their children including reading; (Malin et al., 2014a; Sayer, 2015) than fathers did in the past. Time-diary data reveal that fathers in the 1990s spent more time with their children on both routine activities and fun activities than fathers in the 1970s and 1980s (Sayer et al., 2004). Studies have shown that resident fathers report spending more time on interactive care with children on the weekends rather than on weekdays (Hook & Wolfe, 2012). Increases in mothers' labor force participation could help to explain the overall increase in time fathers spend with children. With more mothers working outside of the home, the day-to-day parenting has to be shared between parents, and so fathers find themselves doing more of the child care at home. This increased time spent with children has the potential to improve father–child interactions and promote bonding, which could in turn further increase time spent together and improve child outcomes.

Another possible explanation for increased paternal investments of time with children is that fathers see themselves as more than just providers. Studies with small groups of fathers report that fathers see themselves as parents capable of (and wanting) loving relationships with their children, which require investments of time. Even fathers who work long hours seem to nonetheless make time to be with their children. A participant in one of our qualitative studies recounted just this scenario. He believed that being a good father meant both supporting children financially *and* spending time with them. He felt mortified that working long hours was not permitting him to "be there" for his child. To address this conflict, when he got home from work at 11pm, he and his partner woke their child so that she could spend time with her dad. Many fathers prioritize time spent with children over other important routines, such as bedtime, or engaging in leisure activities (Aldoney & Cabrera, 2016).

There is also an indication that fathers' time spent with children is of high enough quality to benefit children's development. Small-scale studies that have observed fathers interacting with their children during play have found that fathers use higher-quality language (e.g., more diverse words) and when they read to their children they use higher-quality strategies (e.g., use more *wh*-questions, labels) than mothers, which are significantly related to better language skills (Malin et al., 2014b; Pancsofar & Vernon-Feagans, 2006; Rowe et al., 2004). For all these reasons, it seems important to further investigate whether paternal investments of time might be another conduit through which money matters for children's development.

3.1.3 Conclusion

A deeper analysis of the studies discussed above leads to several distinct conclusions. First, with a couple of exceptions, the bulk of the literature on why money matters for children's well-being is based on nonexperimental studies (Troller-Renfree et al., 2022). Experimental data have shown that changes in parents' income are causally related to increases in preschool-age children's achievement (Duncan et al., 2011) and brain activity (Troller-Renfree et al., 2022). But whether these effects are seen across the childhood period or materialize as cognitive outcomes remain empirical questions. Second, to date, the effect sizes across studies, although of practical importance, are relatively small. This suggests that although money is important for children's well-being, why it matters for their development is more hypothetical than certain. These findings also suggest that things other than money might be just as important (or more important) for children's development. Third, some studies find that money matters because it changes the home experiences of children but disagree on which experiences: investing in learning materials, spending time reading, or both? This is an important question that needs to be resolved. Fourth, the largest associations between household income and child outcomes occur in early childhood (e.g., Duncan et al., 2010; Shay et al., 2023; Votruba-Drzal, 2006). Early investment in children's lives is an indisputable conclusion and should be prioritized. Fifth, associations between income and children's outcomes are seemingly stronger for children in low-income compared with children in high-income families, though not everyone agrees (Dowsett et al., 2008; Maurin, 2002).

3.2 THE MONEY STORY FOR NONRESIDENT FATHERS

Fathers who do not live with their children (aka nonresident fathers, or sometimes inaccurately referred to as "absent" fathers) entered public awareness in full force in 1997 with the publication of *Fatherless America* by David Blankenhorn. According to this influential book, effective fathering was possible only when fathers lived with their children. If they did not live with children and failed to pay child support, they were "deadbeat" dads whose absence caused irreparable damage to children. In this book, we take the view that fathers who do not live with their children can nevertheless have a positive impact in their lives through their financial and emotional support.

Though there are similarities between the way the money story operates in resident families and the way it operates in nonresident families, there are also differences, ranging from minor to significant. As with resident families, when nonresident fathers provide more financial support (money), mothers can invest more money in the goods and services that help children develop. Mothers living with higher-earning resident fathers are likely to use the extra income to purchase stimulating, educational toys and experiences and invest more time in learning activities, which can then help children develop the skills they need to succeed in school and beyond. A minor difference in the operation of the money story in nonresident families is the items purchased by the mothers of children with nonresident fathers who provide more financial support. Since total household income in nonresident families is typically lower than in resident families, mothers in nonresident families are likely to direct more of their income toward necessities, such as food and housing, than mothers in resident households. For example, informal financial support significantly reduces food insecurity in nonresident families (Nepomnyaschy et al., 2012). Such reductions are positively associated with children's well-being (Nepomnyaschy et al., 2014). Another minor difference might include the quality of the neighborhood where children of nonresident fathers live. Neighborhood amenities are among the items a British study (Violato et al., 2011) includes in the "consumption bundle" parents in the UK purchase to improve child well-being. Although recent studies indicate that such amenities are particularly important in explaining the income, employment, college attendance, marriage, and teenage fatherhood outcomes of boys (Chetty & Hendren, 2018), there are no USA studies that test the FIM by examining how expenditures on housing quality or neighborhood amenities are associated with child development.

Because of the FSM, there is a significant difference between the way the money story operates in resident and nonresident families. Recall that some empirical evidence shows that higher earnings of fathers in resident families improves children's well-being because such earnings can reduce maternal stress and harsh parenting, and promote greater responsiveness in mothers' interactions with their children. In the absence of conflict, this pathway should operate in the same way when nonresident fathers provide more financial support. However, the literature on nonresident fathers accounts for the possibility that more financial support from nonresident fathers, whether formal or informal (Argys et al., 1998; Nepomnyaschy et al., 2012), is associated with children's skills differently from the way other sources of household income are associated with children's skills (Argys et al., 1998). Nonresident fathers may pressure mothers to allocate more of the formal child support they provide toward child-related expenditures by using visitation to monitor expenditures or by threatening to withhold informal support (Argys & Peters, 2003; Weis & Willis, 1985). Monitoring or withholding financial support may also result in increased interparental conflict, maternal stress, or negative parenting (McLanahan et al., 1994; Nepomnyaschy & Garfinkel, 2010). Alternatively, to maintain positive (and sometimes ongoing romantic) relationships with the fathers of their children and encourage fathers' involvement, mothers may also voluntarily spend more financial support from nonresident fathers on children than they would spend other sources of income (Argys et al., 1998; Cabrera et al., 2008; Mincy et al., 2016; Nepomnyaschy & Garfinkel, 2010).

Unfortunately, policies intended to improve outcomes for children in low-income families with nonresident fathers focus on the formal financial support that fathers provide, to the virtual exclusion of cash and in-kind material support. For steadily employed fathers, this means that child support payments are automatically deducted from their wages. As a result, only fathers with unstable employment have the option of providing financial support through the formal system or through informal arrangements, but doing so involves trade-offs. Thus, fathers who are unstably employed can provide financial support informally, but if they do so they risk accumulating child support arrears. Recent studies show that arrears can easily accumulate because of interest and penalties imposed by states (Sorensen, 2004); are associated with children's socioemotional problems (Nepomnyaschy et al., 2021) and fathers' mental health and alcohol problems; and reduce the work hours of fathers with high arrears-to-income ratios (Robbins et al., 2022; Um, 2019). This means policy can place the "money story" in opposition to the "love story" for unstably employed nonresident fathers.

As documented by rich historical literature, the emphasis on the money story arose following the demise of the male presumption in child-rearing after divorce, which had prevailed since the colonial era (Coltrane & Hickman, 1992; Elam, 1985; Mostofi, 2004). More specifically, the Industrial Revolution drove fathers away from agricultural production and cottage industries and into factories. As a result, mothers assumed control of the home sphere, including primary responsibility for child rearing. Under these circumstances, allowing divorced fathers to retain near exclusive control of child-rearing was no longer feasible; nor did many divorced fathers seek such control. Instead, courts and state legislators concluded that after a divorce the interests of children were best served by having mothers continue in their primary caregiving role. However, until World War II, few married (White) women worked outside the home. Even with the help of parenting programs, which arose to assist divorced mothers in their new roles, gaining primary responsibility for children without the requirement that divorced fathers provide financial support from their fathers (which was uncommon until the late 1920s), was a hollow victory (Polikoff, 1981).

Thus began several decades of effort by mothers' advocates, targeting the judiciary and state legislators, to secure adequate and reliable financial support from divorced fathers. Besides attempting to delay these efforts, divorced fathers' advocates demanded that their constituents have the right to visit their children and retain some rights to influence critical decisions regarding their children (e.g., schooling, religious participation, and so on). The former demand ultimately met little resistance from mothers' advocates, as increased visitation (and involvement) in critical child-rearing decisions after divorce could result in greater involvement of fathers in many aspects of child rearing. Doing so relieved single mothers of some of the burden of child-rearing and enabled them to take advantage of increasing opportunities to participate in textiles and other industries that were open to female employment. Neglected in this evolving consensus were efforts to help divorced fathers to make the best use of the time they spent with their children during visitation.

3.2.1 Data and Methodological Considerations for Studying the Money Story among Nonresident Fathers

To monitor the performance of the child support enforcement system, lawmakers require a lot of data to be collected about child support payments, custodial families, and children. For example, the federal government requires states to report information about child support collections to Congress every year. The Bureau of the Census conducts an annual survey, called the Current Population Survey (CPS) of a representative sample of US households about income, earnings, employment, and hours of work, along with other characteristics associated with children's well-being. Using the biennial child support supplement to the CPS (CPS-CSS), researchers can estimate associations between formal child support receipt and children's well-being. In addition, every four months the Survey of Program Participation (SIPP) collects data from a representative sample of the population on income, employment, and participation in public-benefit programs, including child support payments by nonresident fathers. These longitudinal data enable researchers to make more confident statements (versus those that are available from the CPS-CSS) about cause-and-effect relationships between child support payments and measures of child well-being (Mellgren, 1992).

Besides government reports and surveys, a few surveys periodically undertaken mostly by university-based researchers and funded by private and public donors provide primary sources of information about financial and nonfinancial forms of nonresident father involvement and how these affect children's well-being. Some of these surveys collect large representative samples of mothers and (less frequently) fathers and children. These surveys make it possible for researchers to generalize about how much nonresident fathers are involved with their children (financially and otherwise), and the effects of such involvement on child well-being. However, the surveys provide very little information about the quality of financial and nonfinancial involvement. Information about the quality (e.g., regularity or predictability) of financial involvement is important because some expenses (such as rent, utilities, and mortgage payments) must be met on a regular basis. Irregular or unpredictable child support payments could contribute to maternal stress, and thereby to harsh and unresponsive parenting, which adversely affects children's well-being.

3.2.2 *Empirical Evidence for the "Money" Story among Nonresident Fathers*

Several studies find support for hypotheses derived from the FSM model about associations between fathers' financial and other involvement in early childhood, preschool, and school-age measures of child well-being. Studies by Jackson and her colleagues find that fathers' involvement with their twelve-month-old children is positively associated with children's cognitive development when children are three and five years old, through lower maternal stress and/or maternal depression, and improved maternal parenting skills (Jackson et al., 2015). Most of these studies measured paternal involvement when the child was twelve months old and, curiously, not all these studies included financial support among the father-involvement dimensions measured. Collapsing formal and financial support into a single measure, when included, was even more curious because FFCWS included separate measures of these two dimensions of father involvement.

Many nonresident fathers of children twelve months old and younger provide financial support informally, if at all (Nepomnyaschy & Garfinkel, 2010; Sariscsany et al., 2019). Such support is highly correlated with other measures of father involvement, including whether the father visits the mother in the hospital during the pregnancy, whether the father wants the mother to carry the pregnancy to term, the frequency of fathers' visits with the child during the child's early years, the frequency of fathers' expressions of love for the child, and so on (Nepomnyaschy et al., 2014). Therefore, it is not surprising that the measures of father involvement in these studies are positively associated with children's outcomes, through maternal stress, maternal depression, and the quality of maternal parenting. What happens as children get older is difficult to predict because unmarried parents move from informal to formal child support, which is much less likely to be positively associated with other measures of paternal involvement (Argys & Peters, 2003).

Measurement problems cloud the evidence about associations between informal versus formal financial support and the well-being of older children. After accounting for the frequency of visitation, one study of the association between financial support and the well-being of young children, using FFCWS data, found that when nonresident fathers provide median or above-median amounts of informal child support, their children exhibit higher reflective vocabulary skills (Nepomnyaschy et al., 2012). That the study relies upon an objective and widely used measure of such skills makes this finding more reliable than the study's finding about the association between formal support and children's well-being. The study finds that mothers who receive formal support from nonresident fathers are more likely to report that their children are aggressive than mothers who receive informal support from nonresident fathers (Nepomnyaschy et al., 2012). Without objective measures of aggression, it is difficult to ascertain whether the breakdown in parental relationship quality, which precipitates the formal child support order, influences mothers' negative perceptions of her children's behaviors.

Besides FFCWS data, researchers have used other data to understand the association between father involvement and child well-being. One study used data from the National Survey of America's Families (NSAF) 1997 to examine race and ethnic differences in the association between nonresident father involvement, measured by contact and financial support, and the behavior of 6–11-year-old children (Mullins, 2011). Findings show that children who received financial support from their fathers were more likely to exhibit positive behaviors than their counterparts who did not receive financial support, although the association between receipt of financial support and positive behavior was smaller for Black children than for White children.

These findings could reflect racial differences in whether a formal child support order exists or in compliance with formal child support orders for whatever reason. The NSF measures of financial support focus on the frequency with which the father provides financial support (formal or informal), which Mullins (2011) converted into a dichotomous variable (yes or no). There is no indication of how much financial support the father provides. Among low-income, unmarried Black parents, informal arrangements for financial support by nonresident fathers tend to occur before a formal child support order is established (Nepomnyaschy & Garfinkel, 2010; Sariscsany et al., 2019). This may occur because births to unmarried Black mothers who are in romantic but noncohabiting relationships with the fathers of their children are quite common (Mincy et al., 2016). Under these circumstances, nonresident fathers provide financial support for their children informally. However, as children get older informal financial support declines or becomes irregular. Possible reasons include the instability of the father's earnings or a breakdown of the parents' romantic relationship. Thus, mothers either seek assistance from the formal child support enforcement system, or they must sign over their rights to financial support to state child support enforcement agencies as a condition of receiving public assistance. Just because the formal child support enforcement system requires these fathers to support their children, often in an amount higher than was previously provided informally, does not mean fathers are able to do so. In sum, during the first five years of their children's lives, Black nonresident fathers and the mothers of their children are likely to experience a decline in relationship quality while they transition from informal to formal child support orders. Ultimately, the amount of formal financial support fathers provide as their children get older is no greater than the amount that they previously provided informally (Nepomnyaschy & Garfinkel, 2010; Sariscsany et al., 2019).

By contrast, White fathers become nonresident fathers later in their children's lives than their Black counterparts do, because the former are more likely than the latter to be married to or living with the mothers of their children at birth. In addition, once they become nonresident fathers, the higher employment rates and higher earnings of White nonresident fathers means that they pay more formal child support than the Black nonresident fathers who have formal child support orders. Thus, all children covered by formal child support orders have parents with fractured relationships, but the White children covered by such orders receive more financial support, which is positively associated with child well-being.

3.3 CONCLUSION

Both FIM and FSM predict that higher household income makes children in resident families better off. The questions are: How much? And why? Things are a lot less clear about the association between child well-being in nonresident families and fathers' financial support. Mothers may comply with nonresident fathers' wishes about child-related expenditures that help children develop (Argys et al., 1998). Doing so encourages nonresident fathers to provide such support, maintain their relationship with their child's mother, and remain involved with their children. Under these conditions the FIM and FSM operate in the same way and, therefore, financial support from nonresident fathers should increase children's well-being. Mothers may fail to make the child-related expenditures that the fathers prefer, or may object to frequent and unwanted visits from fathers who use such visits to monitor how mothers are spending the money fathers provide (McLanahan et al., 1994; Nepomnyaschy & Garfinkel, 2010). Under these conditions, the FIM and FSM operate in opposite ways. Therefore, the effects of nonresident fathers' financial support on children's well-being are theoretically ambiguous.

Another complexity in understanding the effects of financial support from nonresident fathers on children's well-being is whether that support comes formally or informally. States require mothers on public assistance to sign over their rights to child support to the state, which enforces using the formal child support system. Mothers who raise their children without public assistance can make informal arrangements to receive financial support from the nonresident fathers. Doing so helps them maintain cordial (if not romantic) relationships with the child's father, encourages the father to remain in contact with their child, and enables the father to avoid financial obligations that exceed his ability to pay. If nonresident fathers provide adequate and consistent informal support, having an informal agreement should make FIM and FSM operate in the same way. Therefore, children in nonresident families should be better off (Nepomnyaschy et al., 2012). If nonresident fathers default on their informal agreements, having an informal agreement should make FIM and FSM operate in opposite directions. Therefore, children in nonresident families could be worse off. Finally, formal child support orders are often set above the affordability of low-income or unstably employed nonresident fathers. As a result, many have high arrears (Sorensen, 2004), which can adversely affect nonresident fathers (Um, 2019; Robbins et al., 2022), challenge their relationships with the mothers and their children, and thereby reduce children's well-being. For these reasons, payment of formal child support from nonresident fathers may also be negatively associated with children's well-being (Nepomnyaschy et al., 2014; Nepomnyaschy et al., 2021).

Surprisingly, researchers have not always separated financial support from other kinds of paternal involvement; therefore, the effects of financial support are unobservable (Jackson et al., 2015). Studies that included financial support failed to distinguish between formal and informal support (Choi & Pyun, 2014; Choi et al., 2014). And studies that include financial support and control for other measures of paternal involvement find that informal support positively affects children's well-being, but formal support adversely affects children's well-being. The policy implications of these findings are disconcerting because formal support is either required to reimburse taxpayers for the benefits provided to mothers and children receiving public assistance or are chosen by mothers who do not (or no longer) want informal financial support from the fathers of their children (Nepomnyaschy & Garfinkel, 2010; Sariscsany et al., 2019).

4 The Love Story
Fathers' Emotional Contributions and Children's Development

In contrast to the "money story" discussed in Chapter 3, the "love story" refers to a constellation of positive fathering behaviors that include emotional support, warm and loving interactions, as well as being responsive and attuned to children's needs and interests. As with other constructs, researchers use various measures, including relationship quality, quality of bonding, and quality of time spent with children. Regardless of how it has been measured, a large and growing body of empirical evidence has consistently shown that supportive and loving parenting, especially during the early years, is the most critical driver of child development (NAS report, 2016). This body of literature is mostly based on studies with mothers, but the studies that have included fathers tell a similar story: Fathers' love matters for children's development

There are several key insights from the research on how fathers' loving interactions with their children affect the child's development. First, fathers' parenting behaviors and relationships with their children significantly contribute to their development, both directly and indirectly, through various aspects of the home environment. Second, father–child relationships are unique – that is, they are not the same as mother–child relationships, which means that children forge and develop relationships that are unique to each parent. Third, there is evidence that in some ways fathers are just like mothers, in other ways they are different from mothers, and in yet other ways they complement each other (Cabrera et al., 2014). Some of the differences in behaviors might be in terms of quality (e.g., fathers use higher-quality language than mothers), amount (e.g., fathers engage in a lot more rough-and-tumble play than mothers), and type of parenting behaviors (e.g., fathers encourage their children to take risks more frequently than mothers). But, again, these differences and similarities are specific to a point in time in development, and to a particular outcome. Fourth, father–child relationships have measurable and differential effects on children's development, are dynamic, and change over time. These conclusions suggest that the "love story" of how fathers matter for children's development is not as straightforward as is the "money story." Lack of consensus on what to measure, and how, has produced a "love story" that is riddled with inconsistencies. Nevertheless, the overall theme that emerges is that, even considering these limitations, fathering that is loving and sensitive is beneficial for children's development in measurable and observable ways, over and above mother's loving parenting.

4.1 THE LOVE STORY FOR RESIDENT FATHERS

4.1.1 *Quantity versus Quality of Fathers' Parenting Behaviors*

A classic debate in the early fatherhood research field revolved around *quantity versus quality* of paternal engagement (Pleck, 1997). Is it more important that fathers spend a lot of time with their children (i.e., frequency of contact or interaction), or is it more important that they spend quality time with them (i.e., is the interaction or contact positive or negative?). Indeed, this is the question posed of all working parents. The answer to this question is a central feature of fatherhood research because of its implications for public policies and programs. It is easier to legislate quantity than it is to legislate quality of fathering.

Because there isn't one unified theory of paternal involvement, researchers have measured this construct inconsistently. Theoretically, if fathers' involvement is measured on a continuous scale from less to more involvement, then zero involvement means "father absence." An early study used "father presence" in the home as a measure of involvement (Calderon & Low, 1998). They found that "present" fathers (i.e., those who lived with their children) had children with better language skills than "absent" fathers (i.e., nonresident fathers). But, of course, this approach assumes that fathers who do not live with their children are not involved in their lives at all. We now know that's not true. Since then, measurement of fathering behaviors has evolved to become more attuned to what actual fathers do, regardless of residency.

In contrast, the quality of father–child interactions is typically assessed via surveyed and videotaped parent–child interactions – the gold standard in developmental research. The videotaped interactions are then coded in the laboratory with macro/global codes (i.e., how sensitive is the father to their child's actions) or micro codes (i.e., how many words? What types of words?) by trained and reliable researchers. This method is resource-intensive, costly, and the data are difficult to collect. For all these reasons, there is a lot more information about the quantity of paternal involvement than there is about the quality.

Regardless of measurement issues, at a practical level one can argue that both quantity and quality are important. The empirical evidence, however, is somewhat limited. The few studies that have tested this hypothesis find that quality trumps quantity in explaining children's language skill development (Malin et al., 2014b; Rowe et al., 2016). Malin and colleagues (2014b) found that fathers' quality of reading with their toddlers (measured as using more labels and questions) was more predictive of vocabulary at prekindergarten than quantity of reading. In a similar study, Rowe and her colleagues (2016) also showed that overall quantity of father talk did not relate to children's vocabulary or reasoning skills, but the use of *wh-* questions (a measure of quality) did. Lastly, Thomson and colleagues (2018) found that while the frequency of play was unrelated to children's math skills, fathers who used higher-quality spatial-concept support during block play had children with higher math scores. These findings have important implications for policies designed to encourage fathers and mothers to read to their children: Perhaps parents should be encouraged not just to read more often, but also to read in a high-quality way (i.e., ask *wh-* questions, label pictures, etc.), which increases children's interest in the book and encourages learning of words and concepts (Malin et al., 2014b).

In short, research to settle the quantity versus quality question has been slow in coming, mostly due to methodological and measurement considerations. There is a sense in the field – not entirely backed up by evidence, but rather by commonsense – that both quantity and quality of fathering behaviors are important to children's development. What we can say based on the evidence we have is that it is better to err on the side of encouraging more loving and responsive parenting than less of it.

4.1.2 *Positive Fathering and Children's Development*

Although the term "positive fathering" is vague, it is sometimes used in the literature to denote any parenting behavior that is positive (aka the "love story") or that results in good outcomes for children. Positive behaviors include nurturing and loving interactions and parenting practices such as family routines (eating, bedtime), reading, or engaging in positive discipline.

Fathering and Children's Cognitive Skills. A good source of information to understand the impact of fathering behaviors on children's well-being is the Early Childhood Longitudinal Study-Birth Cohort, a nationally representative study of babies born in 2001 that collected survey and observational data on mothers, fathers, and the home environment of children from birth until kindergarten (National Center for Education and Statistics, 2020: http://bit.ly/4lbxNUc). Studies using this national dataset have shown that fathers who report being frequently engaged in an array of literacy activities (e.g., reading, playing) have children with better cognitive, language, and math skills than fathers who report less involvement (Baker, 2014a; Baker, 2014b; Bocknek et al., 2017; Bronte-Tinkew et al., 2008; Cabrera et al., 2021; Duursma et al., 2008; Duursma, 2014; Duursma, 2016; Lankinen et al., 2020; Sims & Coley, 2016). Because these studies typically measure frequency on a continuous scale, the most we can say is that "more" father involvement is better than "less," but not "how much" father involvement is needed to achieve a certain child outcome. Some studies find that fathers who engage in any type of literacy activity more than three times a week have children with better language skills than fathers who engage fewer times, but we lack well-established thresholds for how much involvement is good enough.

Another area of interest because of its implications for children's academic achievement is paternal involvement in school-related activities (Baker, 2018). Using the Future of Families and Child Well-being Study (FFCWS, N = 1,850), researchers have found that fathers who frequently engage with their children in cognitively stimulating activities (such as reading) at age three have children with better vocabulary knowledge at age nine (Fagan et al., 2022). In Another study of 109 Hong Kong parents of nursery children aged approximately three years, which focused on math skills, researchers found that fathers who reported engaging frequently in number-game activities and used real-life applications to teach number knowledge had children with better number knowledge than fathers who reported less engagement (Liu et al., 2019). These results were found even though the researchers controlled for other factors that contributed to math skills and for mothers' contributions. Cabrera and colleagues (2020) used the Early Childhood Longitudinal Study (ECLS-B) (N = 1,258) and also found longitudinal effects of fathers' early cognitive stimulation (e.g., reading, singing) at twenty-four months and reading and math skills at forty-eight and sixty months.

Using observational measures and aided by global coding measures, a large body of research on father–child relationships has found that fathers who are observed to be sensitive and responsive during play interactions with their children have children with better cognitive and language skills than fathers who are less sensitive or intrusive (Baker, 2017; Black et al., 1999; Bureau et al., 2017; Cabrera et al., 2007; Flippin & Watson, 2015; Feugé et al., 2018; Malmberg et al., 2016; Martin et al., 2007; Meece & Robinson, 2014; Nam & Beyer, 2016; Owen et al., 2013; Park & Dotterer, 2018; Sethna et al., 2017;

Stevenson & Crnic, 2013; St George et al., 2017; Tamis-LeMonda et al., 2004; Towe-Goodman et al., 2014; Webster et al., 2013). Teufl and colleagues (2020) studied a sample of families in Austria and found significant effects for father–child attachment security on children's receptive language skills, as well as effects for father dialogic reading (e.g., asking questions) on children's language skills.

The quality of language used during interactions includes measures of the complexity of parents' speech: How many words fathers used during interactions with their children, what type of words, and other indices of quality. A significant number of studies show that the quality of parents' speech during parent–child interactions predicted children's language development (Duursma, 2016; Fagan & Iglesias, 2000; Leech et al., 2013; Malin et al., 2014a; Malin et al., 2014b; Rowe et al., 2016; Salo et al., 2016; Schwab et al., 2018; Teufl et al., 2020).

Another study with a small sample of bilingual babies and their parents also found that the quality of paternal speech was associated with concurrent parent–infant turn-taking and infant language vocalizations: key aspects of infant language development (Ferjan Ramírez et al., 2022). These findings hold across ethnic and cultural groups. Using an economically and culturally diverse sample of 567 children from the Family Life Project, researchers found that fathers' mean length of utterance and *wh-* questions were significantly associated with vocabulary and math outcomes in kindergarten (Reynolds et al., 2019). Overall, these studies show that fathers who engage in positive parenting behaviors – reading, playing, talking – frequently enough are more likely to have children who have the social and cognitive skills to succeed in school and beyond.

Fathering and Children's Social Skills. Can fathers help their children develop the social skills they need to make and keep friends, be socially engaged, and stay out of trouble? The answer is yes! Fathers who are positively engaged in their children's lives play an important role in their social development (Geller et al., 2012; Malin et al., 2014a). Fathers who report engaging frequently in play and caregiving with their children have children with fewer problem behaviors than fathers who are less engaged (Baker, 2014a; Baker, 2018; Bocknek et al., 2017; Culp et al., 2000; Jia et al., 2012; Lang et al., 2014; Lee & Schoppe-Sullivan, 2017; Levant et al., 2014; McMunn et al., 2017).

The effects of quantity of father engagement on children's social development are not straightforward, as there is evidence of significant contextual effects. Contextual effects are based on the idea that how children turn out depends on multiple influential factors, including the environment in which they grow up. These contextual factors include children's characteristics (such as temperament) and aspects of parenting behaviors. In a study with eighty-five highly educated fathers, Flanders and colleagues (2010) found that fathers who frequently engaged in rough-and-tumble play *and* were less dominant and did not control the physical aggression during play had children who displayed more physical aggression and self-regulation five years later than their counterparts. In another study using a subsample of more than 700 toddlers and their resident fathers from the Early Head Start Research and Evaluation Project, Bocknek and colleagues (2017) found that children who were rated as having high emotional reactivity benefited the most (i.e., showed more self-regulation) when their fathers engaged in moderate amounts of active play but not when they engaged in very low or very high amounts of active play. In another study conducted in rural China, researchers reported that even low levels of paternal involvement were related to a significant increase in cognitive, linguistic, and social-emotional skills, with older children benefiting significantly more than younger children from paternal involvement in all domains (Wang et al., 2022). Several studies find that, overall, children who were securely attached to their fathers also had better social adaptation (Bureau et al., 2017; Diener et al., 2002; Dumont & Paquette, 2013; Feugé et al., 2018; Psychogiou et al., 2018; Volling et al., 2006). Fathers who engage with their children in high-quality interactions help them develop important executive function skills that are important for planful and goal-oriented behavior (Kolak & Dean, 2022).

4.1.3 Negative Parenting and Children's Development

The term "negative fathering" is a broad term that refers to a constellation of parenting behaviors that hinders or even jeopardizes a child's development and results in poor outcomes for children. Examples of negative fathering behaviors include use of harsh discipline, being nonresponsive and mean to children, not showing love and/or attention, and being controlling and intrusive in ways that threaten children's desire to be autonomous and independent. At higher frequencies, negative parenting behaviors can cause (sometimes irreversible) harm (Gershoff, 2002).

Fathers' Intrusiveness and Insensitivity. In general, being intrusive or insensitive means that parents are not respectful of their children's autonomous behaviors during play or that they do not understand the needs of their children. The few studies that have examined the effects of parents' intrusiveness and control have found it to be associated with lower cognitive skills in children (Cabrera et al., 2007; Kelley et al., 1998; Meuwissen & Carlson, 2015; Stevenson & Crnic, 2013). Using a low-income sample, Cabrera et al. (2007) found that fathers' intrusiveness (i.e., not allowing the child to take the lead in play) did not have a significant effect on children's self-regulation but it had a negative effect on language, and that these effects were long-term. In a later study that aimed to understand why intrusiveness was not negatively impacting children, Karberg and colleagues (2019) found that in a sample of low-income families, fathers and mothers did not differ in the frequency of intrusive episodes, but they did differ in how intensively intrusive they were (favoring fathers). Although fathers were more intensely intrusive than mothers, children and their fathers were more likely to exhibit positive affect during these episodes, and fathers' intrusiveness did not adversely affect children (Karberg et al., 2019). Why? The positive and conflict-free interaction might have contributed to children not feeling upset that their fathers were intrusive. When researchers do not code or attend to the emotional valence of the interaction, they typically find that intrusive behavior is negatively related to children's behaviors. For example, Stevenson and Crnic (2013) found that in a middle-class sample (and controlling for mothers' intrusiveness), fathers' observed intrusiveness was related to children's early behavior problems (at ages three, four, and five). And research using data from the Early Head Start Research and Evaluation Study (N = 453, two-parent families; 51 percent girls, aged 24–36 months) showed that paternal insensitivity directly predicted children's poorer self-regulation skills (Oh et al., 2022). These findings are not crystal clear, but they emphasize the importance of harmonious and joyful interactions between parents and their children.

Fathers' Discipline. One of the most important tasks of parenting is the ability to discipline children in positive and developmentally appropriate ways. Discipline is the process of teaching your child what type of behaviors are acceptable and what is unacceptable in specific settings such as home, school, and public spaces. It teaches children to follow the rules and social scripts that conform to the norms and values of their cultural group. The most harmful way to discipline children is by using harsh discipline that includes hitting, physical punishment, and psychological abuse (Gershoff, 2002). The constant use of harsh discipline is consistently and robustly associated with harmful effects on children. Harsh discipline is not effective; instead, it leads to aggression, anxiety, and even substance abuse (Gershoff et al., 2019).

Consistent with findings with mothers and despite the fact that the evidence is not causal, a handful of studies have found that fathers who use harsh discipline have children who exhibit a variety of behavioral problems (Burbach et al., 2004; Cheung et al., 2018; Lee et al., 2011). In a socioeconomically diverse sample of 136 fathers of 1–5-year-old children, Burbach and colleagues (2004) found that the frequent use of corporal and verbal punishment was significantly, and directly, related to child behavior problems. Using a subsample of residential fathers from the FFCWS, Lee and colleagues (2011) found that children's aggressive behavior increased in tandem with fathers' harsh and aggressive behavior, even after controlling for fathers aggressive and nonaggressive discipline strategies. Cheung and colleagues (2018) found that fathers' harsh discipline practices predicted greater adjustment problems in their children, over and above the effects of mothers' discipline practices. Altenburger (2022) studied the effects of fathers' harsh parenting using a family systems perspective and data on 257 participants in the Embedded Developmental Study (N = 257) of the Three-City Study, a longitudinal study of children and families facing economic hardship. They found that resident fathers' harsh parenting predicted decreased levels of self-regulation at later points in development.

4.1.4 Mothers versus Fathers

The jury is still out regarding differences in the quantity of language children hear from their mothers and from their fathers. Although not everyone finds the same (e.g., Cabrera et al., 2007; Malin et al., 2014b; Silver et al., 2023), several studies report that fathers engage less frequently in learning activities at home (i.e., reading) than mothers (Duursma et al., 2008; Ferjan Ramírez et al., 2020; Silver et al., 2023). However, when it comes to quality of engagement, some studies have found that although fathers do not read with their children as often as mothers do, fathers' reading was of higher quality, especially if they had at least a high school education (Duursma et al., 2008; Duursma, 2014). The difference in quality is important for language development. Fathers who use more complex speech than mothers during parent–child interactions have children with better language skills than fathers who use less complex speech (Bingham et al., 2013; Malin et al., 2014; Pancsofar & Vernon-Feagans, 2006). Conica and colleagues (2020) analyzed ten-minute periods of triadic structured play interaction for twenty-one families with two-year-olds. They found that fathers' repetition of the two-year-olds' utterances were correlated with children's vocabulary diversity at four years of age, even after controlling for maternal repetition and children's language abilities at two years.

Other studies have found that fathers have stronger effects than mothers of on children's cognitive development (Malmberg et al., 2016;

Owen et al., 2013). In a study using data from the Family Life Project, Baker, Vernon-Feagans and the Family Life Project Investigators (2015) found that fathers who used more complex language during play had children with better applied problems scores, over and above the effects of mothers' language complexity. Reynolds and colleagues (2019) reported similar findings: fathers' language complexity and use of *wh-*questions (e.g., What's that? Where is the cat?) predicted children's math scores. Foster and colleagues (2016) found that while mothers reported engaging in home learning activities more frequently than fathers, fathers still made a unique contribution to their children's academic skill development. However, in families including a mother with a Bachelor's degree or higher, fathers' involvement was no longer significant.

4.1.5 *Individual Differences*

The research community has long neglected investigating the variation in fathering behaviors within resident two-parent families. It was assumed that resident families were "good" for children in various ways but did not vary very much. However, there is ample variation within resident families in terms of parenting practices and psychological well-being of children. To understand this variability, scholars have studied the factors that are associated with positive and negative psychological outcomes for children in resident families. Several key factors have emerged, the most important of which appears to be the demographic risk that parents pose for their children.

A consistent body of research has repeatedly demonstrated that poverty and its correlates (also called risk factors) such as low levels of education, low income, substance use, and unstable family structures play an important role in the psychological adjustment of children. Risk factors in the family system can be observed at all levels, for both parents and children. Using the ECLS-B, Cabrera, Fagan, Wight, and Schadler (2011) tested the effects of parental risk (i.e., being a teen parent, low education, unemployment) on children's development. They found that having a father who had high levels of risk was adversely and indirectly related to children's general cognitive skills through observed maternal sensitivity. This research has significant implications for interventions that aim to scale up and effectively serve more children of parents who exhibit these risk factors.

4.1.6 Limitations

Much criticism has been directed at the body of research on fathers and children's development. Whereas some of the concerns are valid and should be considered when reading any of the studies detailed herein, other criticisms reflect a double standard in how researchers assess the quality of research on parents.

One of the main problems with developmental research on fathers is low paternal participation in studies. The response rates are typically low (around 60% to 70%); this is reflective of fathers' work schedules, a belief that parenting research is not for them, and lack of time and/or interest. These are valid and serious concerns that need to be acknowledged. These barriers to participation in research, however, can be overcome with appropriate funding. Anecdotal evidence from our laboratory shows that it takes an average of 20–30 hours to secure an appointment with a father to conduct the research session, which is very costly. Many funding agencies are unwilling to fully fund fatherhood research because it is more expensive than research involving mothers. The costs, logistics, and strategies involved in fatherhood research are different and more complex than they are for maternal research. If researchers really want to improve the ecological validity of their studies and include fathers, they must make the case to funders that fathers should not be optional in this research because they are not optional in their children's lives.

Another limitation is that most studies that focus on how the quality of father–child interactions relates to children's development are based on small-scale observational studies, with samples of convenience, and report small to moderate effect sizes (Bocknek et al., 2017; Cabrera et al., 2007). These findings are important, but they are difficult to generalize to the population.

That many studies do not control for maternal effects compounds these problems, because failure to control for these often results in biased estimates of father effects (Cabrera et al., 2006; Nurilla et al., 2017). Studies that exclude maternal controls tend to find statistically significant associations between fathers' parenting behaviors and infants' cognitive ability, whereas studies that include maternal controls tend to find statistically insignificant associations between paternal involvement and infants' cognitive abilities (e.g., Cabrera et al., 2006). Because studies of father effects often rely upon different theories, incomparable data sources, or different measures of the same construct, it is difficult to compare results across studies. For example, studies that have found significant paternal effects on children's cognitive skills used large sample sizes (i.e., >700 participants) and measured general cognitive skills via the Bayley Scales of Infant Development (Cabrera et al., 2007). By contrast, studies that found insignificant father effects on children's cognitive skills measured the latter using a measure of executive function (Nurilla et al., 2017) or utilized a different measure of cognitive ability (Rosman & Yoshikawa, 2001).

Finally, studies of fathering behaviors suffer from the same limitation that compromises parenting research in general – that is, a focus on mechanisms, or *why* parenting or any environmental input matters for children's development. A way to think about this question is to examine the mechanisms or processes that explain why parents' behaviors matter. These mechanisms are often conceptualized either to moderate or buffer associations (moderation analysis) or to mediate and explain why two variables are related to each other. The few studies that have examined mechanisms of influence show that family processes are central to understanding why father engagement matters for children. For example, Cabrera and colleagues (2011) found that both maternal risk (e.g., unemployment) and father risk (e.g., low education) had a negative effect on children's cognitive skills *because* it decreased maternal sensitivity and father engagement (only for social skills). In their studies of fathers and mothers, Jacobvitz and colleagues (2022) found that fathers who were less sensitive with their eight-month-old babies were less sensitive when their children were toddlers, which predicted behavioral problems when children were older. To better inform programs and interventions, research that clarifies why fathering matters, for whom, and under what conditions is urgently needed.

4.2 THE LOVE STORY FOR NONRESIDENT FATHERS

In telling the "love story" for nonresident fathers, we must first think about the "opportunities" that these fathers have to spend enough quality time with their children to form high-quality relationships with them. Nonresident fathers' opportunities to provide emotional support for their children (the "love story") occur when they have contact with their children. During these times, nonresident fathers are engaged in a wide range of activities that can contribute to children's well-being. They interact with children as teachers, advisors, playmates, and disciplinarians, often exercising these roles by cramming as much activity as possible into the limited time available during each visit (Mincy et al., 2014), Thus, the frequency of contact is an important dimension of the love story for nonresident fathers, and we learn much about this dimension from large-sample surveys.

A long literature focuses on racial differences in the frequency of nonresident father–child contact, with most studies showing that Black children generally have more frequent contact with their nonresident fathers than White children (Cabrera et al., 2011; Danziger & Radin, 1990; Mott, 1990). However, this conclusion may be a consequence of the tendency of early studies to take a static view of nonresident father–child contact. According to Cheadle and colleagues (2010), the pattern of nonresident Black children is more likely to exhibit the high-decreasing pattern than the high-stable pattern of nonresident father contact, which is more characteristic of White nonresident fathers.

Our past and preliminary work points to factors, highly correlated with race, that help to reconcile these discordant results. White fathers become nonresident after divorce or the end of a cohabiting relationship. By contrast, many Black nonresident fathers are unmarried but romantically involved with the mothers of their children at birth (Cabrera et al., 2014; Cabrera et al., 2008). These romantic relationships tend to endure until the children reach age five, and sometimes until the age of nine (Mincy et al., 2016). Therefore, residence is a reliable proxy for an ongoing relationship for White, but not for Black, nonresident fathers. Finally, nonresident fathers who remain in romantic relationships with the mothers of their children are more likely to be involved with their children than other nonresident fathers (Ryan et al., 2008).

Even when nonresident fathers are no longer romantically involved with the mothers of their children, several studies show that maintaining a positive relationship with the child's mother is positively associated with nonresident father involvement. This association is strong in studies using multiple measures of father involvement, including: visitation and engagement (what fathers and children do when they have contact) and responsibility (the degree to which fathers take responsibility for meeting children's basic needs) (Castillo & Sarver, 2012). Other attributes that are positively associated with paternal involvement include the father's resources (e.g., his perceptions of the social support available to him from friends and family and his provision of financial support [formal or informal] to his child[ren]). By contrast, fathers with child support arrears are less likely than those without arrears to have contact with their children or to be otherwise involved in their children's lives (Turner & Waller, 2017). Finally, fathers who are prenatally involved with the mothers of their children are more likely to remain involved after their child's birth (Cabrera et al., 2008).

Recall from our discussion of the "money story" that ability to pay child support is an important source of conflict that can diminish nonresident father–child contact. Poorer-quality relationships with mothers explain much of the association between high arrears and lower father–child contact, and both poorer-quality relationships with mothers and poorer paternal mental health account for much of the association between high arrears and low levels of informal support provided by nonresident fathers (Nepomnyaschy et al., 2021).

Finally, although mothers' repartnering is not typically associated with any of the patterns of nonresident father–child contact, more recent studies focusing primarily on never-married nonresident fathers show that children are less likely to have contact with their nonresident fathers when their mothers have repartnered (Bzostek & Berger, 2017; Tach et al., 2010). However, this association is different for Latino versus African American fathers (Karberg et al., 2017). Latino mothers report very few changes in family structure (repartnering) compared to Black mothers.

Our studies also show that relationship status at birth matters. Nonresident fathers who cohabit or were in romantic relationships with the mothers of their children at birth have higher and more stable (though declining) patterns of father–child contact over time than fathers who are in friendly or in no relationship with mothers at birth (Mincy et al., 2016).

4.2.1 Data and Methodological Considerations for Nonresident Fathers' Love Story

While the frequency of contact is an important dimension of the nonresident-father love story, variations in this dimension (e.g., number of days nonresident fathers spend with their children) are not associated with preadolescent well-being (Amato & Gilbreth, 1999). This might occur because measures of frequency of contact do not capture what fathers and children do when they have contact or the quality of the father–child interactions. Another study attempts to close the first gap by using data from the 1997 ECLS-B to examine the role of nonresident fathers' SES in associations between nonresident father involvement and academic achievement of children in grades 3–8 (Nepomnyaschy et al., 2012). Like the study by Jackson and colleagues (2015), this study measures paternal involvement using a scale that combines several dimensions, including involvement in school activities, contact in person or via phone, the distance between the father's and the child's residences, and material involvement (i.e., payment of medical and other bills, and formal child support). Although lower SES nonresident fathers are just as likely to live close to their children as higher SES fathers, the latter are more likely to be involved in every other dimension of father involvement than the former. Furthermore, the multidimensional measure of paternal involvement, which is larger in absolute value for higher-SES fathers, is positively associated with 3rd and 5th grade reading and math scores and negatively associated with grade retention (Jackson et al., 2015). Other studies based on large-sample surveys show that children with fathers who are highly engaged in activities with them performed better on a range of outcomes than children with uninvolved fathers.

4.2.2 *Evidence of Nonresident Father's Love Story*

The best information about the quality of nonresident-father involvement comes from the observations of nonresident father–child interactions by researchers trained to recognize and document the characteristics of parent–child interactions that promote children's well-being. However, these observational studies use smaller and more selective samples than surveys of parents and children, making it impossible to generalize the findings to the larger population.

Most prior studies about what nonresident fathers did when they had contact with their children (hereafter, father engagement) and associations between such engagement and children's well-being used data from Head Start and Early Head Start programs (Fagan, 1996). Since their inception in the 1960s and 1970s, respectively, these federally funded school-readiness programs serving young children in low-income families had a strong emphasis on parental (mostly maternal) involvement. By the 1990s, however, there was growing participation of fathers as well (Fagan, 1996). Because many of the men who were highly involved in the lives of Head Start children were unmarried, surrogate, and/or nonresident fathers, studies based upon Head Start data provided some of the earliest evidence about associations between nonresident-father engagement and children's well-being.

Though information on fathers' residence was available in the Head Start surveys of participants, this information was not always incorporated in studies relying upon these data. In one important exception, Fagan and Iglesias (1999) found that, compared with children not enrolled in Head Start, children of fathers with low levels of participation in Head Start showed increases in behavioral problems over an eight-month period, while children of fathers with high levels of participation in Head Start showed higher increases in mathematics readiness over the same period. Importantly for our purposes, these associations between participation in Head Start and child outcomes were no different for children with resident or nonresident fathers.

Information on fathers' residence was also collected in the Early Head Start Research and Evaluation Project (EHSREP), which assessed the impact of Early Head Start (EHS) on children's school readiness for low-income children (0–2 years old) who were too young to participate in Head Start. Besides collecting data on how frequently EHS fathers engaged in activities that should promote children's well-being and data on outcomes for children at twenty-four, thirty-six, and (approximately) forty-eight months old, EHSREP developers also videotaped father–child interactions. Trained observers used these videotapes to rate the quality of father behavior using a measure called Dads' Parenting Interactions with Children: Checklist of Observations Linked to Outcomes (PICCOLO-D), which incorporated four dimensions (affection, responsiveness, encouragement, and teaching) that promote children's well-being (Anderson et al., 2013).

Using these data, Anderson and colleagues (2013) studied associations between early father–child interactions and later child outcomes. Although the timing of the early interactions and later child outcomes varied, the study found that the quality of earlier father-child interactions (especially fathers' encouragement and teaching behaviors) was positively associated with children's later language skills. With a few exceptions, fathers' affection, responsiveness, encouragement, and teaching during earlier father–child interactions were positively associated with later child behavior. Each fathering behavior during earlier father–child interactions was positively associated with emotional regulation among 48-month-old children. Finally, teaching during father interactions with 36-month-old children was only associated with emotional regulation among 48-month-old children.

Fletcher and colleagues (2013) developed another measure related to the quality of fathering behaviors that should improve child well-being. Unlike the dimensions in PICCOLO-D, this measure focused on rough-and-tumble play, which was more intense when the parent was a father. Their rough-and-tumble play quality scale (RTPQ) measured the quality of such play by the degree to which fathers behavior, child behavior, and the their dyadic interactions displayed warmth, control, sensitivity, winning and losing, physical engagement, and playfulness, along with a prior measure, based on attachment theory, which focused on appropriate, sensitive, reciprocal interactions and the father's ability to challenge the child enough to sustain the child's efforts to solve sedentary tasks. One study selected twenty-five EHSREP (resident and nonresident) father–child dyads that frequently engaged in rough-and-tumble play and examined associations between the quality of EHSREP father–child interactions with their 24- and 36-month-old children, assessed by both the PICCOLO-D and RTPQ scales and later child outcomes (Anderson et al., 2019). It is notable that neither measure was significantly correlated with demographic characteristics (i.e., father's education and residence) and, after controlling for the mother's supportiveness and intrusiveness, both measures showed small (negative) correlations with prekindergarten aggression.

5 Why Does Money Matter for Children's Development?
New Analysis Addressing the Gaps

In this chapter, we address the gaps we identified in the literature (see Chapters 3 and 4) by presenting the analysis of data from the Future of Families and Child Well-being Study (FFCWS; Reichman et al., 2001). As was discussed in Chapter 3, the FFCWS is representative of US cities with populations of 200,000 or more. The first wave of data (1998–2000) was collected at birth (3,711 nonmarital and 1,187 marital). Subsequent waves were collected when children were one, three, five, and nine years old. We conducted new analyses to test new mediational paths to understand why money matters. We test whether household income (financial support from nonresident fathers) influences children's development through its impact on parental investments, parental stress, and children's skills. In the sections that follow, we present this analysis separately for resident and nonresident fathers.

5.1 HOW DOES RESIDENT FATHERS' MONEY MATTER FOR CHILDREN?

We present the results of an analysis we conducted to address some of the gaps we discussed in previous chapters (2, 3, and 4). Overall, our analysis focused on how household income in early childhood matters at the cusp of adolescence (i.e., from early childhood to age nine), when youth undergo dramatic and rapid developmental changes.

Two specific questions guided our analysis. First, we asked whether household income from birth to age one is associated with children's academic attainment (e.g., math, reading, and language) and behavior problems (e.g., aggression) at ages five and nine. We expected that children in households with higher incomes would perform better than children in low-income households. Whether the effects of income during early childhood are observed nine years out is an empirical question that we also explore in this chapter.

Second, we asked *how* does money matter; or, how is the household income available to a child at age one channeled to an observable impact on that child's cognitive (e.g., language skills) and emotional well-being at ages five and nine? We tested three intermediate outcomes or mechanisms that are theoretically believed to explain the association between income and children's well-being. We hypothesized that money would increase parental investments of time and money (the family investment view); increase mothers' emotional well-being (less stress) and improve parenting practices (more engagement in learning activities; the family stress view); and directly increase children's early language skills (the developmental cascade view). We examined two aspects of mothers' parenting: discipline and engaging in learning activities with their children. Due to the limitations of the data, we included just one aspect of fathers' parenting: participating in learning activities; we did not include expressions of warmth and responsiveness for either parent because such data was not collected for fathers and was collected from only a subsample of mothers. We also included a measure of the number of learning materials (such as toys and books) in the home. We conceptualize learning materials and learning activities as investments parents make to ensure their children develop the skills they need to succeed in school. In our study, most of the parenting measures were first observed when children were three years old. We also expected these mediating processes (i.e., parental investments, parental stress, and children's language skills) to differ for cognitive achievement and behavioral problems. We expected that increases in income would be associated more strongly with children's cognitive skills and academic achievement than with behavioral problems.

5.1.1 Data

Our analytic sample included children born to married or cohabitating families with a biological father who lived with them from baseline until age five. It excluded surrogate fathers and biological fathers with weaker commitments to mothers and children, making the sample selective and not representative of all children in two-parent families. We restricted our sample in this way because resident biological fathers have similar parenting behaviors whether or not they are married, but stepfathers and surrogate fathers tend to parent differently than biological fathers. By excluding stepfathers, surrogate fathers, and parenting couples who broke up before their child reached age five, our results eliminated these sources of differences in parenting behaviors and from family instability.

Of 4,898 families participating in the FFCWS, we excluded deceased fathers from birth to age five (N = 113) and fathers who did not live with their children consistently from birth to age five (N = 3,504) for a final analytic sample of N = 1,281 (birth to age five). The issue of selection bias is important, but it is inappropriate to compare the sample to the entire FFCWS sample, which is mostly composed of unmarried mothers. Instead, the question is whether the children whose parents stayed together and completed each survey when the children were born to when they reached age five differed from children whose parents were together at birth but did not stay together or complete the survey until the children turned five.

To examine the selection bias in our sample, we conducted tests to determine whether children whose parents stayed together and completed each survey (our analytic sample) differed from children whose parents were together at birth but did not stay together or remain in the survey (comparison sample, N = 2,914; see Table A.1, Appendix A). In general, our analytic sample is more advantaged than our comparative sample. Table A.1 shows demographic data for our samples of two-parent and comparative families. When compared to the sample of families living together at the birth of their child, the mothers and fathers in our analytic sample were older and more likely to be White. Parents in our analytic sample were more likely to have a college education and higher verbal ability (as evidenced by higher scores on an intelligence test). Finally, our analytic sample earned more money and were more likely to have children of normal birthweight who had easy temperaments. In our analytic sample, White, Black, and Latino fathers were represented evenly; in the comparative sample, African Americans represented almost 40 percent of fathers, Hispanics represented a little more than 30 percent of fathers, and Whites represented approximately 25 percent of fathers. Relative to African American and Hispanic mothers, White mothers are more likely to marry and, in general, have fewer nonmarital births than their counterparts. Focusing exclusively on married and more stable cohabiting partnerships, as we do in this chapter, would increase the proportion of White households, though racial composition alone would not necessarily advantage the sample.

In contrast to the comparison sample, biological parents in our analytic sample invested more in their children and were more likely to have children with high levels of achievement. Aside from the benefits of having two parents, the children in our analytic sample exhibited lower levels of aggressive behaviors. These children also exhibited higher scores for cognitive abilities (receptive vocabulary, which is a measure of words that a person can comprehend and respond to, as ascertained by the Peabody Picture Vocabulary Test). Finally, these children also had higher scores for tests of language and mathematics (as measured by the Woodcock Johnson test) than children in the overall sample. We also analyzed both mothers' and fathers' parenting. A large literature shows differences by socioeconomic status in the types of behaviors parents engage in (Brooks-Gunn & Markman 2005). Although the gap in the types of investments low-income parents make in their children compared to higher-income parents has decreased, overall, parents with more education and income tend to buy more educational toys and books for their children. The former also spend less time on activities such as reading, telling stories, and singing to their children than their better educated and wealthier peers (Berger et al., 2009; Duncan et al., 2011). The quality of these investments also varies, favoring more educated parents. Thus, we expected to find differences in parents' behavior by parental education level.

Finally, while limiting our analytic sample to children living with two biological parents in stable relationships may have reduced the range of parenting behaviors available to study, our analytic sample varied considerably on key independent variables. In particular, variation in total household income in the comparison sample was somewhat larger than variation in total household income in the analytic sample, while fathers' earnings in the former varied less than fathers' earnings in the latter.

5.1.2 Trends in Our Data

5.1.2.1 Parenting in Two-Parent Families at Ages Three and Five

We first focus on basic trends in mothering and fathering behaviors when children were three, five, and nine years old. We identified two aspects of parenting: engaging in learning activities with children and discipline. As stated earlier, the limitations of the data did not allow us to include paternal warmth and responsiveness (such as when fathers respond promptly and sensitively to children's needs). The questions on maternal discipline and how harsh mothers are in disciplining their children were drawn from the Conflict Tactics Scale, a commonly used and valid battery of questions developed to assess parents' physical and psychological aggression toward their children. Mothers and fathers were asked a series of questions about the kinds of learning activities they engaged in with their children, such as how often they read to them, sang to them, or told them stories. We also included a measure of the learning environment at home, including what books and educational toys were in the home.

5.1.2.2 Mothers' Parenting

As expected, mothers' reported frequency of spanking changed as children got older (Figure 5.1). When children were one year old,

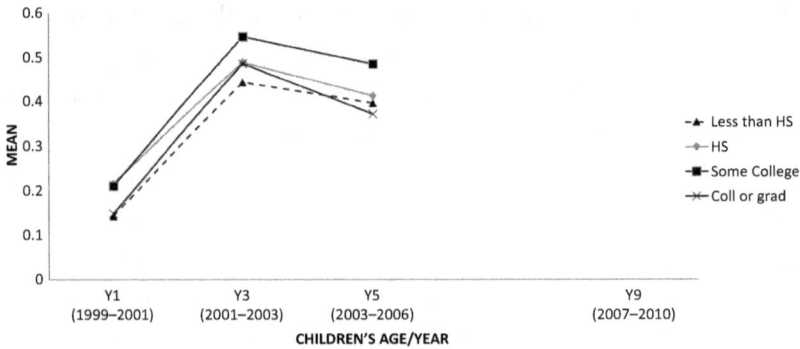

FIGURE 5.1 Mothers' spanking by educational attainment by children's age/year (N = 1,281).

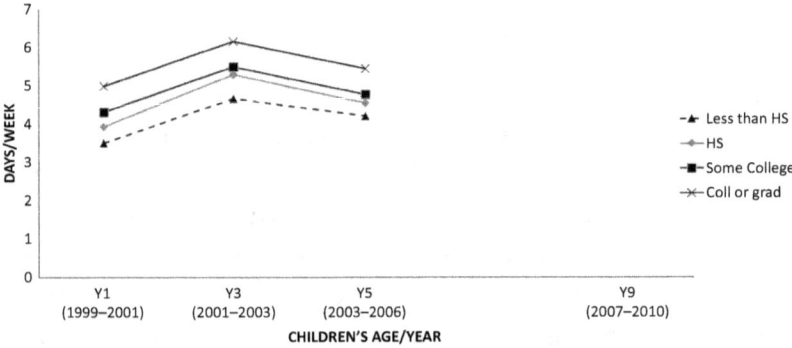

FIGURE 5.2 Mothers' reading to children by educational attainment by children's age/year (N = 1,281).

20 percent of mothers reported spanking them; when children were three years old, spanking increased significantly, followed by a notable decline beginning when the children were five years old. The average probability of spanking did not change by mothers' education levels.

As children get older, the learning activities they engage in with their parents also change. Older children often prefer to read on their own, and parents might encourage more independence by giving children the opportunity to do so. Thus, we expected that learning activities such as reading, telling stories, and singing to children might decline as children aged. We found that across all levels of education, mothers read less often to their children as they moved from age three to age five (Figure 5.2).

Fathers' Parenting. Fathers' parenting behaviors also change as children get older. Approximately 10 percent of fathers reported spanking their one-year-olds frequently (Figure 5.3), and frequency of spanking increased at one and three years old and decreased from ages three to five. The average probability of spanking between fathers with some college education and those with a high school diploma was statistically significant, except for in a one-year follow-up survey.

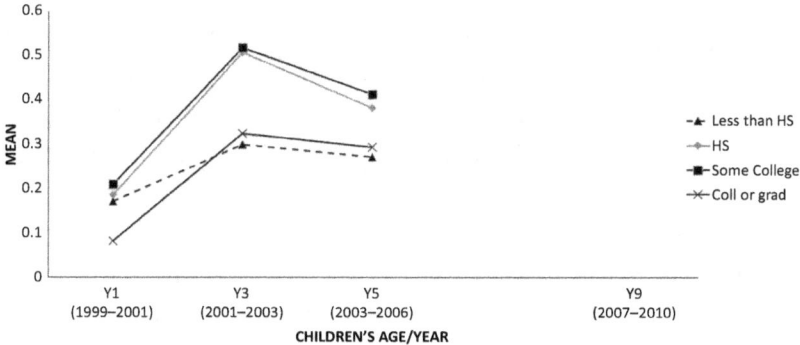

FIGURE 5.3 Fathers' spanking by educational attainment by children's age/year (N = 1,281).

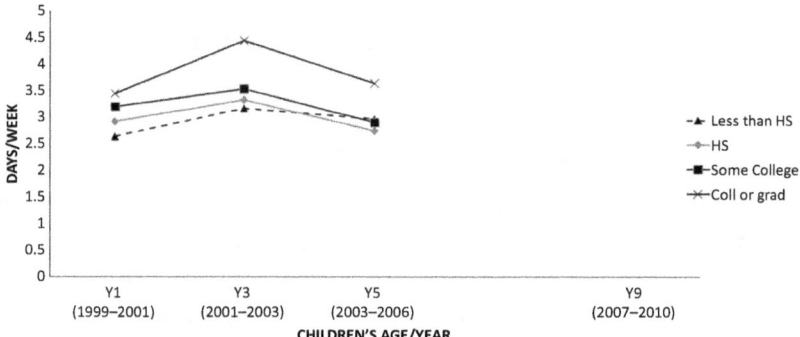

FIGURE 5.4 Fathers' reading to children by educational attainment by children's age/year (N = 1,281).

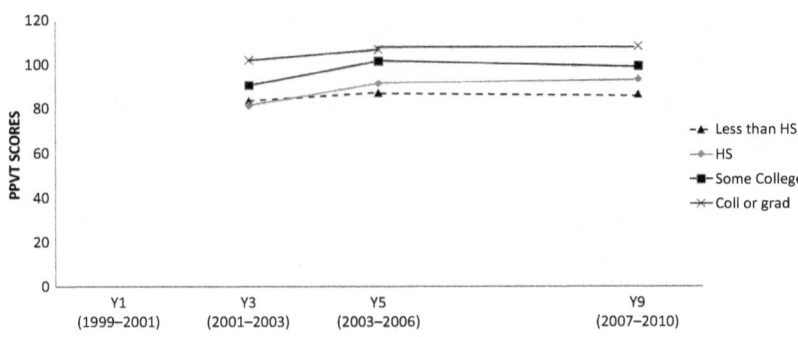

FIGURE 5.5 Receptive vocabulary (PPVT) by educational attainment by children's age/year (N = 1,281).

We also examined the frequency with which fathers engaged in learning activities with their children. Fathers reported reading less often to their children than mothers; they read more with their children from ages one to three, and less when their children reached age five (Figure 5.4).

5.1.2.3 Receptive Vocabulary

Children's vocabulary skills (measured with the PPVT) increased over time due to both maturity and learning experiences (Figure 5.5) and varied by mothers' education levels.

5.1.3 Data Analysis

Why does fathers' money in the early years matter for children's outcomes in middle school? To address this question, we tested a new model with household income as the main predictor (see Appendix A, Figure A.1 for a conceptual model). We use pooled data from surveys conducted when children were born and at age one to estimate the associations between household income and children's vocabulary, academic skills (math and reading), and aggressive behaviors at ages five and nine (see Appendix A at the end of the book for an explanation of the analysis). The path analysis (see Figure A.1, Appendix A) we used to analyze the data enabled us to test a theoretical model of the longitudinal associations among our variables and to test all the associations among our variables simultaneously while accounting for a host of controls. The path analysis was set up as follows: (1) a hypothesized direct path from household income at age one to the three child outcomes for ages five and nine (academic and aggressive behaviors); (2) hypothesized links between household income and our mediators at age three (learning activities for mothers and fathers, learning materials, parenting stress, language skills); and (3) hypothesized links between our mediators and children's outcomes at ages five and nine. Our model tested three premises. First, whether buying more learning toys and increasing the amount of time parents spend in learning activities with their children (investment pathways) explain why household income matters for children's development at ages five and nine. Second, whether reducing maternal stress at age three related to having less money (parenting stress), which in turn improves parenting behaviors, explains why household income matters for children's development at ages five and nine. Finally, we examine whether better children's early language skills, which improve children's later language skills and academic achievement, explain why household income matters for children's development. We controlled for marital birth; mothers' depressive symptoms; fathers' age, race and ethnicity, education, and self-reported cognitive functioning; and children's gender, birthweight, and temperament. We did not control for mothers' race, ethnicity, age, or education because these were highly correlated with fathers' demographic characteristics.

5.1.4 Results: Investment, Family Stress, and Cascade Pathways

Table A.2 (Appendix A) presents a summary of indices for our models. In Table A.2, the "New Model" is our integrated model tested with two-parent families that includes household income, parenting stress, and developmental cascade pathways.

Our new model shows no direct associations between household income and children's vocabulary skills at age five (Table A.2, Appendix A), although there was an association between household income and children's receptive vocabulary at age three (see Figure A.2, Appendix A). However, the pathway from household income to children's vocabulary was mediated through learning materials, an investment mediator, and through receptive vocabulary at age three, a developmental cascade mediator. The indirect association through learning materials explained 13 percent of the total association of the full model, compared to 8 percent that was explained by the indirect association through language skills at age three. The amount of variance explained by our model was 50 percent for PPV5 and 21 percent for aggression. There were no direct or indirect associations between household income and children's aggression at age five (see Table A.2, column 2).

At age nine, household income was not directly and significantly associated with any of the outcomes, providing no evidence of enduring associations across time (Table A.2, column 2). However, there were two mediation associations for each child outcome, excepting aggressive behaviors (see Figure A.3, Appendix A). For receptive vocabulary, math, and reading at age nine, the association with household income was explained (or mediated) by receptive vocabulary at age five, a developmental cascade indicator. There was another significant explanation through learning materials, an investment mechanism, and receptive vocabulary at age five. For receptive vocabulary, the indirect association through learning materials explained 80 percent of the total association of the model, compared to 17 percent explained by the indirect association through language skills at age five. For reading at age nine, the indirect association through learning materials explained 9 percent of the total association of the model, compared to 43 percent explained by the indirect association through language skills at age five. For math, the indirect association through learning materials explained 10 percent of the total association of the model, compared to 46 percent explained by the indirect association through language skills at age five. The amount of variance explained by our model was 56 percent for receptive, 14 percent for aggression, 26 percent for math, and 36 percent for reading.

Overall, our findings are consistent that income in the early years matters for children, especially in the first three years of life, and that these associations are important but relatively small compared to other variables, such as parents' education. Moreover, enduring associations between early income and children's outcomes at ages five and nine seem to be mostly indirect through both investment (learning materials in the home) and cascading mediators (children's early skills). Overall, our findings show that in two-parent families, the long-term associations of early household income on children's development at ages five and nine are channeled through investments in learning materials and children's skills in the early years, which points to the importance of providing enriching opportunities for learning when children are young.

5.2 HOW DOES NONRESIDENT FATHERS' MONEY MATTER FOR CHILDREN?

In this section we report our new analysis for nonresident fathers. For this analysis, we estimate the direct and indirect effects of nonresident father's financial support on children's cognitive and behavioral outcomes at ages five and nine. As we did for the analysis with resident fathers, we draw from family investment, family stress, and cascading developmental perspectives. We (1) assess the direct associations of nonresident father's financial support during early childhood (0–3) to middle-school children's cognitive and behavioral outcomes at age nine; (2) examine the extent to which these associations are mediated by parental investments (i.e., mothers' and fathers' provision of cognitive stimulation in the home), positive discipline, maternal stress, and children's skills at an earlier point in development; and (3) assess whether direct and indirect associations between financial support and middle-childhood outcomes are moderated by whether support is provided formally or informally.

We limit our focus on cash payments given to the biological mother whether or not a formal child support order exists, and children's vocabulary, math, reading, and aggressive behaviors measured at ages five and nine. We focus on age nine because middle childhood is a period marked by important cognitive, emotional, neurological, and social changes that form a strong foundation for later schooling and adulthood. This study extends the literature on how financial support from nonresident fathers influences their children's development in two ways: (1) it allows for, perhaps substantial changes in the (formal or informal) child support nonresident fathers provide during the years that such support should most affect children's development, and (2) it tests key mechanisms (or pathways) that link financial child support and children's outcomes.

We relied on mothers' reports of financial support because these are more reliable than fathers' reports (Sorensen, 1997). To limit bias due to missing data, we used mothers' reports of all variables included in our model. Our analytic sample excludes children with fathers who were unknown (N = 49) or deceased at any wave (N = 113) and children in households not observed at follow-up in-home interviews, when parenting and children's outcomes were assessed, at year three (N = 375), year five (N = 953), and year nine (N = 1,230). Finally, we excluded children with resident fathers at years one and three (N = 1,486). The final analytic sample of nonresident fathers was 692.

5.2.1 Data

Why does nonresident fathers' financial support in the early years matter for children's outcomes in middle-school? To address this question, we tested a new model with nonresident father's financial support as the main predictor (see Appendix B, Figure B.1 for a conceptual model). We use pooled data from surveys conducted when children were born and at age one to estimate the associations between financial support and children's language, academic skills (math and reading), and aggressive behaviors at ages five and nine (see Appendix B for an explanation of the analysis). The path analysis (see Figure 5.B1, Appendix B) we used to analyze the data enabled us to test a theoretical model of the longitudinal associations among our variables and to test all the associations among our variables simultaneously while accounting for a host of controls. The path analysis was set up as follows: (1) a hypothesized direct path from the average of father's formal and informal financial support at age twelve months and thirty-six months to the three child outcomes for ages five and nine (academic and aggressive behaviors); (2) hypothesized links between father's financial support and our mediators at age three (learning activities for mothers and fathers, learning materials, parenting stress, language skills); and (3) hypothesized links between our mediators and children's outcomes at ages five and nine. We focused on the average of father's formal and informal financial support to reflect the assumption that expenditures on children are associated with permanent, rather than transitory, sources of income. Further, we used both continuous and categorical measures of father's financial support (Nepomnyaschy & Garfinkel, 2010). Our model tested three premises: First, whether buying more learning toys and increasing the amount of time parents spend in learning activities with their children (investment pathways) explain why father's financial support matters for children's development at ages five and nine; second, whether reducing maternal stress at age three related to having less money (parenting stress), which in turn improves parenting behaviors, explains why father's financial support matters for children's development at ages five and nine. Finally, we examine whether improved children's early language skills, which improve children's later language skills and academic achievement, explain why father's financial support matters for children's development. We controlled for whether the financial support arrangement was (1) consistently formal, (2) switched from informal to formal, and (3) was consistently formal (the omitted category). We also control for mothers' age, race and ethnicity, education, self-reported cognitive functioning, depressive symptoms, and income (including her earnings and other transfer payments at ages one and three). Father's race, ethnicity, age, and education were excluded from the analysis because these were highly correlated with maternal demographic characteristics, which should be more salient to outcomes for children in female-headed families under the family stress and investment perspectives. We also controlled for children's gender, birthweight, and temperament.

5.2.2 *Descriptive Results*

Mothers in our analytic sample (N = 692) and the overall sample of respondents who responded to the in-home surveys at ages one, three, five, and nine (N = 2199), which were used to measure most of our mediators and outcome variables, differed mainly because of racial composition and, to a lesser extent, education (Table B.1, Appendix B). When compared to the overall sample, our analytic sample included mothers and fathers who were younger, more likely to be Black, foreign-born, and high school graduates. They also had less verbal ability than their counterparts in the overall sample. Mothers in our analytical sample had higher incomes, net of financial support; they scored higher on assessments of depression, were more likely to use harsh parenting, to report food insecurity, and to experience parenting stress, but were less likely to use responsive parenting than mothers in the overall sample. Compared with children in the overall sample, children in our analytic sample were more likely to have difficult temperaments and fewer learning materials such as books and educational toys. They also had lower cognitive skills and achievement in math and reading, but were more likely to exhibit aggressive behavior. Not surprisingly, fathers (but not mothers) in our analytical sample were less likely to be engaged in learning activities with their children.

Average financial support received over the first three years of their children's lives for the analytic sample was $785.85; 28% of the mothers had a formal child support order or award; 50% had no such order or award; and 22% switched from not having an award to acquiring a formal award by age three (Table B.2, Appendix B). A third of our sample (the no-pay group) received no financial support; another third (the low-pay group) received $212/year on average. Of the remaining third, one-half (the middle-pay group) received $991/year, and the remaining half (the high-pay group) received $3,304/year.

Mothers – and, to a lesser extent, children – who were better off (i.e., education levels) received more financial support from nonresident fathers (not shown, results available upon request). For example, 7% of mothers in the high-pay group had a college degree, while college-educated mothers represented, at most, 4% of the mothers in each of the other payment subgroups (results available on request). White mothers were more likely to appear in the high-pay subgroup (39%) than in the other pay subgroups (30–32%). Black mothers were likely to appear in the low- and middle-pay groups (75% and 70%, respectively) than in the subgroups at either extreme of the financial support distribution: no-pay (64%) and high-pay (62%). As with mother's education, mother's household income was also higher in the high-pay subgroup ($31,000) than in the other payment subgroups. Finally, children in the high-pay group were less likely to exhibit aggressive behavior than children in the other pay subgroups.

5.2.3 *Results: Nonresident Fathers' Financial Support and Child Outcomes*

Appendix B explains the measures we used and the analyses we conducted. Table B.3 (a and b) shows a summary of indirect effects and Figure B.1 presents unstandardized parameter estimates of the model with outcomes measured at age nine – the only wave for which we found statistically significant pathways.

At age five, we found no significant indirect effects of financial support on aggressive behavior or reflective vocabulary. Despite evidence (results available on request) that our continuous measure of financial support was significantly associated with lower food insecurity and with more paternal time spent on learning activities, there were no significant direct effects of these variables on aggressive behavior or reflective vocabulary at age five. Similarly, financial support above and below the median was associated with lower food insecurity; financial support above the 75th percentile was associated with higher investments in learning materials; and all categorical levels of financial support were associated with more father's time spent in learning activities.

At age nine, Table B.4 (a and b) shows estimates of indirect effects of financial support on aggressive behavior and achievement at age nine. We found some evidence of indirect effects of financial support on children at age nine (Panel 1): a very small and marginally significant, indirect effect of financial support on aggressive behavior at age nine and small, marginally significant indirect effects of financial support on reading and math achievement at age nine, through children's reflective vocabulary at age five. Again, as expected (results available on request) financial support was significantly associated with lower food insecurity and with more paternal time spent on learning activities, but, with two exceptions, the direct effects of these mediators on children's outcomes at age nine were not significant at conventional levels.

Our categorical results (Table B.4b, Appendix B) are helpful in interpreting the marginally significant indirect effects at age nine. As compared with children who received no support, children who received support above the 75th percentile had higher reflective vocabulary scores at age five, which were then associated with higher reading and math achievement at age nine. The first indirect effect explained 41 percent (= 0.112/0.272) of the total effect of financial support above the 75th percentile on reading achievement; the second explained 27 percent (= 0.097/0.353) of the total effect of such support on math achievement. Thus, our categorical results support the cascading perspective of the effects of financial support on children's achievement. The indirect effects of financial support above the 75th percentile on aggressive behavior at age nine – through maternal stress, harsh discipline, and learning materials – were very small and marginally significant.

Overall, we found no evidence of significant indirect effects of financial support on achievement through the investment (learning materials, mothers' or fathers' learning activities, or food insecurity) mediators. Again, there was evidence of a significant direct effect of financial support on food insecurity and fathers' learning activities, but the direct effects of learning materials on achievement were not significant, while food insecurity had an expected, but only marginally significant, direct effect only on reading achievement ($\beta = -0.7$, $p < 0.06$).

Context Matters: The Role that Formal versus Informal Support Plays on How Money in Nonresident Families Matters for Children. In the previous section, we found associations in the expected direction, though not statistically significant, that support the cascading perspective of the effect of fathers' financial support on reading and math achievement at age nine. In this section, we tested whether these mediating pathways are moderated by financial support arrangements. We hypothesized that the benefits of consistent formal support would be weaker than the benefits of switching from informal to formal financial support, which, in turn, would be weaker than the benefits of consistently informal support. Table 5a shows that financial support arrangements moderated the cascading effect of our continuous measure of financial support on reading and math achievement, but not in the way prior studies suggest. The cascading effects of continuously measured financial support on reading and math achievement were statistically significant when such support was provided under a formal child support order in waves 1 and 3.

5.2.4 Conclusion

Overall, after accounting for maternal education and income, these findings provide some support for the FIM, the developmental cascade, and the money story. We found no significant indirect effects of financial support on aggressive behavior or reflective vocabulary at age five and no evidence of mechanisms that mediated associations between our continuous measure of father's financial support and child outcomes at age nine. However, we found that high levels of financial support (above the 75th percentile) were associated with higher children's reflective vocabulary at age five, which in turn were associated with higher children's math and reading achievement at age nine. Finally, counter to the prediction of the prior studies, we found that, if provided under a formal agreement or order, even small increases in financial support (i.e., our continuous measure) were associated with higher children's reflective vocabulary at age five and higher children's math and reading achievement at age nine.

Our findings are broadly consistent with recent studies that have found small or statistically insignificant effects for nonresident father's financial support on young children, especially when such studies include controls or mediators for paternal contact with children (Adamson & Johnson, 2013; Amato & Gilberto, 1999; Argys et al., 1998; Hawkins et al., 2007; King & Sobolweski, 2006; King, 2006; Knox, 1996; Nepomnyaschy et al., 2012). Our results are inconsistent with recent studies, based upon the FSM that found that maternal stress and parenting behaviors mediated associations between financial support and children's behavior and cognitive skills at age five (Choi & Pyun, 2014; Choi et al., 2014). A primary reason for these discrepant findings is the difference in measures of financial support. Choi and colleagues (2014) included financial support provided during the child's first year, most of which was informal. By contrast, we included average amounts of financial support (whether formal or informal) during the first three years of the child's life. Our measure captures the substantial changes in the arrangements nonresident fathers use to support their children. For example, only 28% of the mothers in our sample had a formal child support award by the child's first birthday. By age three, this proportion had nearly doubled. Another possible explanation for the discrepant results is the measures of parenting behavior used in the two studies. Choi and colleagues (2014) used latent measures of mothers' parenting behavior that combine positive and negative aspects of parenting. We include separate measures to capture positive (responsiveness) and negative (spanning) dimensions of parenting.

Consistent with findings from Nepomnyaschy and colleagues (2012), we found significant direct and indirect effects of financial support on children's outcomes only when such support was high. However, we reached different conclusions regarding the importance of formal support. They found that formal support above the median was negatively associated with children's cognitive development, but we found that the indirect effects of financial support above the 75th percentile on children's academic achievement at age nine were larger when such support was provided formally. These disparate findings could be the result of differences in child outcomes or the measures of financial support arrangements. They studied children's cognitive development at age five; we studied children's math and reading achievement at age nine. Their key independent variable was support provided in a single year; ours was support provided over the first three years. The findings may also differ because they operationalized moderation effects using an interaction term in a single equation model, while the present study used mediated moderation techniques in a path analysis model.

Our results need to be interpreted in the context of the limitations of this study. First, our analytical sample was composed of children who had nonresident fathers during the first three years of their lives and cannot be generalized to the broader population of children. Second, the FFCWS data on aspects of the home environment, family processes, and child outcomes were limited. In particular, we know nothing about the quality of parent–child interactions and FFCWS includes no measure of the degree to which fathers are responsive to children in these interactions. Thus, due to data limitations our findings hold little encouragement for a love story for children with nonresident fathers.

5.3 CONCLUSION

The main difference between the operation of the money story in resident and nonresident families can be best understood through the lens of the FSM. Like their resident-family counterparts, mothers in nonresident families experience less stress when they receive more financial support from nonresident fathers. However, in nonresident families more financial support often means more parental conflict, which increases maternal stress because the courts, rather than the parents, determine the amount of support. Therefore, more financial support from nonresident fathers may be both positively and negatively associated with children's well-being.

Our preliminary analyses address this uncertainty and find significant direct effects of high amounts of father's formal financial support on behavior and achievement at age nine, and significant indirect effects of such support on achievement at age nine, through early language skills. These results raise two points of caution. First, we should be wary about the conclusion that formal child support is harmful to children (Nepomnyaschy et al., 2012). Second, to be helpful, nonresident fathers of young children must provide substantial amounts of formal child support. Unfortunately, nonresident fathers who cannot afford to substantially support their children are precisely the fathers who avoid the formal child support enforcement system. This occurs because they are involved in ongoing romantic, if not cooperative relationships with the mothers of children, who do not cooperate with the formal child support enforcement system (Huang & Pouncy, 2005). This may also occur because of father's inability to meet highly regressive, formal child support obligations (Cancian et al., 2011; Huang et al., 2005). Responsible fatherhood programs increase the number of unemployed or underemployed nonresident fathers who provide some support through the formal system (US Department of Health and Human Services, 2011). However, they do not increase fathers' earnings or child support payments.

However, our analysis also revealed that even small amounts of financial support are associated with significant increases in the time nonresident fathers spend in learning activities with their children. Unfortunately, we know almost nothing about whether fathers of young children are using this time in activities known to increase children's early receptive vocabulary and later academic achievement (Cabrera et al., 2014). Research should observe the quality of nonresident father–child interactions when they are engaged in learning activities and show nonresident fathers which activities benefit children most.

Most policies affecting nonresident fathers are based on studies focusing exclusively on the money story, but we have reviewed the evidence supporting both the "love story" and the "money story." By doing so, we hope to have conveyed the importance of increasing fathers' ability to financially support their children but also their ability to support them emotionally through forging positive, reciprocal, and loving relationships with their children.

There are also differences between how the money and love stories operate in resident and nonresident families, because nonresident fathers spend much less time with their children than resident fathers do. Further, mothers spend much more time with their children than fathers do, especially during the early years. However, mothers in nonresident families are less likely than mothers in resident families to support and encourage father–child interactions.

6 How Does Parental Money and Love and Children's Own Contributions Matter for Children's Development?

In this chapter, we present new analysis on the question that motivated this book: How do both money *and* love matter for children's development? By doing so, we take a slightly different approach from the one we took in Chapter 5. We shift gears to focus on how both household income (the "money story") *and* parenting behaviors from mothers and fathers (the "love story") independently help children develop the skills they need in resident and nonresident families. More specifically, we examined how increases in money (household income or child support) and love (parental engagement) were associated with children's language and social behavior skills over the course of early childhood when children lived with their fathers in two-parent families and when children live in single-parent households and their fathers were nonresident.

In contrast to the analysis we presented in Chapter 5 where we took a parental investment (i.e., parental investments of time and money) approach to understanding child development, for the analysis we present here we take an ecological approach. According to ecological theory (Bronfenbrenner, 1979), parenting is the most proximal influence on children's well-being, and therefore "love" (measured as the quality of parenting; Dunn & Dunn, 1981) is one of the most important contextual characteristics associated with early development. In this perspective, money (i.e., household income) is a distal factor that influences parental love (i.e., parenting behaviors), which, in turn, influences children's development. Experimental and correlational studies with animals and humans have identified key dimensions of the expression of "love" – or, as we measure in this study, parenting behaviors such as cognitive stimulation, physical care, and discipline – that are associated with child development (Dunn & Dunn, 1981). In contrast, in the parental investment model, money is the most influential and proximal factor.

As we have argued elsewhere in this book, parents who are engaged in a variety of activities (such as reading, playing, helping with homework, putting children to bed, and assisting children with eating and other self-care behaviors) make children feel loved and cared for and provide them opportunities for learning, exploring, and asking questions. During interactions with their parents, children learn new words, develop phonological and print awareness, and learn to share, communicate what they need, and develop the social skills necessary to initiate and sustain social interactions with others. The long-term associations between parental behaviors and interactions with children, especially during the early years, and children's skills as children age are less well established. But, overall, evidence suggests that these early parenting behaviors (aka parental love) may have enduring effects on later social and cognitive skills. The links between early parenting behaviors and later development are stronger for younger than for older children (Cabrera et al., 2020; Rodriguez & Tamis-LeMonda, 2011), but there are still significant associations between direct verbal interactions with parents and children's cognitive and social development (Anderson et al., 2021). Specific to the domain of language and cognition, the amount of speech parents direct toward their children before the age of three years accounts for more than half of the variance in children's cognitive performance and vocabulary at three and nine years of age. Further evidence that the associations between home literacy activities and children's development do not diminish over time comes from one study that learning activities with mothers at kindergarten age continued to be associated with the reading and mathematics test scores of 3rd grade children. However, few studies have examined the long-term associations of early learning experiences and mothers' and fathers' parenting behaviors and children's development. In this chapter, we present new analysis that addresses this gap. We expect that parenting activities during the early years would have both concurrent and long-term associations with children's skills over the course of early to middle childhood.

Therefore, we examined the contributions of parental love (measured in this chapter as maternal and paternal engagement in home-based literacy activities such as reading) and money (measured as household income) to the development of aggression and cognitive skills in children from ages three to nine. Although mothers and fathers are influential in how children turn out, children themselves also contribute to determining their behavioral and cognitive trajectories. Thus, we distinguished the contribution of children's early language skills from the learning activities that both parents engaged in at home. Given that parental involvement in two-parent families looks different from parental engagement in single-parent families, in our analysis we explored whether maternal and paternal involvement, household income, and children's skills would differentially relate to the development of behavioral and cognitive skills for children with resident fathers and those with nonresident fathers. Finally, to contribute to our understanding of the long-term or enduring associations of early household income on children's development, in our analysis we examined whether parental involvement at home, household income, and children's language skills continued to be related to the development of skills from the early years (ages three to five) to the later years (ages five to nine), and whether these associations differed over time. To address these questions, we examined children's skills at ages three, five, and nine, drawing on data about children's behavioral problems and language skills (we did not include academic skills such as math and reading because FFCWS did not collect data on these variables before age nine). We assessed children's behavioral problems using maternal reports of aggressive behaviors, and assessed children's receptive vocabulary using the PPVT (Dunn & Dunn, 1981) at ages three, five, and nine.

As in Chapter 5 on how household income (for resident families) and child support (for nonresident families) are associated with children's well-being, this analysis considers how children developed (i.e., how they changed) from ages three to nine – that is, how their behavior problems as well as their scores on a receptive language test changed over time. The availability of data at age three is important because it enabled us to document children's trajectories as well as gain an understanding of important characteristics of the family and the home environment before children entered formal schooling. Having information on mothers, fathers, and children's behaviors since age three enabled us to examine their independent contribution from ages three to nine. We focus on children aged nine because this is the time when most children are in third grade, which is a pivotal time that can predict how children fare in later schooling (Hernandez, 2011; Sparks et al., 2014).

Because children's abilities change as they get older, due to both maturity and everyday learning experiences, it is important to use measures that capture this change but still assess the particular dimension of children's development. Although parenting tends to be stable over time, the particular behaviors and practices parents use to raise their children also change to reflect developmental changes in children. We chose our measures of children's well-being because they could be used with three-, five-, and nine-year-olds. We measured children's aggression by asking mothers a set of similar questions at each age of the child, but also a set of questions that changed with the child's age. For example, all parents were asked questions about their child hitting other children and skipping school. Parents of three-year-olds were asked about children's temper tantrums as well as about how children interacted with their parents, whereas parents of five- and nine-year-olds were asked how their child interacted with peers, whether they physically attacked others, and whether their child skipped school, respectively. To assess children's receptive vocabulary – whether children could name an object by pointing – at ages three, five, and nine, we used the PPVT. The PPVT includes words of increasing difficulty so young children can do well with the easiest words but not with the words that older children identify correctly. We used standardized PPVT scores (M = 1,000, SD = 15) standardized by age.

For the analysis we present in this chapter, our analytic sample included *all children* and their families participating in the FFCWS (N = 4,898). The children were born between 1998 and 2000 in 20 US cities with populations of 200,000 or more (see Reichman et al., 2001). Mothers and fathers were interviewed when children were ages one, three, five, and nine. Parents who were unmarried were oversampled and referred to as "fragile families," meaning that they exhibited multiple risk factors for child-rearing. The term "fragile families" has been deleted from documents – an acknowledgment that this term was disrespectful to families.

6.1 TRENDS IN CHILDREN'S WELL-BEING IN FAMILIES WITH RESIDENT AND NONRESIDENT FATHERS

In the analysis we present here, we are interested in several aspects of children's well-being, including children's aggressive behavior and their receptive vocabulary skills. Because we examined children's outcomes separately for families with resident and nonresident fathers, our measures of children's aggressive behaviors are drawn from a commonly used battery of questions that researchers use to assess children's behavior problems (Achenbach & Rescorla, 2001). To determine children's level of aggression, mothers were asked questions designed to assess broadly externalizing behaviors that include rule breaking and aggressive acts. Children's externalizing behaviors are important to assess because they have long-term negative consequences for children and because they predict lower academic achievement (Masten et al., 2005), less optimal school adjustment (Baker, 2006) and teacher–student relationships (Jerome et al., 2008; Silver et al., 2005), and more substance use (King et al., 2004) and juvenile delinquency (Broidy et al., 2019; Nagin & Tremblay, 1999).

We measured children's receptive vocabulary – a cognitive skill – as gauged by the PPVT, which is appropriate for children as young as three. We assessed receptive skills at ages three and five because of their high relevance to later school achievement (Dunn & Dunn, 1981). In this test, children are presented with a series of cards, each with four pictures, and are asked to point to the picture when the researcher articulates a specific word or phrase. The receptive language cards become more difficult as the test progresses (Dunn & Dunn, 1981).

We began by documenting the trends over time in children's aggressive behaviors and language skills related to children's well-being between ages three and nine, and how these differed by fathers' residential status – our key measure of family structure. As expected from normative patterns of the development of children's behavior, aggressive behaviors between ages three and nine and between ages five and nine decreased over time for children in households with resident and nonresident fathers (see Figure 6.1). This is a typical and expected trajectory. Children with nonresident fathers, however, had consistently higher levels of aggressive behaviors (as reported by their mothers) than children with resident fathers.

Children's scores on the receptive vocabulary are shown in Figure 6.2. These scores are unstandardized and thus differ over time. There is a clear developmental pattern over time by fathers' residential status. Consistent with previous findings, children with

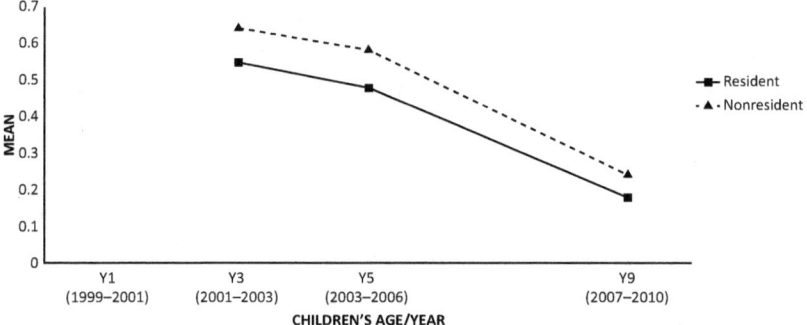

FIGURE 6.1 Children's aggressive scores by fathers' residential status and children's age.

6 HOW DOES PARENTAL MONEY AND LOVE MATTER?

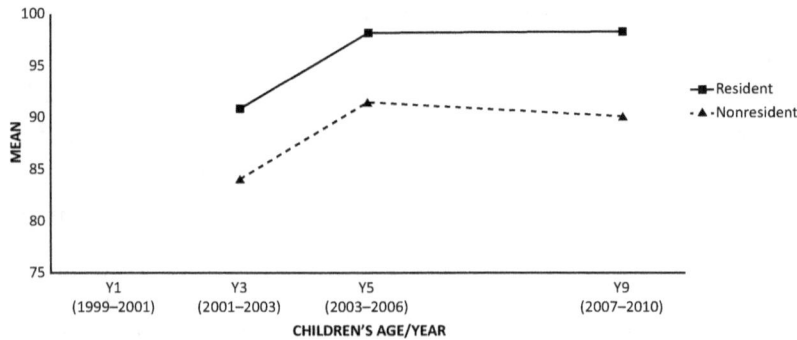

FIGURE 6.2 Children's receptive vocabulary scores by fathers' residential status and children's age.

resident fathers have consistently higher average PPVT scores than children with nonresident fathers, and these differences are statistically significant.

6.2 HOW DO MONEY, PARENTING, AND CHILDREN'S SKILLS MATTER FOR CHILDREN?

To address this question, we tested a model that includes children's aggressive behaviors and language skills at three time points – ages three, five, and nine – and used children's change scores (i.e., subtracting an earlier value from a later value) as the outcome (see Appendix C for an explanation of the latent difference model analysis, and Figures C.1 and C.2 for aggression and Figures C.3 and C.4 for PPVT). We conducted a separate analysis for families with resident fathers and families with nonresident fathers to examine whether the associations of parent and family support on children differed by paternal residency.

6.2.1 Aggressive Behavior

Children's aggressive behaviors for all families and by fathers' type of residency is shown in Table C.1 (Appendix C, see also Figure C.1). For all children in our sample, children's aggressive behaviors increased from ages three to five, and decreased from ages five to nine. Children's average aggression at age three was 7.34 (mean of the intercept). A positive change of 1.60 indicates an increase in aggression from ages three to five, while a negative change of −1.72 indicates a decrease in aggression from ages five to nine. We can attribute these changes to both maturity and experience (Englund et al., 2004).

How do parenting, children's temperament, and family income predict children's aggression in families with resident and nonresident fathers? First, we examined differences in children's aggression between children living in families with resident fathers and children living in families with nonresident fathers. Table C.1 (Appendix C) shows that reported aggression at age three was greater for children living in families with nonresident fathers (M = 8.53, SE = 0.26) than for children living in families with resident fathers (M = 6.45, SE = 0.19). Moreover, the *change* in aggression from ages three to five differed significantly by fathers' residency: Compared to children with resident fathers, children with nonresident fathers had a *greater increase* in aggression from ages three to five (M = 1.42, SE = 0.11 versus M = 1.79, SE = 0.15), but also a *greater decrease* in aggression from ages five to nine (M = −1.58, SE = 0.05 versus M = −1.87, SE = 0.07).

How do children's skills, parenting (aka love), household income (aka money), and other characteristics explain children's development of aggression from ages three to nine in families in which fathers are resident and in nonresident families? We regressed latent intercept factors and difference factors on children's love (parenting), children's temperament, and money (family income; see Appendix C, Figure C.2). Table C.2 shows these associations for children from both types of families.

For children living in families with resident fathers, only maternal involvement (love) at age three was significantly and modestly related to fewer aggressive behaviors at age three, over and above paternal involvement (love). Father involvement, children's language skills, and family income did not contribute significantly to initial levels of aggression at age three. However, the strongest factor associated with children's aggression at age three was the child's temperament, followed by the child's gender (favoring girls). In other words, children's contribution to their own development is greater than money or love.

Levels of maternal involvement at age three were also associated with *change* in children's aggression, although other variables also played a role. Children living with resident fathers and highly involved mothers at age three were more likely to show a significant increase in aggression from ages three to five than children with mothers who were less involved. This finding was small and it stands over and above the fact that increased aggression from ages three to five was also associated with having a mother with depressive symptoms. Being of Latino heritage was a protective factor: Latino parents were less likely than White parents to report increased aggression in their children. *Changes in* aggression from ages five to nine were not related to maternal involvement (either at ages three or five) or to any of our variables of interest. Changes in aggression from ages five to nine were related primarily to child temperament: Children with difficult temperaments showed greater aggression at age three, which was maintained until age five, but children with difficult temperaments at age three were less likely to experience increased aggression between ages five and nine. Overall, for children living in resident families, we found no evidence that children's language skills or fathers' involvement were significantly associated with either initial levels of aggression at age three or with the development of aggressive behaviors from ages three to nine over and above the contribution of other variables, including maternal involvement.

In contrast, for children living in families with nonresident fathers, paternal involvement at age three was significantly and modestly associated with fewer aggressive behaviors at age three. Children's early language skills, family income, and maternal involvement were not significantly associated with children's aggression at age three. However, as with children in families with resident fathers, temperament was the strongest factor associated with children's aggression.

The development of aggression followed a similar pattern for nonresident families: Changes in aggression from ages three to five were associated with high levels of maternal involvement. Decreased aggression from ages three to five was more likely to be associated with high levels of maternal involvement at age three. Larger changes in aggression from ages five to nine were associated with high levels of maternal involvement at age three. Over and above the significant contribution that temperament makes to increased aggression during this period, high levels of maternal involvement at age three were significantly and positively related to increased aggression between ages five and nine but higher levels of household income at age five were more likely to be related to decreases in aggression from ages five to nine. However, these associations were small. Neither paternal involvement nor children's early cognition at ages three and five were associated with the development of aggression in families with nonresident fathers.

6.2.2 *Language Skills*

Overall, children's receptive vocabulary (PPVT) scores increased from ages three to five, and did not significantly change from ages five to nine (see Table C.3, Appendix C). The average receptive vocabulary score at age three (the intercept of the variable at age three) was 87.07. A positive change of 4.09 indicates an increase in vocabulary scores from ages three to five. There was no significant change in receptive language scores from ages five to nine, but there was still significant variance in the factor (10.59), which means that some children increased in scores and some decreased in scores, so, overall, the average change across all these scores is not different from zero.

How do parenting, children's early skills, and household income predict children's language development in families with resident and those with nonresident fathers? First, we examined differences in children's language scores between children living in families with resident fathers and children living in families with nonresident fathers. We regressed latent intercept factors and difference factors on parenting, children's early skills, and family income (see Figure C.4).

As before, we were also interested in examining how parenting, children's skills (in this case, children's executive function skills at ages three and five), and family income were implicated in both receptive language skills at age three and development or changes in receptive language skills from ages three to nine. Table C.4 shows the associations for children from families with resident fathers and children from families with nonresident fathers. Examining differences in the averages of language scores at age three between children with resident fathers and those with nonresident fathers, we found that receptive language scores at age three were greater for children living in families with resident fathers (M = 90.12, SE = 0.86) than for children living in families with nonresident fathers (M = 83.68, SE = 0.72). The change in receptive vocabulary scores from ages three to five also differed significantly by fathers' residency. Children's language scores from age three to five increased for resident and nonresident families. There was no significant difference in the increased scores between resident and nonresident families. There was no significant change in scores from ages five to nine for children living in families with resident fathers, whereas children who lived in families with nonresident fathers had decreased language scores from ages five to nine (M = −0.49, SE = 0.15).

6.2.3 Results: Resident Families

For children in resident families, household income at age three was associated with higher language scores at age three (Table C.4, Appendix C). The association size of household income compared to other variables was smaller. One of the factors that seemed important was race: Children of African American, Asian, and Latino heritage had lower scores at age three than White children. Resident fathers' education levels also played a role, with children scoring higher on the PPVT when their fathers had higher levels of education. Boys were more likely to have lower scores than girls at age three.

But changes in language scores between ages three and five were not associated with any of our variables of interest – household income, parenting, or children's regulatory behaviors – or with any demographic variables. Thus, early parenting and money did not have a significant and enduring association with the development of language during early to middle childhood. The development of language – that is, changes from ages five to nine – were associated with other variables such as gender (favoring boys) and with race/ethnicity and fathers' education. Children of Latino and Asian parents were more likely to show increases in language scores from ages five to nine than children of White parents. Children whose fathers had some college exhibited higher increases in language skills from ages five to nine.

6.2.4 Results: Nonresident Families

For children in families with nonresident fathers, initial levels of language skills at age three were not associated with any of our variables of interest (Table C.4, Appendix C). Other variables (such as children's temperament and low birthweight) were more important. Being African American was the strongest factor associated with lower scores at age three, and children with more difficult temperaments had lower language scores than children with less difficult temperaments.

The development of language skills – that is, changes in language scores from ages three to five – were also not related to any of our variables of interest, although boys were less likely to show an increase in language scores than girls. Further, children who had fathers with some college education were more likely to have increased language scores between age three to five than were children whose fathers had less than high school education. But the development of language in the later years – that is, changes in language scores from ages five to nine – was associated with household income at age five. But these associations were smaller than other variables, such as children's gender. As with resident families, boys in nonresident families were more likely to have increased scores from ages five to nine.

Overall, for families with resident fathers, parental love (maternal involvement) and money (household income) are significantly related to children's aggression and language skills, respectively, at age three – a pivotal point in development. The development of these skills over time progresses on a trajectory of improvement, but it is not associated with money or parental time in these families, with the exception of maternal involvement at age three, which accounts for changes in aggression from ages three to five. In fact, other variables, such as child gender, ethnicity and race, and fathers' education, have stronger and enduring effects on the development of aggression and language skills in resident families (with the last two factors being the most significant). The story here is that in resident families, three-year-old boys are rated as more aggressive and have lower language scores than girls, but, as they get older, being male is no longer associated with increases in aggression and being male is related to higher increases in language scores.

The pattern of how money (household income), love (parenting), and children's early skills matter for children is different for children in families with nonresident fathers and it varies by developmental domain. In nonresident families only love (paternal involvement) is significantly related to less aggression in children at age three. Moreover, early maternal love (mother involvement) and household income at age five are significant contributors to the development of aggression across time. Increased maternal love (i.e., maternal involvement) at age three is significantly related to smaller increases in aggression across time and money (i.e., household income) when children are five is significantly related to smaller changes in aggression from ages five to nine. Other than temperament, no other variable in our model was significantly related to the development of aggression in children in nonresident families.

Neither money, parental love, or children's early skills are significantly related to language skills at age three for children in nonresident families. Recall that children in nonresident families score lower on language skills at age three than children in resident families. The most significant variables related to lower language scores are children's temperament and being of an ethnic minority. However, the development of language skills for children in nonresident families (especially increases in language scores from ages five to nine) is significantly related to money (household income at age five). Boys in nonresident families seem to follow a similar trajectory to boys in resident families, except that boys in nonresident families have lower scores than their counterparts.

In summary, we found important differences in how parental love and money were associated with initial levels of aggression and language at age three, as well as how these factors are implicated in the development of these skills in families with and without resident fathers. As expected, children living in resident families have better language scores and are less aggressive from ages three to nine. These differences exist even though both groups of children show appropriate and expected increases and decreases across time. In both types of families, parental love was significantly related to children's aggression: maternal love was significant for children in resident families and paternal love was significant for children in nonresident families. Money mattered for initial levels of language skills in resident families, but neither money nor parental love was significant for families with nonresident fathers. For children in nonresident families, the strongest factor associated with language difficulties was being Black and being male.

The development of language and aggression also varied by family type. In resident families, the development of aggression was mostly associated with high levels of maternal involvement, whereas the development of language skills was associated with race and child gender. In nonresident families, increasing family income at age five was associated with lowering aggression and improving language scores.

6.3 CONCLUSION

These findings present us with two main take-away messages. First, children's living arrangements – that is, whether they live with their fathers or without – provide an important context for their development. Although the pattern of development of aggression (increases between ages three and five and decreases between ages five and nine) is the same for all children, the *magnitude of the change* is different for children depending on whether they live with their fathers. As our study shows, children living in families with nonresident fathers exhibit greater aggression at age three and had greater increases (ages three to five) but also greater decreases (ages five to nine) than children living in families with resident fathers. Similarly, for language development, children living in families with resident fathers had better language scores at age three and greater increases (ages three to five) than children living in families with nonresident fathers. Another significant finding is that children in resident fathers maintained their vocabulary skills as they got older (ages five to nine), whereas children in nonresident families showed a decrease.

Second, money (household income) and parental love explain the development of language and aggression during childhood differently depending on whether or not children live with their fathers. In families with resident fathers, initial levels of aggression and language skills were significantly related to high levels of maternal love and money (household income), respectively. The development of aggression was weakly related to early levels of maternal involvement. But language development was not related to early parenting or money. These findings are consistent with research suggesting that parents with more resources spend them on their children in ways that promote their cognitive development (Gershoff et al., 2007). Our findings show that this is particularly true for resident families. One of the reasons children in resident families do well might be that they have early access (before age three) to economic resources and have highly involved mothers. Resident families also provide a number of other benefits, not included in these analyses, which can promote social and cognitive development. For example, resident families experience less conflict than families in which fathers are nonresident (McLanahan & Beck, 2010). Our findings suggest that of the multiple factors that play a role in the development of children's cognitive and social skills in resident families, improving family income and supporting maternal love (i.e., positive maternal involvement) might be important targets for programs and policies. Increasing father's education might also be important.

In nonresident families, paternal involvement was significantly related to initial levels of aggression, although the development of it was significantly related to maternal involvement. Money or early parenting were not the most significant factors associated with language skills at age three, but the development of languages skills was significantly related to household income at age five (Davis-Kean, 2005). The parenting resources available to children living in families with nonresident fathers differ from the resources available to children living in families with resident fathers, so it is not surprising that the development of children in these families differs. These findings suggest that children in nonresident families do better when both their mothers and their fathers are highly involved in their lives and when they have access to more economic resources (increased household income), especially for language development. Promoting increased parental involvement and increasing economic resources are important implications of these findings.

These findings should be understood in the context of some limitations. Our study did not include measures of the quality of mother–child or father–child relationships, which is related to early cognitive development. Dimensions of parenting behaviors that have been associated with cognitive development include linguistic and cognitive stimulation (Cabrera et al., 2006) and sensitivity and positive engagement (Blair et al., 2011; Tamis-Lemonda et al., 2004). Furthermore, experimental studies intended to increase maternal support have shown the significance of early sensitive and responsive caregiving for children's cognitive ability (Bernier et al., 2010; Blair et al., 2011; Landry et al., 2006; Matas et al., 1978; Piaget, 1978; Sroufe, 2005). The gold standard of measuring parent–child relationships or sensitivity is through observational methods, which we did not do in our study. Therefore, the measure we used to tap into frequency of behavior may not be sensitive enough to capture the quality of the relationship or parental sensitivity, which can explain why we did not find that fathers' involvement matters for all children. However, our finding that paternal involvement was important for children in families with nonresident fathers suggests that the association might be stronger had we used better measures.

7 Policies and Programs Implicated by Our Findings

Based on the available empirical evidence we have reviewed thus far, and on our own preliminary analysis, we conclude that fathers' contribution to their children's development is *both* financial and emotional. As such, policymakers and program administrators should design and implement policies and programs that support both aspects of fatherhood. In this chapter, we review the status of policies that undergird the "money story." Next, we review existing policies that seem mostly to support the "love story" (i.e. the emotional and engagement aspects of being a parent).

7.1 SOCIAL POLICIES THAT SUPPORT FATHERS

In this section, we describe the status of several policies, initiatives, and programs that affect resident and nonresident fathers and their children. Specifically, we focus on policies that encourage fathers to support their children financially.

7.1.1 *Social Policies that Support Fathers' Financial Responsibilities*

7.1.1.1 *Transfer Payments*

An implication of the empirical evidence reviewed thus far is that resident families use increases in household income to improve the learning environments and maternal responsiveness to young children by reducing maternal stress and harsh parenting. These changes could have long-term associations with children's cognitive skills, academic achievement, and behavior. The primary policy for increasing household income, but not necessarily fathers' earnings, for families (single- and two-parent) with children is the *dependent exemption*, which Congress had allowed to erode by the early 1980s.

It took more than a decade before Congress could agree on one of three strategies to respond to this erosion: increasing the dependent exemption, creating a nonrefundable tax credit, which families with or without tax liability could claim, or a refundable tax credit, which only families that paid taxes could claim. By 1997, Congress resolved this debate in favor of the first option, called the Child Tax Credit (CTC), at $400 per child for middle- and upper-income families. By contrast, the same family (single- or two-parent) would be ineligible for the Earned Income Tax Credit, which policymakers designed to assist low-income families by encouraging work. Subsequent expansions increased the value of the CTC and the number of low-income families that were eligible for the CTC if such families earned enough to encounter tax liability (Crandall-Hollick, 2021).

By 2019, Congressional revisions made the CTC worth $2,000 per child under the age of seventeen for families with earnings of at least $2,500. It remained in full effect for two-parent married families filing jointly with an adjusted gross income of up to $400,000 and for cohabiting and single-parent families with an adjusted gross income of up to $200,000. The Additional Child Tax Credit (ACTC) made a portion of the CTC, up to $1,400, refundable to families that earn $3,000 or more but are taxed at a rate below 15 percent (Shafer et al., 2022).

To assist families hit hard by the COVID-19–induced recession, Congress passed President Biden's American Rescue Plan Act (ARPA) in March 2021, which provided relief to low- and middle-income families until December 2021. Assistance to the latter families with children came in the form of the Expanded Child Tax Credit (ECTC), which added $1,000 per child and an additional $600 for each child under the age of six. Resident families with both parents working were the main beneficiaries of this expansion, especially the additional $600 for children under six. Finally, ARPA provided even greater assistance to low-income families with children by making the CTC fully refundable, which made single mothers eligible for the CTC, in addition to the regular EITC, even if their earnings were too low to incur tax liability.

Finally, ARPA also increased the EITC for low-wage workers not raising children in their homes, nearly tripling the maximum value of the EITC for these workers and allowing 19–24-year-old workers without children to receive the childless EITC for the first time. Nonresident fathers living in households with none of their children benefited from this Expanded Childless EITC (ECTC). Even if they did not pay their formal child support obligations in full, interception of the higher ECTC by the IRS reduced the accumulation of arrears. In prior work, we found that some low-income nonresident fathers welcomed such interceptions because they gave them hope of eventually eliminating their child support debts (Mincy et al., 2014), which were positively associated with their depression and alcohol-abuse problems and negatively associated with their children's well-being (Nepomnyaschy et al., 2021; Um, 2019).

7.1.1.2 *Child Support*

In principle, children need the support of their fathers, even when fathers and children live in different households. Unfortunately, policies intended to improve outcomes for children in low-income families, many with nonresident fathers, focus on the formal financial support that fathers provide, to the virtual exclusion of the cash and in-kind material support (including emotional support) fathers provide for their children, and the parenting and emotional support children need from fathers. In other words, the focus is on the "money story."

The circuitous evolution of child and family policy in the US explains why American family policy focuses on formal child support (the money story) so much more than the love story. Family law in the American colonies followed English common law, which, in turn, borrowed from Roman law, according to which fathers had exclusive rights over all matters relating to children. In the rare case of divorce, the colonies (and later states) or the courts awarded fathers custody of the children. For the most part, the male presumption in custody continued until the mid-nineteenth century.

The demise of said male presumption followed the Industrial Revolution, which moved men away from the family farm or cottage industry, making it impractical for fathers to continue bearing primary responsibility for preparing children with the skills they needed to become responsible citizens. Thus, fathers assumed the breadwinner role by working as wage labor away from home, and mothers took command of the home sphere, becoming the primary caretakers of children (young and old) and thus the main providers of emotional support. The Industrial Revolution also reduced the value of child labor, so preparing children for work was a role required of neither fathers nor mothers. Instead, expanded public – and, in many states, compulsory – education assumed that role. In addition, removing the male presumption of custody became a goal of the women's movement, which also sought to improve the legal status of women in other ways, especially suffrage. Since mothers were the primary caregivers for children in marriage, state laws or the courts presumed this arrangement should continue after divorce, thus establishing a female presumption, which became a short-lived standard by 1920.

The female presumption did not remain a permanent feature of US family law, for several reasons. First, although influential research on children's attachment to their mother during infancy bolstered maternal presumption in custody, not long afterwards other studies established that children formed attachments to their father by the time they were twelve months old. Second, fathers did not passively acquiesce to the loss of the male presumption in custody decisions. Instead, advocacy groups began to form, asserting that the female presumption in custody denied divorced fathers equal protection under the law. Instead, these "fathers' rights groups" lobbied state lawmakers to pass legislation that awarded divorcing parents joint (or shared) legal custody, and found success in some states.

Third, until World War II the gendered division of labor meant that few married (White) women worked outside the home. While married, they and their children were equally dependent on their husband's earnings. Once divorced, the female presumption of custody added financial support to mothers' existing responsibilities to provide direct care for their children. However, requiring divorced fathers to provide financial support for their children was not common until the late 1920s. Before then, the female presumption increased the risk of poverty among many divorced mothers and their children.

The final blows to female presumption occurred over the next forty years. First, the dramatic increase in labor force participation among (even married) women after World War II undermined the argument that mothers were best suited to provide care for children. Once so many of their constituents were working and bearing primary responsibility for children of divorce, feminist groups found common cause with fathers' rights groups who wanted fathers to play a larger role in the lives of children after divorce. If fathers played a greater role in the care of children while married and after divorce, women would enjoy greater freedom in their roles as mothers and full-time workers. Alongside the increasing labor force participation was the even larger increase in divorce by 1960, which had two important consequences. First, rising divorce rates exposed many more children to family breakup, reduced contact with their fathers, and ran the attendant risk of mental health, substance abuse, and related problems, as was documented by increasing evidence. Second, rising divorce rates along with highly variable and poorly enforced child support orders operating across the states left many children in the custody of their divorced mothers who sought public assistance to alleviate poverty. This led to large increases in federal and state spending for the Aid to Families with Dependent Children (AFDC) program.

The Uniform Marriage and Divorce Act of 1970 responded to these changes by supplanting male and female preferences in custody with a new standard, called the *best interest of the child*. To operationalize the new standard, states began to craft new legislation, which provided children with continuity in their parenting arrangements, using legal processes that quickly resolved questions of custody once parents determined to divorce. Implementation of the *best interest of the child* standard paved the way for widespread adoption of joint (or shared) custody across the US. Under joint or shared custody, courts awarded physical custody to mothers in most cases. Children also received a right to financial support from their nonresident parent (most often the father). Judges received wide discretion in determining child support, custody, and visitation. This discretion meant that neither parent could ignore the wishes of the other in matters affecting the child. However, fathers could use their incomes, which were typically higher than the incomes of their wives, to hire attorneys, who negotiated smaller amounts of child support in exchange for less intrusive visitation and interference with mothers' preferences about child rearing (Kelly, 1994). As a result, many divorced mothers were left without the resources they needed to support children, and their children had less contact with their fathers.

Courts responded with education programs designed to teach divorced parents how to reduce the level of conflict to which children were exposed, and to increase positive parent–child relationships (coparenting), the amount of time spent with children, and the quality of parenting by mothers and fathers. Court-mandated or recommended parent education programs typically lasted less than 36 hours, and few were rigorously evaluated. However, independent researchers developed longer, theory-based, parent-education programs for divorced parents and children. These programs led to reduced conflict in high-conflict families and lower repeat litigation and court costs, but increases in the amount of time children spent with divorced, nonresident fathers. To our knowledge, neither court affiliated nor independent programs for divorced parents and their children led divorced fathers to engage in the types of activities during visitation that will have the greatest effects on children's well-being.

Note that this evolution of family law ignored unmarried fathers, mothers, and their children. Instead, most colonies (and, later, states), passed "bastard laws" to sanction men who fathered "illegitimate" children. Such sanctions rarely involved financial support to children, their unmarried mothers, or other caregivers. Not until the 1950s did the Supreme Court partially remove the unequal treatment of children born to married and unmarried parents by recognizing that the latter also had a right to the financial resources of their fathers (Mostofi, 2004). Therefore, state laws also gave courts the authority to require unmarried fathers to pay child support, after establishing that putative fathers were indeed the legal fathers of the nonmarital children that came before them. Unlike divorced fathers, however, states did not give courts the authority to grant unmarried fathers the legal right to have contact with the children during the same proceedings used to establish paternity or a child support order. Therefore, to this day, unmarried fathers in most states must pursue such rights in separate legal proceedings, even after paying child support (Pearson, 2015). Since such legal proceedings require expensive legal representation, and unmarried fathers generally earn less than married fathers, few unmarried fathers have legal rights to visitation. Finally, until recently, few family policies or programs have attempted to ensure that unmarried fathers engage in the activities that benefit children most during visitation.

Since the federal government paid two-thirds of the cost of AFDC, the growth of divorced (and later unmarried) mothers and children receiving AFDC in the 1960s persuaded Congress to abandon its heretofore passive role in child support enforcement. Beginning in 1965, Congress strengthened child support enforcement policy to ensure that parental separation did not result in a loss of income to the child. Persuaded by arguments that the rising feminization of poverty was the result of parental separation, Congress positioned child support enforcement policy to restore the income fathers no longer provided to mothers and children after parental separation. This approach disenfranchised low-income, nonresident fathers, especially those who were unmarried, because many of these fathers (who were disproportionately Black (Mincy, et al., 2014), fully complied with their formal child support payments and provided little or inconsistent informal cash support to the mothers of their children (Mincy and Pouncy, 2003). They did, however, provide in-kind support, which reduced food insecurity in early and middle childhood.

Relationships among income, marital status, and the percentage of income child support orders required nonresident fathers to pay have caused a persistent problem. Historically, higher-income men have been more likely to marry than lower-income men (Lerman, 2010; Mclanahan, 2004). Therefore, the former typically became nonresident fathers following a divorce proceeding in which they were represented by legal counsel. Such representation often results in child support orders that require them to pay a lower proportion of their income in child support than their counterparts who lack legal counsel. The latter could occur following a divorce or legal separation, an informal separation, or a nonmarital birth to a cohabiting or non-cohabiting partner. Before 1975, court proceedings that resulted in child support orders for moderate- and low-income fathers often did not occur unless the mothers of their children sued for child support. Therefore, many moderate- and low-income nonresident fathers provided informal cash or in-kind support or completely avoided supporting their children when mothers could not afford, or chose not to seek, legal counsel to obtain an initial child support order or to enforce an existing order.

However, in 1975 Congress amended the Social Security Act by adding Section IV-D, which created the Federal Office of Child Support Enforcement (OCSE) to coordinate the efforts of state child support enforcement agencies. Section IV-D gave OCSE and its state counterparts the power to undertake several activities to make the collection of child support more certain. For example, under Section IV-D, OCSE required custodial parents (mostly mothers) to assign their rights to child support to the state as a condition of receiving AFDC. Then, to reimburse taxpayers for AFDC benefits paid on behalf of children and their mothers, state child support enforcement agencies sued nonresident fathers for child support. Though attorneys represented state child support enforcement agencies, the nonresident fathers involved in such lawsuits rarely had legal counsel and, until recently, their child support orders were based on the value of AFDC and public benefits provided, rather than the father's ability to pay (Mincy, Jethwani, & Klempin, 2014). Such suits occurred even if mothers were willing, without further recourse, to accept the informal support fathers were able to supply.

Subsequent amendments under Section IV-D, which Congress hoped would increase child support payments and supplement the earnings of mothers leaving welfare for work (Bane & Elwood, 1996) gave child support enforcement agencies new powers to collect child support payments. Among these new powers, the most important was a 1984 provision allowing wage withholding for all child support orders established in 1990 or later (Solomon-Fears, 2013). Child support reforms in 1988, 1993, and (especially) 1996 replaced judicial discretion with administrative procedures needed to establish paternity and set child support orders for nonmarital children, who were becoming a growing share of the AFDC recipients.

These child support reforms exposed more unmarried nonresident fathers to an increasingly aggressive child support enforcement environment. Although, automatic wage withholding dramatically increased child support payments among nonresident fathers who were steadily employed, it caused mounting debts among those with unstable employment (Miller & Mincy, 2012). Federal law also allowed states to charge interest and penalties on unpaid child support, which tended to concentrate mounting child support debt on the lowest-income fathers. Recent studies showed that nonresident fathers with annual incomes of less than $10,000 owed 70 percent of child support arrears (Sorensen et al., 2007). Nonfinancial penalties (e.g., suspension of drivers' and occupational licenses and incarceration) also tended to increase employment instability and reduced hours of work among low-income nonresident fathers. Hence, aggressive efforts by child support enforcement authorities to collect state debts rarely resulted in more payments to lower-income mothers and children. Instead, hours of work decreased among nonresident fathers with arrears that were high in relation to their income (Miller and Mincy, 2012). Mounting child support debt was also associated with increases in depressive symptoms and alcohol abuse (Um, 2019; Robbins et al., 2022).

Black men have also been disenfranchised by the options for securing support from nonresident fathers that child support enforcement policies and practices have ignored, because they are more likely than other nonresident fathers to sustain romantic relationships with the mothers of their young children (Cabrera et al., 2008) and to provide hands-on care for their nonresident children (e.g., bathing, dressing, diapering, playing, and enjoying meals together). Further, in-kind support is positively associated with visitation. However, only recently have child support policymakers begun to endorse counting informal and in-kind support toward child support obligations. Failing to do so made child support enforcement incongruent with the informal arrangements to meet children's needs, given the instability of earnings among low-income fathers. Such incongruence might explain why mothers of their children preferred not to engage the fathers of their children in the formal child support enforcement process (Sorensen and Zibman, 2001; Vogel, 2020a). Though the AFDC reforms dramatically reduced the proportion of single mothers receiving AFDC (Ziliak et al., 2000), the legacy of the child support enforcement program remains. Only two-thirds of the child support cases enforced by federal and state authorities involved children currently receiving public assistance (Tollestrup, 2019).

Unpaid child support affects custodial parents, children, and taxpayers. Only 66 percent of the child support due is ever collected, and only 44 percent of custodial parents receive all the child support due to them (Tollestrup, 2019). Further, because of assortative mating, many young, less educated, nonresident fathers have children by custodial mothers with the same profile, who depend upon public benefits to support their children. To replenish funds used to provide these benefits, states require mothers to sign over their rights to child support to the state, which mounts concerted efforts to collect child support from nonresident parents. However, it is difficult to distinguish fathers who refuse to pay from those who are unable to do so.

Launched in 1994, Parents Fair Share (PFS) was the first responsible fatherhood (RF) program designed to enable the courts to distinguish between nonresident fathers who could pay and those who could not (Doolittle & Lynn, 1998). By assigning all fathers who claimed they were unable to pay to a low- or no-paying service program intended to prepare them for work, judges could flush out those whose claims were untruthful. After identifying fathers falsely claiming they were unable to meet their child support obligations, which increased child support payments, PFS focused on job readiness, job searches, and placement-and-retention services for the low-income nonresident fathers in need.

However, low-income nonresident fathers need more comprehensive workforce services than PFS or its successors provided (Berger et al., 2021; Vogel, 2020a, b). First, nearly thirty years after PFS began, few RF programs serving low-income nonresident fathers offer a comprehensive range of wraparound services that address the multiple employment barriers affecting their ability to meet their child support obligations. These issues may include substance abuse, unstable housing, prior incarceration, limited transportation options, and mental or physical health challenges. Second, many nonresident fathers who can find and keep a job earn too little to meet child support obligations that involve multiple orders, imputed earnings, or interest charges and other financial penalties for past amounts due.

7.1.2 Social Policies that Support Fathers' Relationships

7.1.2.1 Healthy Marriages Initiative
Increases in the rates of divorce and nonmarital births (Lerman, 1996; Thomas and Sawhill, 2002) were primarily responsible for the substantial increases in child poverty in the quarter century prior to the 1996 welfare reform legislation, called The Personal Responsibility and Work Opportunity Reconciliation Act (PROWRA). Of special

concern were the racial/ethnic and spatial concentrations in large cities of children at risk of experiencing poverty, unemployment, and welfare dependence as adults (Sawhill & Chadwick, 1999). This evidence persuaded Congress to assert that marriage was the foundation of a successful society and was critical to the interests of children. This assertion formed the foundation for the three specific goals of PROWRA: to reduce reliance on government assistance among low-income parents by promoting job readiness, employment, and marriage; to prevent and decrease out-of-wedlock pregnancies under PROWRA; and to support the formation and stability of two-parent families.

The Administration for Children and Families (ACF) funded and implemented the Healthy Marriage Initiative (HMI), which aimed to promote stable and healthy relationships by providing low-income married couples with access to couple and relationship education (CRE) services (Hawkins et al., 2022; McLanahan & Sawhill, 2015). If successful, the initiative would reduce the number of married couples that divorced, the number children in female-headed families, and the number of nonresident fathers. As a result, more children would rely upon the income of two parents, rather than the income of a single mother and a nonresident father, who contributes only part of his income to the household in which his children reside.

The core components of this initiative included promoting positive emotional connections between couples and teaching couples to engage in relationship problem-solving and develop communication skills. These efforts to stabilize marriages would hopefully stem the tide of divorce and the proportion of children in single-parent and dependent families, especially among African Americans, which was largely responsible for the Black–White gap in marriage rates that began to accelerate in the 1960s (Mclanahan & Sawhill, 2015). The hope was that strong marital relationships would trickle down to relationships between parents and their children, improving child well-being.

Thus far, rigorous evaluations of three flagship, multi-site, HMI programs have been completed, targeting unmarried or married couples with or expecting children. Intervention participants were randomly assigned to a skills-based healthy marriage and couples relationship education programs, sometimes along with support services. The first intervention, called Building Strong Families (BSF), served expectant unmarried couples. The second flagship HMI intervention, called Supporting Healthy Marriage (SHM) served low-income married couples with children. The third, and more recent HMI intervention, called Parents and Children Together (PACT), served expectant couples or couples including a parent with at least one child. Results of the impacts of these HMI programs on measures of marital or relationship quality improved over the decade (2010–2020) in which researchers developed and evaluated these programs. In only one of the sites, BSF treatment-group couples scored no higher than control-group couples on several measures of relationship quality or relationship stability. Researchers generally found that SHI had similar effects on measures of relationship quality and marital stability. However, all sites offering one curriculum showed small positive effects on these outcomes. However, PACT treatment-group couples scored higher than control-group couples on measures of relationship and coparenting quality and, most significantly, on marital stability. Unfortunately, none of these flagship HMI programs showed significant impacts on child well-being – the ultimate motivation for Congressional support for healthy marriage and couple relationship education programs.

Researchers have also completed rigorous evaluations of ACF-funded HMI programs operated by local organizations that chose their own external evaluators. A meta-analysis of these local HMI programs that served mostly couples found that treatment-group participants scored slightly higher than control-group participants on measures of relationship skills and quality; even smaller differences between treatment- and control-group participants on coparenting quality; and no significant differences between treatment- and control-group participants on intimate partner violence, parenting, or child well-being (Hawkins et al., 2022). Results of the rigorous evaluation of the most recent flagship, multi-site, HMI intervention, begun in 2015, called Straightening Relationship Education and Marriage Services (STREAMS), are not yet available.

Some critics argue that the modest effects of HMI programs on marriage rates and the null effects on child well-being are due to a mismatch between the demographic characteristics of the couples served and the corollary characteristics of those who participated in the design and pilot-testing of the curricula (Hawkins, 2019). The former are predominantly low-income Black, Hispanic, and White couples, while the latter were primarily White middle-class couples. Elsewhere, we have argued that the failure was due to the absence or weakness of service components that addressed the poor employment and earning prospects of Black and Latino males (Mincy, 2001). As a result of these labor market conditions, male–female employment and earnings gaps in communities of color have been declining for decades (Mincy & Pouncy, 2003).

Since the 1960s, when the Black–White gap in marital dissolution began to accelerate, these declines in male–female labor market gaps have diminished the marriage incentives in Black communities. As a result, the Black–White marriage gap accelerated in the midst of a diminishing cultural imperative for heterosexual marriage that has prevailed since the 1970s. In recent decades, similar labor market trends have been playing themselves out for all workers with less than four years of college, especially in rural areas, with corollary consequences for class differences in marriage rates. Whether HMI programs can stem the tide in marital dissolution without more attention to these underlying trends is doubtful.

7.1.2.2 *Responsible Fatherhood Programs*

Besides HMI programs, ACF has funded responsible fatherhood (RF) programs since 2006. Researchers focused PFS singularly on increasing child support payments using a two-step process. First, it gave courts a tool to distinguish fathers who refused to pay from those who were unable to pay. Second, it attempted to increase employment and earnings (hereafter, economic self-sufficiency) of the latter, through participation in employment services. While RF programs funded by ACF were intended to improve economic self-sufficiency, ACF soon added other goals, including increasing fathers' involvement with children, positive parenting skills, and improving relationships with the mothers of their children. Given these diverse goals, it is not surprising that RF programs have had mixed reviews, showing greater impacts on interactions involving children than on those involving adults.

Rigorous evaluations of the early ACF-funded RF programs showed that treatment-group fathers scored higher than control-group fathers on their knowledge about child development, nurturing behaviors (e.g., encouraging child to talk about their feelings), engagement in critical child development activities (e.g., reading, bathing, feeding, and rough-and-tumble play). However, the former scored no higher than the latter on outcomes requiring adult cooperation (e.g., visitation, coparenting relationships with the mothers of their children) or on employment, earnings, and provision of financial support.

The null impacts of RF programs on coparenting relationships are perplexing and difficult to reconcile with a recent meta-analysis of RF programs, targeting low-income fathers but not restricted to those funded by ACF. This study found that RF programs with enough documentation to facilitate comparisons across studies show that impacts on coparenting relationships are larger and more likely to be significant than impacts on other goals of RF programs. On the other hand, the null impacts of RF programs on employment, earnings, and financial support were documented.

The earliest RF programs tried to achieve RF goals by working exclusively with fathers. Some critics argued that doing so neglected opportunities to exploit the five domains that, according to family systems theory, influenced child development: (1) the quality of couple/coparenting relationships between the parents; (2) the quality of relationships between each parent and the child; (3) each parents' adjustment, including personality and mental health; (4) relationship patterns emerging from each parents' family of origin; and (5) life stressors and social supports arising from outside the nuclear family. To make their case, these critics developed a sixteen-week intervention, called Supporting Father Involvement (SFI), operating through these domains serving three groups of low-income, Mexican American and White married or cohabiting fathers. The first group received a high-dose version of SFI in a group format with their partners. The second group received a low-dose version of SFI in a group format with their partners. The final group received SFI in a group format serving fathers only. Results showed that the strongest increases in father involvement, the most resilient couple relationships following birth, and the best reports of child behavior occurred when fathers participated in the high-dose couple group. Fathers participating in the fathers-only group format also reported stable children's problem behaviors, while those in the low-dose couple-group format reported increases in children's behavioral problems. A follow-up study showed similar results, even though this study added a site located in an urban setting with mostly Black parents, who were less likely than parents in the first study to be married or cohabiting and less likely to have all children in common.

After rigorous evaluations of several programs modeled after SFI showed significant impacts on outcomes related to several family systems theory domains, ACF funded a similar intervention, called True Dads, which was designed by the developers of SFI. To address ACF priorities and the stressors arising from unemployment and underemployment, True Dads added an optional two-week employment program to the usual SFI-like curricula focused on family systems theory domains. True Dads required all participating fathers to secure the participation of a coparenting partner who was the mother of at least one of the fathers' children. Rigorous evaluation showed small, negative impacts on depressive symptoms, destructive communication, and intimate partner violence; positive impacts on father's employment; but no impacts on life stressors, parenting quality, or children's behavior.

The results of RF programs based upon family systems theory offer some encouraging signs about the potential benefits of integrating couples/coparenting relationship education into ACF-funded RF programs. Perhaps as a result, the most recent request for proposals for ACF funding of RF programs require applicants to use a curriculum like those used in CRE programs.

However, such integration runs the risk of blurring the lines between HMI and RF initiatives in a way that poorly serves children with nonresident fathers and their parents. Proponents of such integration are explicit about the focus of their work on couple relationships, a focus that favors resident families. For example, among the fathers True Dads recruited, 78 percent were married to or cohabiting with the mothers of their children. Though the average incomes of the treatment- and control-group fathers in True Dads (less than $9,000 in 2016) was low enough to place them below the poverty line for single-person households, they managed to sustain their unions prior to True Dads. As the developers of True Dads hypothesized, such low levels of earning were likely to be a source of stress in the relationships between fathers and their married or cohabiting partners. Though True Dads was able to help these resident families respond to those stresses with less intimate partner violence and negative communications, it did not diminish the stress couples experienced given such low earnings.

It is surprising that only 37 percent of the fathers assigned to True Dads' treatment group elected to participate in the voluntary work program, and that half of those who elected not to participate were, in fact, unemployed. Managing these and other stresses reduces the likelihood that couples break up. However, low-income fathers whose unions dissolve because of such stressors become nonresident fathers who are subject to formal child support obligations. Even in states with modest child support guidelines, a nonresident father with one child must pay 17 percent of his income in child support. It is doubtful that a two-week voluntary job search and resume writing program, such as the one offered by True Dads, would enable these fathers to meet their obligations and cover their other basic expenses, even if accompanied by other services available at employment resources centers.

Finally, it would be difficult to incorporate the optional work program used in True Dads into an initiative targeting nonresident fathers who had difficulty meeting their child support obligations. As PFS demonstrated, initiatives targeting such fathers need a mandatory employment program to flush out fathers falsely claiming they were unable to meet their child support obligations.

7.2 CONCLUSION

This chapter reviews policies and programs in four domains (transfer payments, child support enforcement, healthy marriage, and responsible fatherhood) that affect the money and the love resident and nonresident fathers provide to their children. The most important transfer-payment policies (the CTC and the EITC) are intended to incentivize work by parents and prevent families from being taxed into poverty. Child support enforcement policy has been primarily concerned with recovering the cost of benefits provided to single mothers and children. These policies have worked well for the children of nonresident fathers who are securely attached to the workforce. However, for those with fathers who are weakly attached to the workforce, child support enforcement policy more likely results in large, uncollectible debts, which harm nonresident fathers and children. Healthy marriage and responsible fatherhood programs are intended to encourage and sustain well-functioning relationships by teaching parents relationship skills that will be helpful in the home (and workplace). Legislators assume that children will be better off as a result. However, thus far this remains an untested assumption even among children of married couples. Further, few attempts have been made to encourage strong parental relationships among unmarried parents who are not cohabiting or no longer romantically involved.

Finally, responsible fatherhood programs were originally intended to increase economic self-sufficiency among nonresident fathers with little prior work experience. However, in recent years the line between responsible fatherhood and healthy marriage has become blurred and funding levels available to these programs are insufficient to overcome the significant employment barriers many nonresident fathers with limited employment experience face.

In the next chapter, we propose that changes in four domains increase the money and love resident and nonresident fathers provide to their children and the impact of money and love on their children's well-being. More specifically, we propose: (1) changes in the CTC and EITC that would provide stronger work incentives, more tax relief, and even higher income to resident and nonresident fathers; (2) a child support enforcement policy that would increase employment and employment stability among low-skilled nonresident fathers and the opportunities available to them to spend time with their children; (3) major rethinking of healthy marriage services targeting nonresident fathers who are no longer romantically involved with the mothers of their children; and (4) changes in responsible fatherhood programs that would more effectively address the employment barriers faced by many nonresident fathers and enable participants in responsible fatherhood programs to gain access to workforce development programs that can increase their earning capacity.

8 Implications for Policy and Program Change

The theoretical and empirical literature we reviewed and presented in Chapters 2 to 6 suggests that children need both the financial and the emotional support of their fathers. This chapter recommends changes in the way the policies and programs reviewed in Chapter 7 affect the financial and emotional support fathers provide. We recommend changes in the way the following policies and programs: (1) increase financial support to resident and nonresident families by making permanent the temporary changes to transfer programs that Congress made in response to the COVID-19 pandemic; (2) increase the focus of HMI programs on improving child well-being; (3) provide coparenting relationship education to eligible RF-program graduates and their coparenting partners and increase the focus on improving child well-being; and (4) incorporate informal financial support or right-sized child support orders for nonresident fathers lacking recent, stable employment experience and parenting-time orders into standard child support enforcement policy.

8.1 TRANSFER PAYMENTS

Congressional responsiveness to the 2020 COVID-19 pandemic had many of the desired effects on resident and nonresident families. First, child poverty, food insecurity, and material hardship were lower among families who received the expanded CTC in the first two months of eligibility than for families who were eligible to receive the CTC monthly. Resident families with two working parents benefited more from these changes than nonresident families, because the former generally had higher incomes than the latter and families with annual incomes of at least $75,000 were more likely to qualify for the CTC. Some observers believe that the larger benefits available to higher-income families explain why expansions of the CTC had no adverse effects on employment or positive effects on parental mental health or well-being (Glasner et al., 2022). Nevertheless, because of concerns about inflation, Congress failed to pass the Biden Administration's Build Back Better legislation in 2018, which would have made the ECTC permanent features of our tax structure to support children. Hopefully, progress in reducing inflation, which is already occurring, will persuade members of Congress to make these changes permanent.

8.2 HEALTHY MARRIAGE INITIATIVE

While HMI programs have had statistically significant impacts on couple relationship quality, relationship skills, mental health, and coparenting, their small or null impacts on parenting and marital stability suggest that they are not realizing their Congressional intent (Hawkins et al., 2022). As a result, some critics conclude that ACF should discontinue its support for HMI programs. Two other shortcomings bolster this view. First, the dearth of evidence of the impacts of HMI programs on child well being. Second, the dearth of rigorous evaluations of HMI programs on marriage, parenting, or relationship stability in communities of color, where declines in marriage have been the most severe. Proponents, by contrast, argue that the impacts of HMI programs on relationship quality and stability are similar to the impacts of long-standing, federally funded programs, such as Head Start, and home-visiting programs. Between these two extremes there are at least three middle-ground positions toward which HMI programs have already begun to move.

The first involves including impacts on child well-being in future rigorous evaluations of the effects of HMI programs. Ultimately, the justification for HMI programs was that reducing divorce and marital stability would positively impact child well-being. After two decades there is some evidence in favor of the proximal outcomes (e.g., couple relationship quality, relationship skills, and coparenting) of HMI programs. Therefore, it is time that rigorous evaluations test the distal outcomes – namely, various dimensions of child well-being – as well.

The second involves two steps: First, developing HMI programs that link CRE services, the core of HMI programs, with more robust efforts to improve employment and earnings among less-educated men, including men of color. These labor market barriers contributed to the growth in marital instability in the 1960s. In more recent decades, the same trends also reduced incentives for marriage in working-class communities and communities of color. It should not be surprising that HMI programs that pay minimal attention to these barriers have had little success in working-class communities (McClanahan & Sawhill, 2015). Even if such linkages were unable to increase marriage rates or relationship stability, they could still improve the prospects for coparenting quality and children's well-being.

To do so, HMI programs would also have to provide more direct support for fathers to become engaged in activities that improve child development, including (but not restricted to) children's behavior. Doing so would follow the example of Head Start and Early Head Start programs, described below (see Sections 8.3 and 8.5), which have helped men improve school readiness among toddlers and young children with equal effect, despite variations in the biological or residential relationships between these men and the children with whom they are involved. Presently, these large, federally funded programs reach children in poor families and involve nonresident fathers, but there is little coordination with child support enforcement. Increasing such coordination would connect the "love story" and the "money story" story.

8.3 RESPONSIBLE FATHERHOOD PROGRAMS

Extending programs based on family systems theory, such as SFI and True Dads, to fathers who can secure the participation of their coparenting partners has already begun to blur the distinction between HMI and RF programs, because most of the fathers served by these programs are married to or cohabiting with the mothers of their children. Developers of these programs have little confidence in the potential of these services to effectively serve nonresident fathers and mothers who cannot or will not participate together. As a result, these programs serve mostly married or cohabiting couples (Cowan et al., 2014). Fortunately, other family systems researchers and practitioners engaged in community-based participatory research with nonresident fathers and the mothers of their children do not share this skepticism. Instead, they advocate or are developing interventions designed to improve coparenting quality, father engagement, and child well-being among nonresident fathers and their children (McHale et al., 2012).

Family systems theory posits interdependence of outcomes for mothers, fathers, and children, which is not restricted to nuclear families. Instead, researchers who have used this theory as the basis of their interventions have imposed the nuclear family as an operating constraint for reasons that are not clearly specified.

Researchers could engage nonresident fathers and the mothers of their children (their coparenting partners) in an intervention designed to improve coparenting quality and increase father engagement with children in activities that improve children's well-being, although it would be naïve to expect that identifying such parenting pairs is an easy task. We know from the RF programs emphasizing economic self-sufficiency and child support compliance that many nonresident fathers face substantial and co-occurring barriers to employment (e.g., substance abuse, learning disabilities, and prior incarceration). Many of these barriers are also likely to compromise their ability to function as parents and coparents. Engaging these fathers in coparenting programs might require investment in wrap-around services that would make the cost–benefit of such programs infeasible. Other nonresident fathers (or their coparenting partners) may be unwilling to participate in such programs because their toxic relationships with the other parent are a barrier to coparenting quality that they do not believe can be overcome. These are possible reasons why coparenting interventions with nonresident fathers and their coparenting partners have not yet been developed and tested.

However, practitioners who are close to populations with high proportions of nonresident fathers do not have the luxury of allowing these barriers to block their efforts to improve child well-being in these populations by engaging nonresident fathers. Instead, they are beginning to develop two-stage coparenting programs to engage unmarried nonresident fathers and their coparenting partners. During the first stage, they use existing fathers-only RF programs serving nonresident fathers to screen for candidates who would pass the inclusion restriction for True Dads. At the same time, they are reviewing the literature on mothers-only programs in search of ideas that would make coparenting programs with unmarried nonresident fathers more appealing to mothers (Pearson et al., 2020). They are also developing mothers-only programs of their own to screen for coparenting partners of the fathers they are serving in fathers-only RF programs. These mothers-only programs give mothers opportunities to process, and in some cases resolve, the remaining grievances they have against the nonresident fathers of their children. After identifying mothers for whom past grievances are no longer barriers to participation in a coparenting intervention, practitioners enroll these mothers and the fathers of their children in the third stage. This third stage involves a replication of True Dads with greater attention to the employment barriers that compromise employment and coparenting relationships. Currently, such efforts are in the pilot stage and involve little participation of the academic community. Thus, these efforts have limited prospects of attracting funding for pilot studies, which might provide the evidence for (or against) replication and expansion of these efforts (Personal communication with Dr. Jeffrey Johnson, President of The National Partnership for Community Leadership, February 2023).

Federally funded Head Start and Early Head Start programs aim to improve school readiness for children under six years of age in low-income families. These programs are especially appropriate for engaging nonresident fathers, because so many have children in low-income families. Since their inception, family engagement has been the hallmark of Head Start and Early Head Start, which provide funds to local programs to provide services that promote early learning and development, health, and family well-being. Though there are still wide variations across states, Head Start– and Early Head Start–funded programs are increasingly engaging resident and nonresident fathers, surrogate fathers, and father figures, especially in child-development services (Pearson & Wildfeuer, 2022). Nonresident fathers have long participated in these programs, and studies using data from these programs show that associations between father–child interactions and child outcomes do not depend upon father's residence (Anderson et al., 2013). As a result, more (and more rigorous) pilot studies of the effects of nonresident father–child interactions, including those involving fathers in shared and dialogic reading, on children's well-being could help to produce the evidence policymakers need to determine if public investment in such interventions is warranted.

Policymakers could also use the federally funded Healthy Start program, which aims to reduce infant mortality and other negative birth outcomes, to prepare fathers to engage in early literacy efforts. Like Head Start and Early Head Start, Healthy Start funds services through local agencies. However, under the new funding guidelines the Healthy Start program requires every Healthy Start–funded project to serve fathers and male partners affiliated with the women, infants, and children the project serves. Agencies that apply for funding under Healthy Start must specify plans for recruitment and paternal engagement in their applications and, if successful, must report progress on achieving paternal involvement during pregnancy and afterwards, until children reach age two. Finally, the National Head Start Association provides training and technical assistance to local healthy start programs on fatherhood for Healthy Start programs, including a national summit, and a Fatherhood Academy, which provides training sessions on father engagement programming.

Besides improving the health of infants and young children by helping local programs to recruit and engage fathers, Healthy Start might also lead to more recruitment and engagement of nonresident fathers in early education and literacy programming for two reasons. First, nonresident fathers who are engaged in the lives of their children during the early years tend to remain involved afterwards (Cabrera et al., 2011). Second, local Healthy Start programs often collaborate with Early Head Start programs (personal communication with Kenn Harris, Senior Project Director, National Institute for Children's Health Quality, February 2023).

8.4 CHILD SUPPORT

Current child support enforcement policy emphasizes the "money story" – namely, nonresident fathers must fully comply with child support orders set according to state guidelines. Many ACF-funded RF programs have been focused on increasing fathers' economic self-sufficiency and, consequently, child support to children. Rigorous evaluations show that few RF programs designed to achieve these goals have significant impacts (Avellar et al., 2018; Avellar et al., 2011; Holmes et al., 2020; Soloman-Fears & Tollestrup, 2016). Parents Fair Share (PFS), the most well-known of the studies we cite show that such programs enable courts and child support administrators to distinguish nonresident fathers who refuse to pay child support from those who are unable to do so (Miller & Knox, 2001). By requiring fathers who claim the latter to participate in employment services, the courts can increase the cost of noncompliance for those whose claims are false, thereby inducing them to pay the required amounts. Adding this innovation of the 1990s to standard child support enforcement policy is the core of subsequent RF programs focused on self-sufficiency. This addition should continue so that children with stably nonresident fathers who can pay child support at middle to high levels, which prior studies show is associated with better child outcomes.

What about nonresident fathers who cannot pay and their children? Chapter 7 showed that the most recent ACF-funded RF program focused on economic self-sufficiency and child support payments combined modest relief from coercive child support practices with job search and placement services. However, this combination of services was not sufficient to increase employment, earnings, and child-support payments by nonresident fathers with co-occurring employment barriers (Cancian et al., 2022; Noyes et al., 2018; Vogel, 2020). Instead, these fathers needed jobs-skills training and wraparound services.

Rules governing federal subsidies to states for child support enforcement do not allow states to incorporate the cost of such employment and related wraparound services. Therefore, many states do not incorporate the PFS innovation into their standard child support enforcement policies, which rely upon automatic wage withholding plus coercion to increase the consistency and amount of child support payments. Automatic wage withholding is ineffective for nonresident fathers lacking steady employment. Even if states temporarily reduce financial penalties, interest charges, and the risk of incarceration for nonpayment, their standard child-support enforcement policies do not result in higher formal child support payments to custodial mothers and children. Nor do they result in the recovery of the costs of benefits state and federal governments provide to mothers and children. Instead, these policies concentrate arrears among fathers with limited ability to pay what they owe to the state and federal governments that provide benefits to mothers and children.

Many studies have shown that arrears were concentrated among low-income nonresident fathers (Mincy & Sorensen, 1998; Sorensen et al., 2007; Sinkewicz & Garfinkel, 2009). The comprehensive reforms of the cash assistance program (now called Temporary Assistance to Needy Families; TANF), along with reforms of the child support enforcement system in 1996 further concentrated arrears among low-income nonresident fathers. By these reforms, Congress hoped to substitute increased earnings by mothers and child support payments from fathers for the public benefits, especially cash assistance, on which many single-parent families depended. Within a decade, the number of single mothers who were working rather than receiving cash assistance increased so much that child support orders signed over to the government also fell, as did the quantity of child support owed to the government but not paid by nonresident fathers (Sorensen, September 2021). By 2021, child support orders set at least fifteen years earlier were nearly 70 percent of TANF arrears and 43 percent of non-TANF arrears (Sorensen, September 2021). These findings supported the earlier findings that nonresident fathers with limited ability to pay owed much of the TANF arrears and that these arrears were uncollectible. Said differently, the child support reforms of 1996 did not supplement the earnings of working single mothers as Congress intended. Instead, these reforms increased the concentration of arrears among low-income nonresident fathers, resulting in depression, alcohol abuse, and lower hours of work among fathers and reductions in well-being for their children (Nepomnyachy et al., 2021; Robbins et al., 2022; Um, 2019).

Many fathers whose arrears accumulate over time face employment instability, and have low wages and little education or work experience, often because they are young. Substance abuse problems and histories of incarceration add to these employment barriers. African American and Hispanic fathers are overrepresented among low-income nonresident fathers with arrears as they make up most cases in the child support enforcement system (Mincy & Sorensen, 1998; Robbins et al., 2022).

Child support orders initially set substantially above their ability to pay are a primary reason that arrears accumulate among low-income nonresident fathers. This occurs because magistrates who set these child support orders often lack the information they need to set appropriate child support orders. This can occur for several reasons: (1) periods of incarceration make documentation of recent earnings impossible; (2) housing instability means that they never received a summons to appear in court, where they would have the opportunity to provide information about their income; (3) after receiving a summons, some fathers don't respond because of fears of the justice system; (4) some fathers have child support orders for the children of two or more mothers receiving cash assistance, the sum of which is far above their ability to pay; (5) some fathers face difficulties when they request downward modifications of their child support obligations after changes in their economic circumstances (Ha et al., 2010; Haney 2018; Robbins et al., 2022).

The Federal Office of Child Support Enforcement (hereafter, OCSE) attempted to address these challenges by sponsoring the Child Support Noncustodial Parent Employment Demonstration (CSPED). CSPED operated in eighteen sites located in eight states around the country, so there was wide variation in child support policy regimes. The demonstration offered RF programs the opportunity to relieve participants of coercive child support enforcement practices and provided participants with a variety of employment-related services. Relief took the form of review and possible modification of child support orders if appropriate, temporary relief from coercive child support enforcement sanctions while participants participated in the program, and reduction of arrears at the state's discretion. Employment-related services included job readiness, search, placement, retention, and replacement services following a layoff; short-term skills training, on-the-job training, vocational training, and education directly related to employment; and work supports such as transportation assistance. The goal was to determine if this combination of relief and services would increasing child support compliance by lowering child support orders or increase participant employment stability, earnings and satisfaction with child support enforcement practices (Noyes et al., 2018).

While the variety of available relief and services was quite broad, the dosage of these services was quite modest. Interestingly, almost all participants with current child support orders had these orders reviewed to determine if a downward modification was appropriate. However, few were successful in receiving such a modification.

A possible reason was that 70 percent of CSPED recipients were formally incarcerated. However, CSPED began in 2012 and only four of the eight states that participated in CSPED permitted nonresident fathers to use incarceration as a reason to request a downward modification. Had CSPED been implemented after 2016, changes in economic circumstances due to incarceration would have been considered in requests for downward modification in all of the CSPED sites. Ultimately, CSPED led to substantial increases in the proportion of clients who reported satisfaction with child support enforcement services. Nevertheless, there were only modest (5–6 percent) reductions in child support orders, and child support payments (4–5 percent), and no significant increase in child support compliance or earnings (Cancian et al., 2022).

Debt accumulation and related problems inspired federal child support enforcement rules in 2016 that reduced the likelihood that state CSE policies continued to concentrate arrears among low-income nonresident fathers. These rule changes, called *Flexibility, Efficiency, and Modernization in Child Support Enforcement Programs* (US Department of Health and Human Services, 2016), encouraged states to adopt child support guidelines based on the incomes of both parents, which usually resulted in lower child support orders. The 2016 rule changes also required states to adopt self-support reserves or low-income adjustments that set child support orders below state guidelines for qualified nonresident fathers. The 2016 rule changes also prohibited incarceration for child support noncompliance unless states verified that child support orders were within nonresident fathers' ability to pay. As a result of the administrative burden associated with such verification, incarceration for noncompliance rarely occurs, although other sanctions, such as interest and penalties on arrears, continue. Finally, the 2016 rule changes eliminated a long-standing obstacle faced by low-income nonresident fathers who sought downward modifications of their child support orders. Until this rule change, many states treated declines in income due to incarceration as voluntary unemployment, a change in economic circumstances that nonresident fathers could not use to support their petitions for a downward modification; now, they can.

Besides these requirements, OCSE rules also encourage states to offer arrears compromise programs. Such programs reduce up to 100 percent of state-owed arrears if nonresident fathers meet certain conditions. Currently, several states offer arrears compromise programs, although the conditions under which nonresident fathers may qualify for the compromise vary widely. For example, some compromise programs require nonresident fathers to pay current child support in full for six months, after which arrears owed to the state fall by 25 percent for each month that nonresident fathers pay current support in full. Because many nonresident fathers continue to face employment instability, such stringent conditions result in underutilized compromise programs.

Although OCSE continues its attempts to reduce the concentration of arrears among low-income nonresident fathers, the discretion available to states in specifying the conditions under which nonresident fathers may qualify for such relief is an ongoing problem. For example, the 2016 federal rule changes require all states to have self-support reserves or low-income adjustments in the child support guidelines. In twenty states these mechanisms are available for nonresident fathers with incomes at or above the poverty line; in the twenty other states, these mechanisms are only available to nonresident fathers with incomes below the poverty line. Such discretion is critical because of a recent federal rule change that allows states to fund employment services for nonresident fathers with the federal subsidy states receive to fund their child support enforcement activities (Tollestrup & Landers, 2024; Braswell, 2025).

Responsible fatherhood programs and some child support enforcement administrators have long sought this rule change, for several reasons. First, it could free up the limited funds RF programs outlay to provide employment services for their clients. Second, some of these services are the soft- and pre-employment skills clients with limited work experience need to qualify for the hard-skills training typically provided by workforce development agencies funded by the US Department of Labor. Third, acquiring these hard skills is key to the higher-paying jobs these clients need to support themselves and meet their child support obligations. Fourth, it would provide child support administrators with the resources they need to implement the PFS strategy for flushing out fathers falsely claiming they were unable to meet their child support obligations.

To meet the child support obligations, nonresident fathers with limited ability to pay need two things. First, employment services that increase their earnings enough to pay their current and future child support orders. Second, relief from child support enforcement practices, such as interest charges on their existing arrears. After fifteen years of trying, ACF has still not identified RF programs that satisfy both conditions, perhaps because satisfying the first condition would be extremely costly. One approach is to just keep on trying.

A simpler way is to blend aspects of the money story and love story in three steps. First, if both parents agree, recognize informal financial support from nonresident fathers with limited means instead of formal payments (Turetsky & Waller, 2020). Or, if the custodial parent prefers, allow the below-median levels of formal child support that many nonresident fathers currently pay without the extensive wraparound services required to increase child support payments to the levels required by current guidelines.

Second, supplement the household income available to single-parent families by making permanent the provisions of the ECTC that, as we discussed earlier, increase the CTC and make it fully refundable. Third, redirect government expenditures used to pilot part employment and wraparound services intended to enable low-income nonresident fathers to comply with the child support orders imposed by current guidelines. Instead, use these expenditures to pilot new services, building upon Head Start and Early Head Start.

These new services would attempt to improve child development by increasing nonresident father engagement, nonresident father–child relationships, and the quality of interactions between low-income nonresident fathers and their children.

Finally, there may be more effective ways than coercion to ensure greater child support compliance by nonresident fathers lacking the ability to pay. Many unmarried nonresident fathers refuse to pay the full amount due because doing so does not guarantee access to their children. This is a result of the injustice they feel because child support enforcement forces them to comply with the "money story" but plays no role in the "love story." Recognizing this problem, federal policymakers are already funding several states to experiment with alternative strategies intended to increase child support compliance by addressing visitation and access problems.

Recall that even after paternity establishment, unmarried fathers had no right to see their children unless they obtained visitation orders through separate litigation, which was often prohibitively expensive. In 1996, Congress authorized a $10 million visitation and access program that allowed child support enforcement administrators in selected states to help unmarried parents develop parenting plans, which included specific provisions to facilitate nonresident fathers' access to their children. Nearly half of the parents assisted under this program were unmarried parents with annual incomes below $30,000. Though no rigorous evaluations were conducted, a review of these programs suggested that they increased child support compliance and parent–child contact (Pearson, 2015).

Since then, several states are using OCSE funds to pilot efforts to help unmarried parents obtain parenting-time (visitation) agreements and to incorporate successful efforts along these lines into standard child support enforcement policy. In some states, like Michigan and Indiana, this occurred by assisting unmarried parents to reach a mutually agreeable parenting plan after establishing paternity, using mediators, facilitators, or printed information (Pearson, 2015).

Preliminary studies of these efforts suggest that they add minimally to the cost of child support enforcement programs but increase child support payments (Pearson, 2015). In other states, such as Texas, a judge imposes a standard and legally enforceable custody and parenting-time order on unmarried parents at the same time the judge imposes a child support order (Brustin & Martin, 2015; Waller & Emory, 2018). Increases in child support payments without additional child support costs have persuaded the Texas state legislator to make standard parenting-time orders state law once paternity is established for nonmarital children (Brustin & Martin, 2015; Waller & Emory, 2018).

There are three reasons why we encourage continued experimentation and evaluation of incorporating parenting-time orders into standard child support procedures. First, prior efforts along these lines have always been attentive to excluding families in which there is a risk of intimate partner violence. There is every reason to believe that future efforts will continue this tradition (Pearson, 2015). Second, besides employment and related wraparound services, formulas determining the share of state child support enforcement costs paid by the federal government do not allow states to incorporate the cost of services related to access and visitation, including parenting-time orders. If rigorous evaluations show positive impacts of parenting-time orders on child support payments, the federal government is likely to allow states to incorporate the cost of including parenting-time services, or states may be encouraged to pay for such services on their own. Finally, as we showed in Chapter 7, court-ordered education programs designed to reduce conflict among divorcing parents occurred after family courts took responsibility for reducing the adverse consequences of high-conflict divorce on the children of divorcing parents. Should parenting-time orders have positive impacts on the well-being of children of unmarried parents, courts might assume a similar responsibility to require similar services for the unmarried parents of children subject to parenting-time orders. In turn, researchers working on improving court-ordered education programs for divorcing parents could apply similar methods to reduce conflict among unmarried parents under parenting-time orders.

Such an effort is sorely needed now that more than two-thirds of all children are born to unmarried parents, who are less likely to be a will, and engaged in high-quality relationships than their married counterparts (Brown et al., 2017).

8.5 INCREASE FATHERS' PARTICIPATION IN PARENTING PROGRAMS: EARLY HEAD START PROGRAMS

Furthermore, in the same way programs can use shared and dialogic reading programs for children with mothers and resident fathers, programs can use books for nonresident father–child reading, which contain information valuable to nonresident fathers while also bestowing the benefits of reading to children. For example, books may contain information on positive coparenting skills, providing useful knowledge to fathers while at the same time benefiting children. Researchers who are incorporating shared and dialogic reading into early childhood education programs for the children in resident families have been slow to extend these services to nonresident fathers and their children (Chacko et al., 2018). This is not surprising because the logistics required to ensure that fathers and children are simultaneously available to practice shared or dialectic reading are manageable when fathers are resident. This set of logistics becomes much more difficult when fathers are nonresident, because many factors (e.g., the child's nap times, the father's work schedules, uncertain relationships between nonresident fathers and the mothers of their children) may interfere with scheduling joint nonresident father–child reading times.

8.6 CONCLUSION

Previous research leaves many unanswered questions about how fathers' income matters for children's development. For example, most studies on the effects of income on children's well-being collapse fathers' earnings with other sources of income and include single- and two-parent families in the same sample. These approaches are inadequate because fathers' financial contributions to household income mean different things for children growing up in resident versus nonresident families, and the association between income and child outcomes may depend on the source of income.

Fathers who live with their children contribute about two-thirds of household income, while nonresident fathers who provide support split their incomes between at least two households. Formal child support from nonresident fathers represents close to half of the income in poor, single-mother households that receive it, whereas informal financial support, which nonresident fathers often provide when children are young, represents only a small fraction of the income received by poor, single-mother households. As a result, household income in resident households and financial support in nonresident families may be differently associated with children's outcomes.

In this book, we have explored how fathers' money and love are associated with children's short- and long-term behavioral, cognitive, and academic outcomes. We have also separately reviewed the literature about children living in resident families and those living with their mothers but not their fathers from birth to middle childhood. Our results show that children in two-parent families have lower levels of aggressive behavior and higher cognitive scores than children living in nonresident families. Incremental increases in total household income in two-parent families are associated with cognitive skills and academic achievement scores close to national norms. These parents have enough total income to provide the necessities that support their children's cognitive development in the early years. Moreover, these parents provide a cognitively stimulating home environment by buying books and educational toys for their children. Together, early cognitive skills and a stimulating home environment appear to facilitate later cognitive and academic skills. We found no evidence that time spent by fathers in learning activities with their children explains why higher household income (or fathers' earnings) is associated with improved children's outcomes.

Stably nonresident fathers contribute far less to household income than stably resident fathers, so incremental increases in financial support, even when provided informally, have still smaller direct associations with children's well-being. However, nonresident father's financial support at or well above middle levels is associated with children's outcomes. Such large amounts of financial support may enable mothers to pay for necessities, which, in comparison to children who receive no support, improves children's early (and later) language skills and academic achievement. However, we found no evidence that single mothers use large amounts of nonresident fathers' financial support to invest in their children's learning environments. Nonresident fathers who provide more financial support are also more engaged in learning activities with their children than fathers who provide little financial support. However, higher levels of engagement in learning activities cannot explain why higher amounts of financial support are positively related to children's outcomes.

Fortunately, the states now have the discretion to use federal subsidies for their child support programs to pay for employment services for nonresident fathers who are unable to meet their child support obligations. States that choose to do so can distinguish nonresident fathers who refuse to pay from those who are unable to pay, focus coercive efforts to collect on the former, and provide soft-skills and pre-employment services to the latter. This, in turn, enables low-income nonresident fathers to qualify for hard-skills training provided by workforce development agencies, which are funded by the US Department of Labor. This type of training would help low-income nonresident fathers experience the earnings increases that would, in turn, enable them to meet the higher levels of child support obligations, which are associated with improvements and child well-being.

Based on our findings, we recommend that Congress pass a fully refundable Young Child Tax Credit that would provide an additional

$1,000 for each child under five years of age. Such an increase in household income would help stable two-parent families increase the cognitive skills of their children, and help single-parent families with stably nonresident fathers reduce their children's aggressive behavior. We also recommend that states expand parenting-time orders at the same time that unmarried fathers who are nonresident at birth establish paternity and receive child support orders. Since the process of establishing child support orders now begins with paternity establishment, such an expansion could increase the involvement of nonresident fathers in the lives of children when they are young, which, according to our results, is associated with lower levels of aggressive behavior in children. Thus, experimental studies of parenting-time orders established near the birth of the child should be undertaken to examine the effects of such orders on children's outcomes. Efforts to raise the employment rate and earnings of young, low-skilled nonresident fathers, who are most likely to be nonresident at birth, are unlikely to result in child support payments that are high enough to increase children's well-being. Nevertheless, these efforts should continue, and should be combined with efforts to engage fathers and the mothers of their children in setting the financial and nonfinancial arrangements by which they will jointly support their children. To the extent that parents treat the resulting arrangements as voluntary, even smaller increases in regular child support may improve children's well-being. However, we find no evidence to support the adoption of paternity leave policies like those in many industrialized European countries because we find no evidence that stably resident fathers' involvement has significant direct or indirect associations on children's well-being.

Finally, children benefit when they spend time with their mothers and fathers, including nonresident fathers. To facilitate increased involvement, we recommend the expansion of parenting-time orders when unmarried fathers establish paternity for very young children. However, the benefits can be enhanced by what parents and children do with this time. Researchers are beginning to incorporate shared and dialogic reading programs involving mothers and fathers in resident families in early childhood education programs. The logistics that are necessary to identify common times for children and nonresident fathers to read, and which are amenable to mothers and fathers in nonresident families, are more difficult than the logistics of such arrangements in resident families. Nevertheless, policymakers should support the development of evidence-based practice along these lines and encourage similar efforts targeting nonresident fathers and young children.

Methodological Appendices

APPENDIX A: Chapter 5 Resident Fathers

MEASURES

Children's aggressive behaviors (as reported by mothers) at ages five and nine were measured with the Child Behavior Checklist (CBCL; Achenbach & Edelbrock, 1991). During the in-home survey, mothers were asked when their children were five to rate nineteen items (α = 0.85) and when their children were nine to rate twenty items (α = 0.88) (e.g., "child is cruel, bullies, or shows meanness to others") on a 3-point scale (1 = not true, 2 = somewhat true, 3 = very true). The items were summed to create the aggression variable.

Children's academic achievement was assessed with two subscales of the Woodcock Johnson Achievement Test-Revised (W-J; Woodcock & Johnson, 1989): the applied problems that assess math skills (α = 0.85) and reading (α = 0.80, Reichman et al., 2001).

Household income was assessed via a constructed measure of household income provided by FFCWS. We used household income from multiple years (baseline and one-year follow-up survey) because single-year measures are unreliable (Berger et al., 2009). We deflated household income to 2006 dollars using the Consumer Price Index, then transformed the result using a logarithmic scale to smooth the distribution, and divided the result by 0.10 so the variance of our household income variable was similar to the variance of other continuous variables (Kline, 2011).

Fathers' earnings were measured with father' reports of their own earnings. Fathers were asked how many hours per week they worked in the past twelve months (work hours/weeks). Then, they were asked how much they earned based on the hours/weeks they reported (wage rate). We derived the fathers' yearly earnings measure by multiplying those work hours/weeks by the wage rate. Similar to the procedure for household income, we used paternal earnings from multiple years (baseline and one-year follow-up survey). The average fathers' earnings variable was top coded at $200,000. Then, we deflated average paternal earnings to 2006 dollars using the Consumer Price Index, transformed the result using a logarithmic scale to smooth the distribution, and divided the result by 0.10 so the variance of our household income variable was similar to the variance of other continuous variables.

Investment Model Constructs

Families' investment in children was assessed with two sets of indicators: expenditures on learning materials and investments of time spent with children in stimulating activities. We did not include other expenditures (e.g., child care) that parents can buy because they do not mediate these links (Guo & Harris 2000; Yeung et al., 2002). *Learning materials* were assessed when children were three years old using a subscale of eight items (e.g., "How many push or pull toys does your child have?") from the Home Observation for Measurement of the Environment (HOME; Bradley et al., 1994). Each item was scored 0 for none, 1 for 1–2, 2 for 3–4, and 3 for 5 or more. The items were then summed and averaged as a measure of learning materials ($\alpha = 0.75$). *Learning activities*, assessed when children were aged 1–3 years, refers to parents' time spent in activities that promote learning (such as frequency of reading, telling stories, and singing per week). Items were coded (0 for none to 7 for every day) and averaged ($\alpha = 0.86$ for fathers and 0.85 for mothers).

Maternal responsiveness, assessed when children were three years old, was based on mothers' responses to eight questions (e.g., "Parent encourages child to contribute") from the subset of the full HOME scale (Bradley et al., 1994). These items were summed and averaged; $\alpha = 0.81$.

Family Stress Constructs

Maternal stress was assessed when children were three years old using four items (e.g., "Being a parent is harder than I thought it would be") from the Parenting Stress Index-Short Form (PSI-SF; Abidin, 1997). Score range was 0 to 3, with higher scores reflecting more stress; $\alpha = 0.81$.

Maternal harsh discipline was assessed when children were three years old using items (e.g., "Spanked him/her on the bottom with your bare hand") from the Conflict Tactics Scale (Straus et al., 1998). Scores were summed; $\alpha = 0.81$.

Developmental Cascade Constructs

Receptive vocabulary was assessed using the PPVT; Dunn & Dunn, 1981) at the home visit when children were three and five years old. Higher scores indicate higher vocabulary; α = 0.81.

Demographic Controls

Mothers reported all control variables at baseline unless otherwise noted. Characteristics of the children included gender (1 = male, 0 = female), temperament ("often fusses and cries," "gets upset easily," "reacts strongly when upset"; 1–5), marital birth (1 = child born in marriage, 0 = child born out of marriage), and low versus normal birthweight (1 = less than 2,500 grams, 0 = equal to or greater than 2,500 grams). Characteristics of the mother included depressive symptoms (we used constructed FFCWS variable 1=depressed, 0=not depressed, measured when the children were one year old), number of children mother had at baseline, and mothers' employment status at baseline ("unemployed," "employed part-time," "employed full-time"). Characteristics of the father included age, race and ethnicity, education, and cognitive functioning as reported by the father (0 = low to 15 = high; Wechsler Adult Intelligence Scale-Revised [WAIS-R]; Wechsler, 1981). We excluded mothers' race, ethnicity, age, and education from the analysis because these were highly correlated with paternal demographic characteristics. For the model with fathers' earnings, we controlled for all variables stated earlier, as well as for mothers' income and transfers, which we called "other income." Other income (including mothers' earnings and transfers) was coded as household income minus fathers' earnings. We controlled for other income so our estimates of the direct and indirect associations between fathers' earnings were independent of the associations with other components of household income.

MISSING DATA ANALYSIS

To understand the extent to which missing data may present problems in our analyses, we performed a missing value analysis. Findings from a missing data analysis using the analytic sample (n = 1,281) suggest that there are 101 missing data patterns in which more than 40 percent had missing data. The variable with the greatest number of cases with missingness was PPVT at age five. This overall level of missingness is handled successfully with full-information maximum likelihood (FIML), which uses all observed variables to infer data that is missing at random (MAR; Graham, 2003). Data are MAR when there is no relation between the propensity for missing data on the variable in question and the observed values of that same variable after removing the association with other variables (Schafer & Graham, 2002). The assumption that the missingness mechanism is MAR seems plausible in this context.

ANALYTIC PLAN

We conducted an observed variable path model analysis adjusting for multivariate nonnormality using robust standard errors as recommended by Finney and DiStefano (2013) using M*plus* 8 (Muthén & Muthén, 2011) to test the main associations between household income and children's outcomes at age five (language and aggression). We conducted a second but identical model with children's outcomes (math, reading, and language) measured at age nine. The goodness of fit of the model to the data is suggested when the chi-square is nonsignificant, the comparative fit index (CFI) is greater than 0.95 (Hu & Bentler, 1999), and the root-mean square error of approximation (RMSEA) is less than 0.06 (Browne & Cudeck, 1993). Little (2013) suggests a somewhat more generous cutoff (CFI: < 0.85 is poor fit, 0.85–0.90 is mediocre, > 0.90 is acceptable; RMSEA: > 0.10 is poor, 0.10–0.08 is mediocre, < 0.08 is acceptable). We used FIML to handle missing data assumed to be MAR.

Path analysis, subsumed under a more general modeling framework known as structural equation modeling (SEM), is preferable to multiple regressions because it allows for simultaneous tests of all the associations among constructs; the direct and indirect associations of all predictors can be assessed while accounting for the control variables. This enabled us to assess the theoretical derived, longitudinal associations among our variables of interest.

First, we tested a new model with main associations between household income and children's language and aggression at ages five and nine with three mediational pathways: parental investment (such as learning materials and activities), family stress mechanisms (maternal stress and maternal harsh parenting), and developmental cascades (e.g., children's language at age three). Second, we tested the new model but *with* fathers' earnings instead of household income. All models based on household income controlled for mothers' report of baseline child gender, temperament, maternal depressive symptoms, number of children, mothers' employment status and fathers' age, mothers' race and ethnicity, mothers' education levels, marital birth, marital status, and father-reported cognitive functioning. The model based on fathers' earnings controlled for the same variables, as well as for maternal earnings and transfers. The analysis included only observations with valid data on children's outcomes.

Overall Fit of Model

The model fit was evaluated by comparing each theoretical model (0) with a theoretical saturated model (x). The chi-square goodness of fit test for each model was statistically significant ($p < 0.001$). However, the chi-square goodness of fit test may not be exactly true, especially when sample sizes exceed 400 (Kenny & West, 2008). Because our sample includes more than 700 observations, we applied two commonly used alternative fit indices. The rule of thumb for acceptable levels is that the value of RMSEA should be less than 0.08 (MacCallum et al., 1996) and the standardized root mean square residual (SRMR)

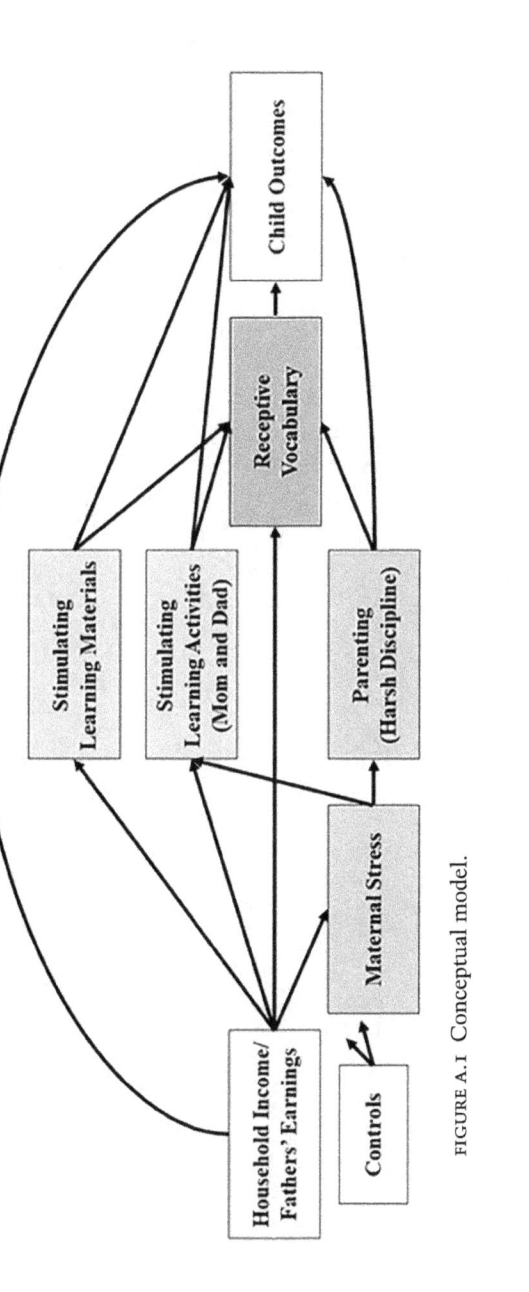

FIGURE A.1 Conceptual model.

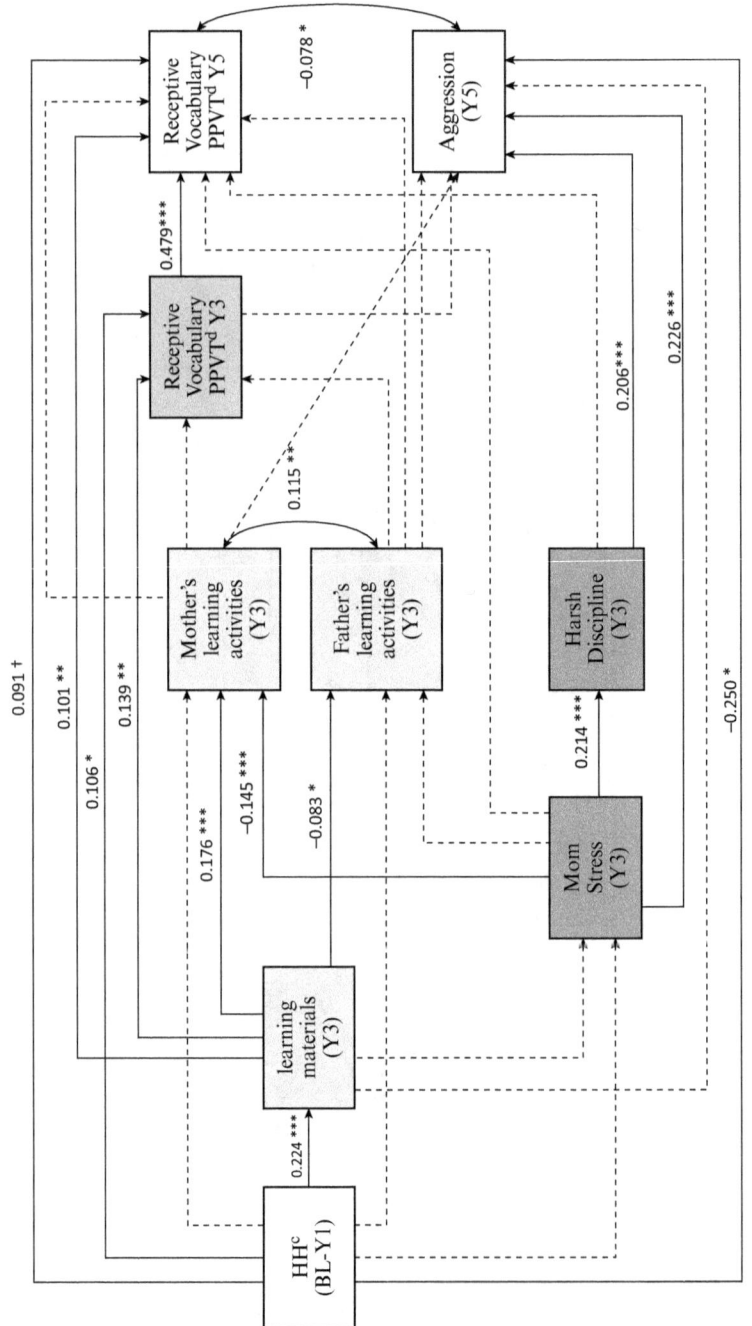

FIGURE A.2 Path analysis for age five model.

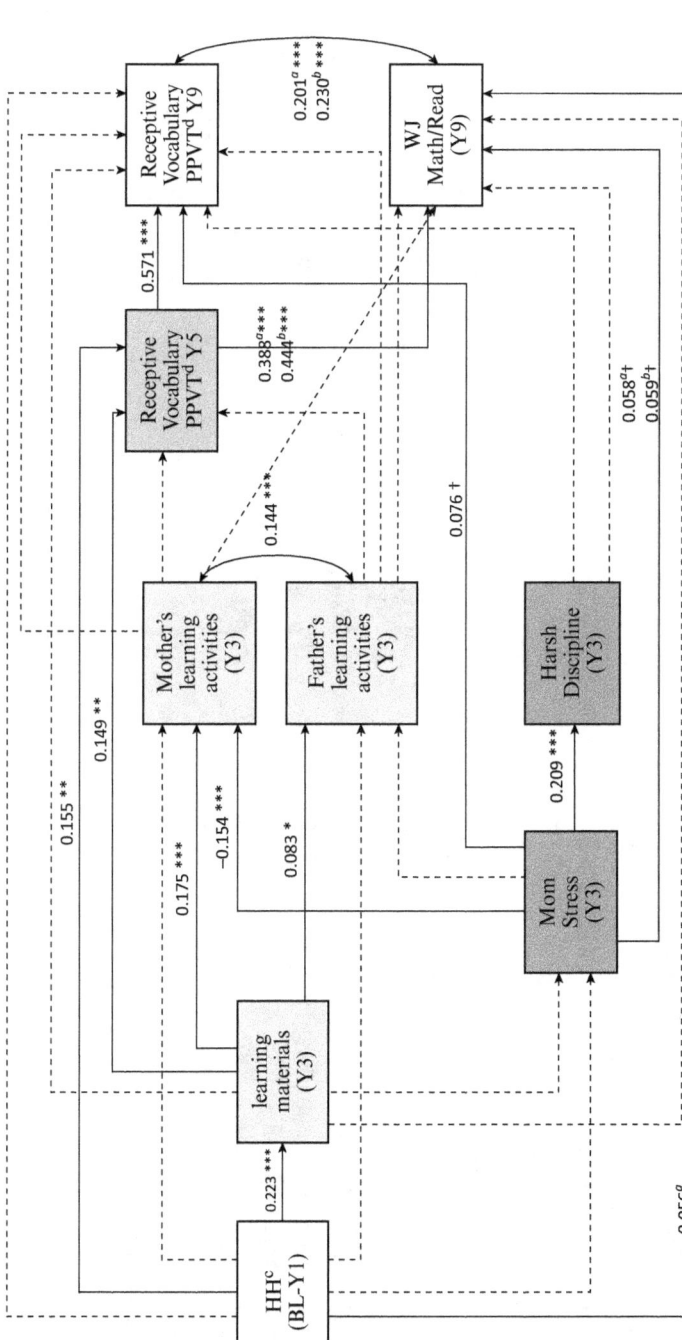

FIGURE A.3 Path analysis for age nine model.

Note: For simplicity, the control variables are not shown but they were included. The solid lines indicate significant pathways and the dotted lines represent nonsignificant paths.

[a] Results for Woodcock Johnson Math scores; [b] Results for Woodcock Johnson Reading scores; [c] Logged household income; PPVT: Peabody Picture Vocabulary Test. Results for Aggressive Behavior Outcome in age nine model are omitted due to space limitations.

† $p < 0.1$, * $p < 0.05$, ** $p < 0.01$, *** $p < 0.001$ (two-tailed).

Table A.1 Unstandardized descriptive statistics, N = 1,281

Baseline demographic/socioeconomic characteristics (range)	Comparative sample 2,914			Analytic sample 1,281		
	M/%	(SD)		M	(SD)	t/chi
Child characteristics						
Male	52%	(0.50)		53%	(0.50)	
Low birthweight	8%	(0.27)		6%	(0.24)	*
Temperament (1–5)	2.77	(1.03)		2.67	(1.00)	**
Born in marriage	40%	(0.49)		58%	(0.49)	***
PPVT at year 3 (40–137)	86.36	(16.19)		90.13	(18.04)	
PPVT at year 5 (40–139)	93.76	(15.81)		97.44	(16.94)	
Woodcock Johnson reading (1–136)	92.86	(14.26)		96.13	(13.60)	
Woodcock Johnson math (1–152)	97.93	(16.52)		102.52	(16.30)	
Father characteristics						
Age in years (15–80)	28.79	(7.03)		30.15	(6.85)	***
Less than high school education	30%			23%		***
High school diploma	32%			26%		
Some college	23%			27%		

				Sig.
College degree	15%		24%	***
White	26%		36%	
Black	37%		28%	
Hispanic	32%		31%	**
Other	5%		5%	
Born in US (0–1)	76%	(0.43)	74% (0.44)	***
Intelligence (WAIS-R) (0–15)	6.69	(2.81)	6.95 (2.89)	
Paternal employment – not working	17%		11%	
Paternal employment – part-time	10%		8%	
Paternal employment – full-time	73%		81%	
Paternal stress			1.21 (0.64)	
Paternal spanking			0.32 (0.34)	
Learning activities (0–7)	3.51	(2.08)	4.09 (1.81)	
Mother characteristics				
Age in years (15–80)	26.30	(6.06)	27.74 (6.10)	***
Less than high school education	30%		22%	***
High school diploma	28%		26%	
Some college	26%		27%	
College degree	16%		26%	
White	28%		37%	***
Black	36%		26%	
Hispanic	31%		31%	
Other	5%		5%	

Table A.1 (cont.)

Baseline demographic/socioeconomic characteristics (range)	Comparative sample 2,914		Analytic sample 1,281		
	M/%	(SD)	M	(SD)	t/chi
Born in US (0–1)	0.78	(0.41)	0.74	(0.44)	**
Intelligence (WAIS-R) (0–15)	6.98	(2.74)	7.30	(2.79)	***
Maternal employment – not working	29%		29%		
Maternal employment – part-time	27%		25%		
Maternal employment – full-time	44%		46%		
Depressive symptoms (0–1) (measured at Y1)	0.14	(0.35)	0.11	(0.31)	***
Number of children mother has	2.12	(2.12)	2.06	(1.17)	
Maternal stress (0–3)			1.21	(0.64)	
Maternal harsh discipline (0–5)			1.25	(0.83)	
Maternal spanking (0–1)			0.39	(0.35)	
Learning activities (0–7)	5.12	(1.62)	5.22	(1.56)	
Household characteristics					
Household income (div. by $10,000)	3.69	(3.56)	5.68	(4.49)	***
Fathers' earnings (div. by $10,000)	3.37	(2.94)	4.25	(2.36)	***
Learning materials (0–3)	2.17	(0.54)	2.23	(0.51)	

Note: Means (standard deviations, in parenthesis); Comparative: Parents who are living together (married or cohabiting) at birth, excludes deceased fathers; Analytic: Parents consistently resident from birth to age five.

[a] Temperament: High scores mean difficult temperament.

* $p < 0.05$, ** $p < 0.01$, *** $p < 0.001$ (two-tailed)

Table A.2 *Summary of indices for the investment and new models at ages 5 and 9 based on household income and father's earnings*

	Year 5			Year 9			
	PPVT receptive vocabulary	Aggressive behaviors		PPVT receptive vocabulary	Aggressive behaviors	WJ [a] – math	WJ [a] – reading

Panel 1: Investment and stress model with household income

Age 5 model
R^2 for outcome: 0.325 / 0.211
χ^2 (*df*): 1350.43 (140)*** / RMSEA [b]: .044 / SRMR [c]: .003

Age 9 model
R^2 for outcome: 0.339 / 0.137 / 0.155 / 0.221
χ^2 (*df*): 2616.78 (189)*** / RMSEA [b]: .044 / SRMR [c]: .002

Panel 2: New model (family investment, parental stress, developmental cascade) with household income

Age 5 model
R^2 for outcome: 0.504 / 0.212
χ^2 (*df*): 1665.81 (164)*** / RMSEA [b]: .034 / SRMR [c]: .004

Age 9 model
R^2 for outcome: 0.562 / 0.137 / 0.260 / 0.356
χ^2 (*df*): 3110.53 (215)*** / RMSEA [b]: .026 / SRMR [c]: .002

Table A.2 (cont.)

Panel 3: New model (family investment, parental stress, developmental cascade) with fathers' earnings

Age 5 model
R² for outcome   0.500   0.216   0.563   0.135

χ²(df): 693.504 (51)*** / RMSEA [b]:.099 / SRMR [c]:.039

Age 9 model
R² for outcome   0.260   0.354

χ²(df): 5.155 (2) / RMSEA [b]:.035 / SRMR [c]:.003

Note: [a] WJ = Woodcock Johnson; [b] RMSEA; [c] SRMR = standardized root mean square residual
†$p < 0.1$, *$p < 0.05$. **$p < 0.01$. ***$p < 0.00$

APPENDIX B: Chapter 5 Nonresident Fathers

DATA AND SAMPLE

We used data from the Future of Families and Child Well-being Study (FFCWS), formerly known as Fragile Families and Child (Reichman et al., 2001). FFCWS is a national study that followed a cohort of 4,898 children born between 1998 and 2000 in twenty US cities with populations of 200,000 or more (see Reichman et al. 2001). Both mothers and fathers were interviewed when children were ages one, three, five, and nine. Unmarried-parent families were oversampled and are referred to as fragile families, meaning that they exhibited multiple risk factors for child-rearing and vulnerability to the parents and children (Reichman et al., 2001).

MEASURES

Children's aggressive behaviors (mother reported) at ages five and nine were measured with the Child Behavior Checklist (CBCL; Achenbach, 1992). *Children's academic achievement* was assessed with two subscales of the Woodcock Johnson Achievement Test-Revised (W-J; Woodcock & Johnson, 1989): the applied problems that assess math skills and reading (Reichman et al., 2001).

Nonresident Fathers' Financial Support was measured when the child was twelve and thirty-six months old. We measured both the amount provided and the financial support arrangement. Following Berger, Paxson, and Waldfogel (2009), we assumed that expenditures on the home environment depended upon permanent income, so we used the average formal and informal support provided when the child was twelve and thirty-six months old to measure the amount provided. Whatever the arrangement, we averaged the amounts provided at twelve months and thirty-six months, after adjusting the result for inflation, and made other transformations so that the variance of our financial support variable was like the variance of other continuous variables (Kline, 2011). Following Nepomnyaschy and Garfinkel (2010), we allowed associations between financial support and children's outcomes to be nonlinear by creating categorical versions of our (average) financial support variable: no pay (= 1 if father provided no financial support at twelve months and thirty-six months, = 0 otherwise); low pay (= 1 if average financial support was below the sample median, = 0 otherwise); middle pay (= 1 if average financial support was above the sample median, but below the 75th percentile, = 0 otherwise); and high pay (= 1 if average financial support was above the 75th percentile, = 0 otherwise). To create dichotomous measures of the financial support arrangement we used mothers' responses to the question "have a formal child support award/agreement," assessed at twelve and thirty-six months. *Consistently formal* (= 1 if the mother responds yes at both twelve and thirty-six months, = 0 otherwise). *Switching* from informal to formal (= 1 if the mother responds "no" at twelve months and "yes" at thirty-six months, and = 0 otherwise.) The omitted category, *consistently informal* (= 1 if the mother responds no at twelve months and thirty-six months, and = 0 otherwise).

Measuring Constructs for Our Theoretical Perspectives

Family investment in children was assessed with four sets of indicators: responsiveness, expenditures on learning materials, food insecurity, and investment of time spent with the child in stimulating activities. We did not include other expenditures (e.g., childcare) that parents can buy because they have been found not to mediate these links (Guo & Harris, 2000; Yeung et al., 2002). *Learning materials* were assessed at age three using a subscale of eight items (e.g., How many push or pull toys does your child have?) from the HOME scale (Bradley et al., 1994). Each item was scored 0 for "none," 1 for "1–2," 2 for "3–4," and 3 for "5 or more."

Child food insecurity was assessed by the Children's Food Security Scale (CFSS), an eight-item subscale of the US Household Food Security Survey (Coleman-Jensen et al., 2013). The primary caregivers were asked to complete the survey on children's food insecurity status when the focal child was three, five, and nine years old. In this study, the child food insecurity was assessed at age three. Each item was coded 1 if the primary caregiver reports "often" or "sometimes," and 0 if she/he reports "never true." The item scores were then summed and standardized.

Family stress was assessed with four sets of indicators. Parental stress variables were assessed with three indicators: maternal stress, harsh discipline, and positive discipline. *Developmental cascade* was assessed using a measure of reflective vocabulary, the PPVT; Dunn & Dunn, 1981) at the three- and five-year in-home visits. Higher scores indicate higher vocabulary.

Demographic Controls

Control variables. All control variables were mother reported at baseline, unless otherwise noted. Characteristics of the child included gender (1 = male, 0 = female), temperament ("often fusses and cries," "gets upset easily," "reacts strongly when upset"; 1–5), and low versus normal birth weight (1 = less than 2,500 grams, 0 = equal to or greater than 2,500 grams). Characteristics of the mother included age, race and ethnicity, education, and mother-reported cognitive functioning (0 = low to 15 = high; Wechsler Adult Intelligence Scale-Revised; WAIS-R [Weschler, 1981]), depressive symptoms (used constructed FFCWS variable 1 = depressed, 0 = not depressed) and mother's income, including her earnings and other transfer payments at ages one and three. Father's race, ethnicity, age, and education were excluded from the analysis because these were highly correlated with maternal demographic characteristics, which should be more salient to outcomes for children in female-headed families under the family stress and investment perspectives.

ANALYTIC PLAN

To test our hypotheses, we conducted a measured variable path analysis adjusting for multivariate nonnormality using robust standard errors as recommended by Finney and DiStefano (2013). Path analysis allows for simultaneous tests of all the associations among constructs. In addition, it enables us to test underlying hypotheses about the direction of associations between variables invoked by each of the three theoretical perspectives on child development (e.g., fathers' financial support, learning materials, learning activities, food insecurity, maternal responsiveness, maternal harsh discipline, and maternal stress) (Alwin & Hauser, 1975). Only observations with valid child outcome data were included in the analyses. Yeung and colleagues (2002) argued that associations among constructs suggested by the family stress and investment perspectives were difficult to disentangle, and, therefore, future research should involve models that integrated these two perspectives. Findings from Cabrera and colleagues (2017), who added the cascading perspective to their study of the effects of fathers' earnings on children's well-being, support models that integrate mediators drawn from multiple perspectives. Therefore, we estimated a model including mediators and controls from these all three perspectives.

Table B.1 *Unstandardized descriptive statistics*

Demographic/ socioeconomic Characteristics (range)	Full Sample 2199		Analytic sample 692			
	M%	(SD)	M%	(SD)	Range	t/chi^2
Mother characteristics						
Age in years	25.232	(6.04)	23.811	(5.60)	14–47	***
% Less than high school degree	31%		37%		0–1	
% High school degree	30%		34%		0–1	
% Some college	27%		26%		0–1	
% College degree	12%		3%		0–1	
% White	23%		12%		0–1	

Table B.1 (cont.)

Demographic/ socioeconomic Characteristics (range)	Full Sample 2199 M%	(SD)	Analytic sample 692 M%	(SD)	Range	t/chi^2
% Black	50%		68%		0–1	***
% Hispanic	24%		19%		0–1	
% Other	3%		1%		0–1	
% Born in US (0–1)	88%		94%		0–1	***
Intelligence (WAIS-R)	6.859	(2.66)	6.336	(2.56)	0–15	***
CIDI	0.164	(0.37)	0.220	(0.41)	0–1	***
Household income (excluding financial support)	24,060	(19,665)	22,219	(18256)	0–200,000	*
Father characteristics			23.811			
Age in years	27.690	(7.18)	25.703	(6.67)	15–80	***
% Less than high school degree	31%		36%		0–1	
% High school degree	36%		43%		0–1	***
% Some college	22%		19%		0–1	
% College degree	11%		3%		0–1	
% White	20%		8%		0–1	
% Black	53%		70%		0–1	***
% Hispanic	24%		19%		0–1	
% Other	3%		2%		0–1	
% Born in US (0–1)	85%		92%		0–1	***
Intelligence (WAIS-R)	6.580	(2.71)	6.276	(2.48)	0–15	**
Child characteristics						
% Male	52%		54%		0–1	
% Low birthweight	10%		11%		0–1	
Temperament	2.804		2.957	(1.12)	0–5	**
Parent behaviors/family processes						
Learning materials	2.165	(0.54)	2.069	(0.54)	0–3	***
Learning activities (fathers)	3.476	(1.91)	2.236	(1.89)	0–7	***

Table B.1 (cont.)

Demographic/ socioeconomic Characteristics (range)	Full Sample 2199		Analytic sample 692		Range	t/chi²
	M%	(SD)	M%	(SD)		
Learning activities (mothers)	4.939	(1.41)	4.863	(1.41)	0–7	
Responsiveness	0.878	(0.20)	0.853	(0.21)	0–1	**
Harsh discipline	1.449	(0.90)	1.577	(0.93)	0–6	**
Parental stress (mother)	1.226	(0.59)	1.322	(0.62)	0–3	***
Food Insecurity	0.344	(0.91)	0.467	(1.15)	0–8	**
Children's behavioral outcomes						
Aggressive behaviors at year 5	10.901	(6.36)	11.730	(6.57)	0–36	**
Aggressive behaviors at year 9	4008	(4.66)	4.414	(4.67)	0–36	*
Children's receptive vocabulary						
PPVT at year 3	86.263	(16.20)	84.033	(15.78)	40–137	**
PPVT at year 5	93.698	(15.91)	91.424	(15.12)	40–139	***
Children's academic skills						
Woodcock Johnson reading	92.831	(14.28)	91.431	(13.88)	1–136	*
Woodcock Johnson math	97.899	16.53	96063	(15.85)	1–152	*

*$p<0.05$ **$p<0.01$ ***$p<0.001$.

Table B.2 *Financial support payments by analytical sample nonresident*

Method of financial support payments	%	Mean	SD
Consistently formal payments	28%		
Switching (informal to formal)	22%		
Consistently informal payments	50%		
Amount of financial support paid by father			
Continuous financial support variable		$784.85	$1406.77
No financial support paid	33%	$0.00	$0.00
Payment below the median level	33%	$73.87	$39.78
Payment at median but below the 75th percentile	17%	$212.51	$156.00
Payment at or below the 75th percentile	17%	$991.30	$282.94

Table B.3a *Summary of indirect effects (continuous father's financial support)*

	B	SE
Effect from father's financial support [a] to aggressive behaviors year 9		
Total effect	−0.238	0.117
Specific indirect effect		
Support [a] → maternal stress → harsh discipline → aggression at year 9	−0.008	0.005
Direct effect	−0.229	0.13
Effect from father's financial support [a] to WJ math at year 9[b]		
Total effect	0.364	0.122*
Specific indirect effect		
Support [a] → PPVT age 5[c] → WJ math at year 9[b]	0.094	0.052
Direct effect	0.239	0.111

Table B.3a (cont.)

Effect from father's financial support [a] to WJ read at year 9[b]		
Total effect	0.360	0.128
Specific indirect effect		
Support [a] → PPVT age 5[c] → WJ read at year 9[b]	0.108	0.060
Direct effect	0.231	0.115*

Note: Unstandardized coefficients are shown
[a] Support = Father's financial support (continuous scale). [b] WJ Math = Woodcock Johnson Math, [b] WJ Read = Woodcock Johnson Reading, [c] PVT = Peabody picture vocabulary test *$p<0.05$ **$p<0.01$ ***$p<0.001$.

Table B.3b *Summary of indirect effects (categorical father's financial support)*

	B	SE
Effect from father's financial support [a] to aggressive behavior year 9		
Total effect	−0.284	0.115 *
Specific indirect effect		
Support (PayMax) [a] → maternal stress → harsh discipline → aggression at year 9	−0.009	0.005
Support (PayMax) [a] → learning materials → maternal stress → harsh discipline → aggression at year 9	−0.001	0.000
Direct effect	−0.261	0.123 *
Effect from father's financial support [a] to WJ math at year 9[b]		
Total effect	0.351	0.115 **
Specific indirect effect		
Support (PayMax) [a] → PPVT age 5[c] → WJ math at year 9[b]	0.099	0.050 *
Direct effect	0.213	0.104 *
Effect from father's financial support [a] to WJ read at year 9[b]		
Total effect	0.271	0.114 *

Table B.3b (cont.)

Specific indirect effect		
Support (PayMax)[a] → PPVT age 5[c] → WJ read at year 9[b]	0.116	0.057 *
Direct effect	0.124	0.106

Note: Unstandardized coefficients are shown
[a] Support (PayMax) = Father provided financial support above the 75th percentile. [b] WJ Math = Woodcock Johnson Math, [b] WJ Read = Woodcock Johnson Reading, [c] PVT = Peabody picture vocabulary test **$p<0.05$ **$p<0.01$ ***$p<0.001$.

Table B.4a *Moderated mediation of indirect effect (continuous father's financial support at age nine)*

	Support → PPVT5[c] → WJ Read 9[b]			Support → PPVT5[c] → WJ Math 9[b]		
Moderator	Indirect effect	SE	P	Indirect effect	SE	p
Always	0.123	0.073	0.094	0.109	0.065	0095
Informal	0.233	0.103	0.023*	0.206	0.092	0.025*
Always Formal	−0.119	0.12	0.323	−0.105	0.107	0.324
Switching						

Table B.4b *Moderated mediation of indirect effect (categorical father's financial support at age nine)*

	Support (PayMax)[a] → PPVT5[c] → WJ read 9[b]			Support (PayMax)[a] → PPVT5[c] → WJ math 9[b]		
Moderator	Indirect effect	SE		Indirect effect	SE	p
Always	0.118	0.071	0.095	0.102	0.062	0.098
Informal	0.149	0.081	0.065	0.129	0.07	0.066
Always Formal	0.066	0.088	0.452	0.058	0.077	0.453
Switching						

Note: Unstandardized coefficients shown
[a] Support = Father provided financial support above the 75th percentile.
[b] WJ Math = Woodcock Johnson Math [b] WJ Read = Woodcock Johnson Reading [c] PVT = Peabody picture vocabulary test **$p<0.05$ **$p<0.01$ ***$p<0.001$.

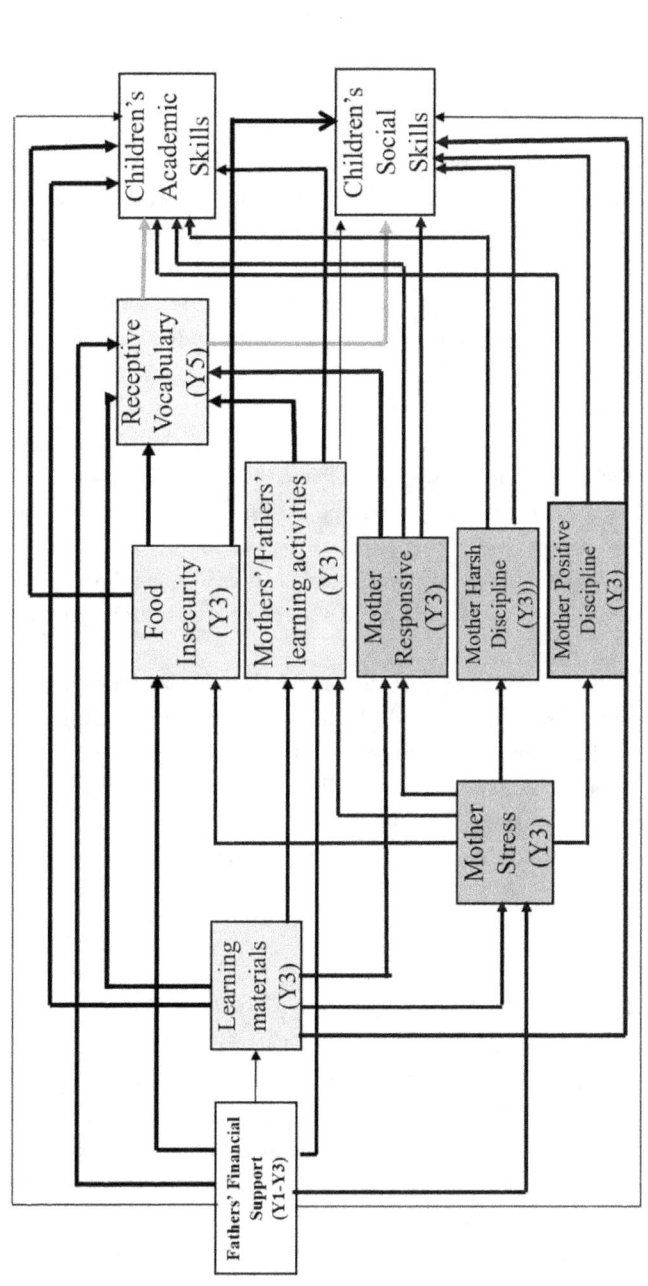

FIGURE B.1 New theoretical model.

APPENDIX C: Chapter 6

DATA AND SAMPLE

We used data from the Future of Families and Child Well-being Study (FFCWS), a national study that followed a cohort of 4,898 children born between 1998 and 2000 in twenty US cities with populations of 200,000 or more (see Reichman et al., 2001). Both mothers and fathers were interviewed when children were aged one, three, five, and nine. Unmarried-parent families were oversampled and are referred to as "fragile families," meaning that they exhibited multiple risk factors for child-rearing and vulnerability to the parents and children (Reichman et al., 2001). The FFCWS enables researchers to compare fragile families to traditional two-parent families.

In the parent interviews, we collected information on demographic and socioeconomic characteristics, parenting attitudes and behaviors, and mental/physical health status. In in-home interviews, we collected information on children's cognitive and noncognitive development, health, and home environment. A fifteen-year follow-up was conducted with parents and children (now teenagers) in 2014.

Less than 5 percent of information on all study variables was missing, and this level of missingness was handled with full-information maximum likelihood (FIML), a statistical method that uses all observed variables to infer missing data when it is missing at random (MAR; Collins et al., 2001; Graham, 2003). Data are MAR when the probability of missingness depends on other variables (including observed variables), but does not depend on the values of items that are missing (Rubin, 1976).

MEASURES

Children's aggressive behaviors (reported by mothers) at ages three, five, and nine were measured using the aggressive subscale of the Child Behavior Checklist (CBCL; Achenbach, 1992). The CBCL is widely used and has acceptable validity and reliability ($\alpha = 0.87$) in various population samples (Rescorla et al., 2007). Mothers were asked to rate each aggressive item on a three-point scale: 1 = not true, 2 = somewhat true, 3 = very true. There were fifteen items at age three ($\alpha = 0.88$), nineteen items at age five ($\alpha = 0.85$), and twenty items at age nine ($\alpha = 0.88$). Examples of questions include "child is cruel, bullies, or shows meanness to others," "child physically attacks people," and "child has temper tantrums or a hot temper." The aggressive items were then summed to create the aggression variable. For a detailed description of these measures, see the User's Guide to the FFCW (https://ffcws.princeton.edu/documentation).

Children's receptive vocabulary. Drawing from cascading models that early skills are the foundation of later skills, we included a measure of language skills using the PPVT, a measure of receptive (hearing) vocabulary for Standard American English that also provides a quick estimate of verbal ability or scholastic aptitude that has high relevance to school achievement (Dunn & Dunn, 1981). In the in-home interview, children were administered the PPVT at three, five, and nine years of age. Higher scores indicate increased levels of language skills. The PPVT was designed for use with individuals ages 2.5–40 years. The English language version of the PPVT-Revised consists of 175 vocabulary items of generally increasing difficulty. The child listens to a word uttered by the interviewer and then selects one of four pictures that best describes the word's meaning.

Children's executive function. At age three, we used the Walk-A-Line task (motor control) to measure children's executive function. During Walk-A-Line, children are asked to walk a six-foot line (marked by masking tape on the floor) three times and in each instance are prompted to walk more slowly than the previous time. This task is often used as a measure of inhibition (a component of executive function) and yields high levels of interrater reliability (ICC = 0.98; Smith-Donald et al., 2007). At age five, we used the Leiter International Performance Scale-Revised, which is a nonverbal intelligence test that measures logical ability for children and adolescents. We used the sustained attention task, an aspect of executive function. The task administered require children to match or point to a response to a series of images or game-like tasks, making it appropriate for children of younger ages who may have limited language skills.

Parent involvement. In each survey, mothers and fathers were asked about the frequency with which they engaged in activities with their children. Types of activities were adjusted to match children's developmental stage, replacing items on caring behaviors at age three (e.g., assisting the child with eating, putting the child to bed) with items involving outdoor activities at age five. The response range was from 0 to 7 times per week.

Household income. We gauged household family income by asking mothers, "In the past 12 months, what was the total income of your household from all sources before taxes and other deductions? Please include your own income and the income of everyone living with you. Please include the money you have told me about from jobs and public assistance programs, as well as any sources we haven't discussed, such as rent, interest, and dividends." Family income includes child support payments.

Other children's characteristics included gender (0 = female, 1 = male) and low birthweight (1 = < 2,500 grams, 0 = > 2,500 grams). Our measure of temperament consisted of three items that were asked to mothers: "child often fusses and cries," "child gets upset easily," and "child reacts strongly when upset." (Mean = 2.82, 1–5, higher scores mean more difficult temperament.)

Demographic characteristics. All background variables were from information reported at baseline, unless otherwise noted. Fathers' characteristics included age, education level, race, and number of children. We also included whether the mother had depressive symptoms, as measured by the Composition International Diagnostic Interview-Short Form (CIDI-SF; Kessler et al., 2006). Mothers' age, education level, and race were excluded from the analysis because of high correlation with paternal demographic characteristics. We also controlled for fathers' cognitive functioning (0 = low to 15 = high, as indicated by the WAIS-R).

DATA ANALYSIS

Using *Mplus* (Muthén & Muthén, 1998–2010), children's aggressive behaviors at three points – ages three, five, and nine – were fitted into a latent difference score model (LDS). A LDS analysis is an extension of a latent growth curve model, and is appropriate with data in which many respondents have been measured repeatedly over time. While a latent growth curve model estimates the average intercept and average slope from the starting time to an ending time, LDSs are modeled at each time of measurement, and the change in variables is modeled using latent growth parameters. Latent intercept variables represent children's cognition and aggression test scores at age three, and latent change variables represent changes between each part of adjacent points (Figures C.1 and C.3). Figure C.1 shows that latent variables of change in children's aggressive behaviors from ages three to five were loaded at 2, representing the growth for two years. Latent variables of change in aggressive behaviors from ages five to nine were loaded at 4, representing the growth for four years. All latent variables were allowed to covary above and beyond the effects of covariates structured in the analysis. The variance of the intercept parameter represented variation in the initial status of aggressive behaviors among children at age three, and variance of the latent difference parameter indicated the variability of the rate of change across children.

Then, latent intercept factors and difference factors were regressed on fathers' involvement at ages three and five, mothers' involvement at ages three and five, household income at ages three and five, and children's PPVT scores at

APPENDIX C 175

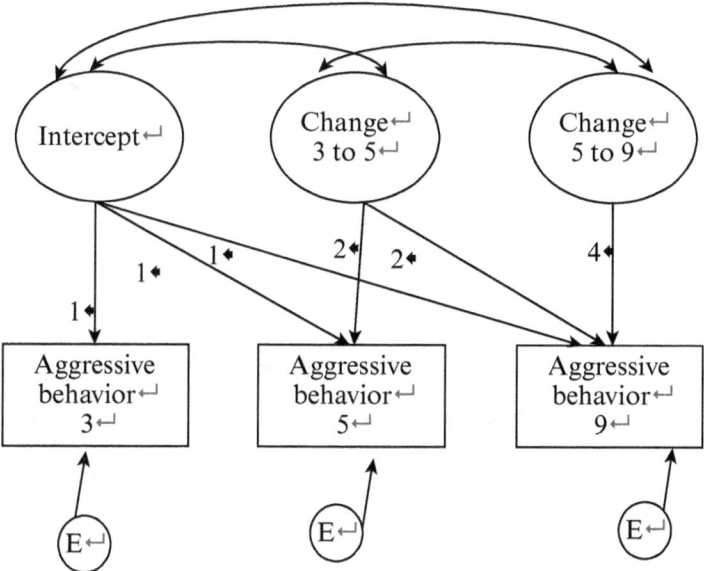

FIGURE C.1 Latent difference score model of children's aggressive behaviors.

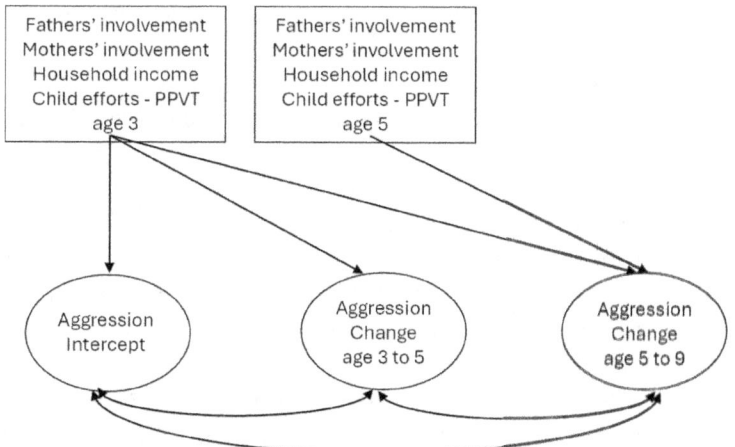

FIGURE C.2 Regression analysis model with covariates[a].
[a] Controlling for children's gender; fathers' age, race, and education; number of children in the household, and mothers' depression.

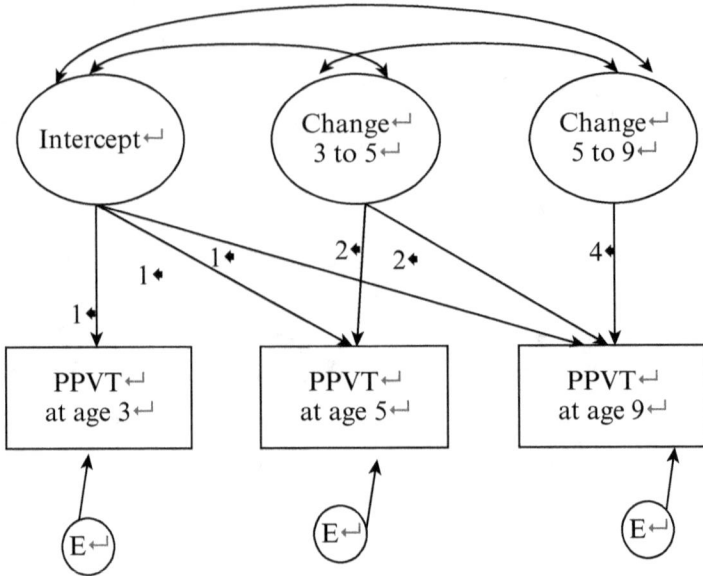

FIGURE C.3 Latent difference score model of children's PPVT scores.

ages three and five, controlling for parent and family characteristics (Figure C.2). We analyzed families of resident and nonresident fathers separately to examine whether the effects of parent and family support on children differed by paternal residency.

Figure C.3 shows that latent variables of changes in children's PPVT scores from ages three to five were loaded at 2, representing the growth for two years. Latent variables of changes in PPVT scores from age five to nine were loaded at 4, representing the growth for four years. Latent intercept factors and difference factors were regressed on paternal involvement at ages three and five, maternal involvement at ages three and five, household income at age three and five, and child's executive function scores at age three and Leiter scores at age five, controlling for parent and family characteristics (Figure C.4).

Figure C.3 shows that latent variables of change in children's aggressive behaviors from ages three to five were loaded at 2, representing the growth for two years. Latent variables of change in aggressive behaviors from ages five to nine were loaded at 4, representing the growth for four years. All latent variables were allowed to covary above and beyond the effects of covariates structured in the analysis. The variance of the intercept parameter represented variation in the initial status of

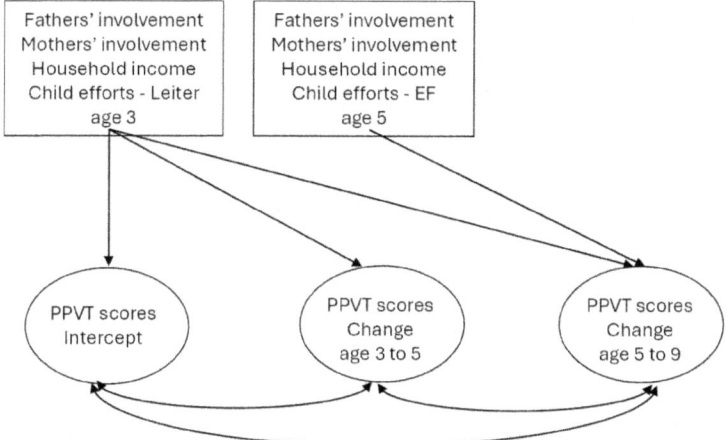

FIGURE C.4 Regression analysis model with covariates[a].

aggressive behaviors among children at age three, and variance of the latent difference parameter indicated the variability of the rate of change across children.

Then, latent intercept factors and difference factors were regressed on paternal involvement at ages three and five, maternal involvement at ages three and five, household income at ages three and five, and children's PPVT scores at ages three and five, controlling for parent and family characteristics (Figure C.4). We analyzed families of resident and nonresident fathers separately to examine whether the effects of parental and family support on children differed by paternal residency. We also examined gender differences.

Figure C.4 shows that latent variables of changes in children's PPVT scores from ages three to five were loaded at 2, representing the growth for two years. Latent variables of changes in PPVT scores from age five to nine were loaded at 4, representing the growth for four years. Latent intercept factors and difference factors were regressed on paternal involvement at ages three and five, maternal involvement at ages three and five, household income at age three and five, and child's Leiter scores at age three and executive function scores at age five, controlling for parent and family characteristics (Figure C.4).

For simplicity, covariances between the latent variables, as well as covariances of predictors with each other and at different time points, are not shown in the figure.

Table C.1 *Means and variances of latent factors of children's aggressive behaviors*

	All		
	Means	SE	p
Aggression			
Intercept	7.34	0.16	***
Change 3 to 5	1.60	0.09	***
Change 5 to 9	−1.72	0.04	***
Variances			
Intercept	24.74	1.38	***
Change 3 to 5	7.50	0.45	***
Change 5 to 9	1.99	0.12	***

	Resident			Nonresident			Res vs Non[a]
	Means	SE	p	Means	SE	p	p
Aggression							
Intercept	6.45	0.19	***	8.53	0.26	***	*
Change 3 to 5	1.42	0.11	***	1.79	0.15	***	*
Change 5 to 9	−1.58	0.05	***	−1.87	0.07	***	*
Variances							
Intercept	18.29	1.49	***	29.76	2.18	***	*
Change 3 to 5	5.85	0.50	***	9.32	0.77	***	*
Change 5 to 9	1.54	0.12	***	2.43	0.21	***	*

Note: Two-tailed test; a significant difference between groups at the level of 0.05.

*** $p< 0.001$, ** $p< 0.01$, * $p< 0.05$.

Table C.2 Coefficients from the structural model of aggression, by resident versus nonresident fathers

Resident father families	Intercept at age 3				Change 3–5				Change 5–9			
	Beta	p	b	SE	Beta	p	b	SE	Beta	p	b	SE
Fathers' involvement at 3	-0.03		-0.26	0.37	0.28		0.28	0.25	-0.01		-0.03	0.13
Fathers' involvement at 5									-0.02		-0.04	0.06
Mothers' involvement at 3	-0.11	*	-1.39	0.56	0.10	*	0.69	0.31	-0.02		-0.06	0.16
Mothers' involvement at 5									0.00		-0.01	0.06
Family income at 3	-0.09		-0.08	0.06	0.01		0.01	0.03	0.01		0.00	0.02
Family income at 5									-0.05		-0.01	0.01
PPVT at 3	-0.01		0.00	0.01	-0.04		-0.01	0.01	0.01		0.00	0.00
PPVT at 5									0.06		0.00	0.00
Demographic controls												
Boys	0.08	*	0.72	0.36	-0.04		-0.19	0.21	0.03		0.08	0.11
Temperament	0.27	***	1.22	0.20	0.01		0.03	0.12	-0.16	***	-0.20	0.05
Low birthweights	-0.02		-0.30	0.83	-0.06		-0.06	0.40	0.02		0.08	0.21
Fathers' age	-0.09		-0.06	0.03	0.05		0.02	0.02	-0.03		-0.01	0.01
Race (ref. White)												
African American	0.04		0.41	0.44	-0.06		-0.33	0.27	-0.05		-0.13	0.14
Latino	0.04		0.34	0.52	-0.13	*	-0.67	0.32	0.00		0.01	0.16

Table C.2 (cont.)

Resident father families	Intercept at age 3			Change 3–5			Change 5–9		
	Beta	b	SE	Beta	b	SE	Beta	b	SE
Asian and others	0.02	0.46	0.68	-0.01	-0.09	0.37	0.04	0.24	0.21
Fathers' education									
High school	-0.01	-0.08	0.63	-0.09	-0.52	0.40	0.07	0.19	0.20
Some college	-0.05	-0.48	0.63	-0.09	-0.49	0.42	0.06	0.16	0.20
College degree or more	-0.06	-0.58	0.71	-0.15	-0.80	0.46	0.13	0.36	0.21
Number of children	0.07	0.26	0.20	-0.03	-0.07	0.15	-0.03	-0.03	0.06
Fathers' WAIS-R	0.07	0.10	0.07	-0.03	-0.03	0.05	-0.02	-0.01	0.02
Mothers' depression	-0.02	-0.30	0.59	0.11	0.92	0.45	0.01	0.04	0.22

N = 614; Chi-square = 459.746, df = 66; RMSEA= 0.026; CFI = 0.992; SRMR = 0.008.

Table C.2 Continued

Nonresident father

	Intercept at age 3				Change 3–5				Change 5–9			
	Beta	p	b	SE	Beta	p	b	SE	Beta	p	b	SE
Fathers' involvement at 3	−0.12	*	−0.50	0.25	0.05		0.12	0.15	0.02		0.02	0.08
Fathers' involvement at 5									−0.02		−0.02	0.06
Mothers' involvement at 3	−0.03		−0.34	0.46	−0.13	*	−0.82	0.31	0.12	**	0.40	0.15
Mothers' involvement at 5									0.03		0.07	0.07
Family income at 3	−0.04		−0.11	0.13	−0.07		−0.11	0.06	0.02		0.01	0.03
Family income at 5									−0.07	**	−0.06	0.02
PPVT at 3	−0.10		−0.04	0.02	−0.02		0.00	0.01	0.09		0.01	0.01
PPVT at 5									0.02		0.00	0.00
Demographic controls												
Boys	0.01		0.06	0.51	−0.03		−0.19	0.30	0.06		0.19	0.14
Temperament	0.21	***	1.02	0.24	0.03		0.07	0.13	−0.14	**	−0.19	0.06
Low birthweights	0.05		0.80	0.72	0.00		0.02	0.50	−0.03		−0.14	0.22
Fathers' age	0.04		0.03	0.05	0.02		0.01	0.03	−0.07		−0.02	0.01
Race (ref. White)												
African American	−0.08		−0.98	1.24	−0.02		−0.15	0.71	0.00		0.00	0.35
Latino	−0.05		−0.75	1.36	−0.04		−0.34	0.78	0.01		0.04	0.38
Asian and others	−0.08		−2.94	2.24	0.03		0.64	1.60	−0.03		−0.31	0.65

Table C.2 (cont.)

Nonresident father	Intercept at age 3				Change 3–5				Change 5–9			
	Beta	p	b	SE	Beta	p	b	SE	Beta	p	b	SE
Fathers' education												
High school	-0.03		-0.33	0.60	-0.02		-0.13	0.34	0.06		0.17	0.17
Some college	-0.07		-0.96	0.72	0.06		0.49	0.45	0.03		0.11	0.23
College degree or more	-0.07		-2.76	2.74	0.03		0.66	0.91	0.03		0.29	0.30
Number of children	0.04		0.16	0.25	-0.10		-0.20	0.12	0.06		0.06	0.07
Fathers' WAIS-R	0.04		0.08	0.14	-0.05		-0.06	0.08	0.05		0.03	0.04
Mothers' depression	0.07		0.96	0.62	-0.01		-0.10	0.36	0.05		0.19	0.18

N = 551; Chi-square = 381.544, df = 66; RMSEA = 0.036, CFI = 0.981, SRMR = 0.009.

Table C.3 *Means and variances of latent factors of children's PPVT scores*

	All		
	Means	SE	p
PPVT			
Intercept	87.07	0.57	***
Change 3 to 5	4.09	0.27	***
Change 5 to 9	−0.19	0.11	
Variances			
Intercept	303.51	15.95	***
Change 3 to 5	62.95	43.31	...
Change 5 to 9	10.59	0.57	...

	Resident			Nonresident			Res vs Non[a]
	means	SE	p	means	SE	p	p
PPVT							
Intercept	90.12	0.86	***	83.68	0.72	***	*
Change 3 to 5	4.37	0.39	***	3.82	0.38	***	
Change 5 to 9	0.08	0.15		−0.49	0.15	**	*
Variances							
Intercept	344.24	27.85	***	247.92	18.10	***	*
Change 3 to 5	59.09	5.51	***	65.39	6.29	***	
Change 5 to 9	10.51	0.83	***	10.55	0.76	***	

Note: two-tailed test; a significant difference between groups at the level of 0.05.

*** $p < 0.001$, ** $p < 0.01$, * $p < 0.05$

Table C.4 Coefficients from the structural model of receptive vocabulary scores, by resident versus nonresident father

Resident father	Intercept at age 3				Change 3 to 5				Change 5 to 9			
	Beta	p	b	SE	Beta	p	b	SE	Beta	p	b	SE
Fathers' involvement at 3	0.05		2.22	1.56	-0.06		-1.11	0.89	-0.07		-0.47	0.36
Fathers' involvement at 5									0.02		0.09	0.21
Mothers' involvement at 3	0.06		3.21	2.32	-0.03		-0.74	1.25	-0.07		-0.66	0.46
Mothers' involvement at 5									0.00		-0.01	0.25
Family income at 3	0.16	**	0.66	0.23	0.01		0.02	0.11	-0.10		-0.07	0.05
Family income at 5									0.03		0.02	0.04
Executive function at 3	0.04		0.14	0.19	-0.07		-0.11	0.10	0.07		0.05	0.04
Leiter scores at 5									-0.02		-0.01	0.01
Demographic controls												
Boys	-0.13	**	-4.80	1.49	0.09		1.33	0.72	0.12	**	0.76	0.29
Temperament	0.02		0.38	0.78	-0.08		-0.61	0.41	0.01		0.04	0.16
Low birthweights	0.01		0.47	2.89	0.00		0.10	1.51	0.00		-0.05	0.61
Fathers' age	-0.03		-0.07	0.14	0.04		0.04	0.06	0.06		0.03	0.03
Race (ref. White)												
African American	-0.20	***	-8.19	1.91	0.05		0.83	0.92	0.01		0.07	0.36

Latino	-0.18	**	-7.26	2.37	-0.13	-2.17	1.12	0.17	**	1.21	0.44
Asian and others	-0.11	**	-9.42	3.19	0.08	2.94	1.52	0.10	**	1.50	0.52
Fathers' education											
High school	0.12	*	4.96	2.41	0.00	0.04	1.22	0.07		0.55	0.48
Some college	0.21	***	8.51	2.27	-0.13	-2.19	1.12	0.14	*	1.04	0.46
College degree or more	0.21	**	8.70	2.76	-0.13	-2.16	1.35	0.13		0.97	0.59
Number of children	-0.02		-0.37	0.58	-0.06	-0.36	0.32	-0.05		-0.14	0.17
Fathers' WAIS-R	0.09		0.56	0.33	0.03	0.07	0.17	0.01		0.01	0.06
Mothers' depression	0.00		-0.12	2.65	0.01	0.26	1.44	0.06		0.60	0.44

N = 614; Chi-square = 846.8, df = 66; RMSEA = 0.087; CFI = 0.952; SRMR = 0.022.

Table C.4 Continued

Nonresident father	Intercept at age 3				Change 3 to 5				Change 5 to 9			
	Beta	p	b	SE	Beta	p	b	SE	Beta	p	B	SE
Fathers' involvement at 3	0.05		0.63	0.68	−0.01		−0.09	0.37	−0.01		−0.03	0.18
Fathers' involvement at 5									−0.06		−0.17	0.16
Mothers' involvement at 3	0.04		1.18	1.41	0.04		0.61	0.76	−0.04		−0.24	0.31
Mothers' involvement at 5									0.03		0.20	0.18
Family income at 3	0.04		0.29	0.43	0.09		0.37	0.19	−0.07		−0.11	0.10
Family income at 5									0.09	*	0.15	0.07
Leiter scores at 3	0.02		0.04	0.14	−0.05		−0.06	0.06	0.07		0.04	0.04
Executive function at 5									0.06		0.02	0.01
Demographic controls												
Boys	0.02		0.49	1.40	−0.17	***	−2.71	0.74	0.21	***	1.39	0.31
Temperament	−0.16	**	−2.09	0.62	0.07		0.48	0.33	−0.03		−0.09	0.13
Low birthweights	−0.10	*	−4.60	2.17	0.11	*	2.68	1.20	−0.03		−0.34	0.41
Fathers' age	0.05		0.10	0.17	−0.08		−0.09	0.10	0.14		0.07	0.04
Race (ref. White)												
African American	−0.30	***	−10.81	3.02	−0.02		−0.34	1.66	0.07		0.56	0.76
Latino	−0.16	*	−6.81	3.33	−0.11		−2.30	1.80	0.15		1.31	0.84
Asian and others	−0.02		−1.71	4.64	−0.01		−0.38	2.32	0.04		0.86	1.23

Fathers' education									
High school	0.03	0.97	1.67	0.07		1.09	0.92	-0.03	-0.23	0.37
Some college	0.03	1.38	2.42	0.19		3.98	1.35	-0.05	-0.39	0.55
College degree or more	0.04	4.25	4.36	0.04	**	2.30	1.79	-0.05	-1.18	0.92
Number of children	-0.04	-0.39	0.82	0.07		0.37	0.35	-0.11	-0.23	0.17
Fathers' WAIS-R	-0.01	-0.06	0.39	0.02		0.07	0.20	0.04	0.05	0.08
Mothers' depression	-0.03	-1.28	1.89	0.07		1.35	1.01	-0.04	-0.32	0.40

References

Abidin, R. R. (1997). Parenting stress index: A measure of the parent–child system. In C. P. Zalaquett & R. J. Wood (Eds.), *Evaluating stress: A book of resources* (pp. 277–291). Scarecrow Education.

Achenbach, T. M. (1992). *Manual for child behavior checklist/2-3 and 1992 profile*. University of Vermont.

Achenbach, T. M., & Edelbrock, C. (1991). *Child behavior checklist (Vol. 7)*. University of Vermont Department of Psychiatry.

Achenbach, T. M., & Rescorla, L. A. (2001). *Manual for the ASEBA school-age forms & profiles*. University of Vermont, Research Center for Children, Youth, and Families.

Adams, G. (2018). *A historic boost to childcare funding means states can start to realize the potential of the Childcare and Development Block Grant*. Center for Law and Social Policy, The Urban Institute. https://bit.ly/42XdMsV.

Adamsons, K., & Johnson, S. K. (2013). An updated and expanded meta-analysis of nonresident fathering and child well-being. *Journal of Family Psychology, 27*(4), 589.

Ainsworth, M. D., & Bell, S. M. (1970). Attachment, exploration, and separation: Illustrated by the behavior of one-year-olds in a Strange Situation. *Child Development, 41*(1), 49. https://doi.org/10.2307/1127388.

Albarran, A. S., & Reich, S. M. (2014). Using baby books to increase new mothers' self-efficacy and improve toddler language development. *Infant and Child Development, 23*(4), 374–387.

Alderson, D. P., Gennetian, L. A., Dowsett, C. J., Imes, A., & Huston, A. C. (2008). Effects of employment-based programs on families by prior levels of disadvantage. *The Social Service Review, 82*(3), 361–394. https://doi.org/10.1086/592360.

Aldoney, D., & Cabrera, N. J. (2016). Raising American citizens: Socializations goals of low-income immigrant Latino mothers and fathers of young children. *Journal of Child and Family Studies, 25*(25), 3607–3618. https://doi.org/10.1007/s10826-016-0510-x.

Alm, J., & Melnik, M. I. (2005). Taxing the "family" in the individual income tax. *Public Finance and Management, 5*(1), 67–109.

Altenburger, L. E. (2022). Resident and non-resident father involvement, coparenting, and the development of children's self-regulation among families facing economic hardship. *Frontiers in Psychology, 13*, 785376.

Alwin, D. F., & Hauser, R. M. (1975). The decomposition of effects in path analysis. *American Sociological Review, 40*, 37.

Amato, P. R., & Gilbreth, J. G. (1999). Nonresident fathers and children's well-being : A meta-analysis. *Journal of Marriage and the Family*, 557–573.

Ananat, E., Glasner, B., Hamilton, C., & Parolin, Z. (2022). Effects of the expanded Child Tax Credit on employment outcomes: Evidence from real-world data from April to December 2021 (NBER Working Paper No. w29823). National Bureau of Economic Research.

Anderson, N. J., Graham, S. A., Prime, H., Jenkins, J. M., & Madigan, S. (2021). Linking quality and quantity of parental linguistic input to child language skills: A meta-analysis. *Child Development, 92*(2), 484–501.

Anderson, S., Roggman, L. A., Innocenti, M. S., & Cook, G. A. (2013). Dads' parenting interactions with children: Checklist of observations linked to outcomes (PICCOLO-D). *Infant Mental Health Journal, 34*(4), 339–351.

Anderson, S., St. George, J., & Roggman, L. A. (2019, December). Measuring the quality of early father–child rough and tumble play: Tools for practice and research. *Child & Youth Care Forum, 48*(6), 889–915.

Argys, L. M., & Peters, H. E. (2001). Interactions between unmarried fathers and their children: The role of paternity establishment and child-support policies. American Economic Review, 91(2), 125–112

Argys, L. M., & Peters, H. E. (2003). Can adequate child support be legislated? Responses to guidelines and enforcement. *Economic Inquiry, 41*(3), 463–479.

Argys, L. M., Peters, H. E., Brooks-Gunn, J., & Smith, J. R. (1998). The impact of child support on cognitive outcomes of young children. *Demography, 35*(2), 159–173.

Arsenault, K., & Stykes, J. B. (2019). Moving past dichotomies of fathering roles: A new approach. *Jou rnal of Marriage and Family, 81*(3), 747–759. https://doi.org/10.1111/jomf.12548.

Aughinbaugh, A., & Gittleman, M. (2003). Does money matter? A comparison of the association of income on child development in the United States and Great Britain. *The Journal of Human Resources, 38*(2), 416–440. https://doi.org/10.2307/1558750.

Avellar, S., Covington, R., Moore, Q., Patnaik, A., & Wu, A. (2018). Parents and children together: Effects of four responsible fatherhood programs for low-income fathers. OPRE Report Number 2018-50. Office of Planning, Research, and Evaluation, Administration for Children and Families, US Department of Health and Human Services.

Avellar, S., Dion, R. M., Clarkwest, A., Zaveri, H., Asheer, S., Borradaile, K., Angus, M. H., Novak, T., Redline, J., & Zukiewicz, M. (2011). Catalog of research: Programs for low-income fathers. OPRE Report # 2011–20. Office of Planning, Research and Evaluation, Administration for Children and Families, US Department of Health and Human Services.

Baker, C. E. (2014a). Mexican mothers' English proficiency and children's school readiness: Mediation through home literacy involvement. *Early Education and Development, 25*(3), 338–355. https://doi.org/10.1080/10409289.2013.807721.

Baker, C. E. (2014b). Parenting and cultural socialization as predictors of African American children's science and social studies achievement. *Journal of African American Studies, 18*, 92–107. https://doi.org/10.1007/s12111-013-9257-2.

Baker, C. E. (2017). Father-son relationships in ethnically diverse families: Links to boys' cognitive and social emotional development in preschool. *Journal of Child and Family Studies, 26*(8), 2335–2345. https://doi.org/10.1007/s10826-017-0743-3.

Baker, C. E. (2018). When daddy comes to school: Father–school involvement and children's academic and social–emotional skills. *Early Child Development and Care, 188*(2), 208–219.

Baker, C. E., Vernon-Feagans, L., & The Family Life Project Investigators. (2015). Fathers' language input during shared book activities: Links to children's kindergarten achievement. *Journal of Applied Developmental Psychology, 36*, 53–59. https://doi.org/10.1016/j.appdev.2014.11.009.

Baker, J. A. (2006). Contributions of teacher-child relationships to positive school adjustment during elementary school. *Journal of School Psychology, 44*(3), 211–229.

Bane, M. J., & Ellwood, D. T. (1996). *Welfare realities: From rhetoric to reform.* Harvard University Press.

Becker, G. S. (1991). *A treatise on the family.* Harvard University Press.

Becker, G., & Tomes, N. (1986). Human capital and the rise and fall of families. *Journal of Labor Economics, 4*(3), 1–39.

Belsky, J. (1984). The determinants of parenting: A process model. *Child Development, 55*(1), 83–96. https://doi.org/10.2307/1129836.

Bergen, D. (2021). The role of toys in promoting children's development. In B. Bergen (Ed.), *The handbook of developmentally appropriate toys* (pp. 1–10). Bloomsbury.

Berger, L. M., Cancian, M., Guarin, A., Hodges, L., & Meyer, D. R. (2021). Barriers to formal child support payment. *Social Service Review, 95*(2), 312–357.

Berger, L. M., & McLanahan, S. S. (2015). Income, relationship quality, and parenting: Associations with child development in two-parent families. *Journal of Marriage and Family*, 77(4), 996–1015.

Berger, L. M., Paxson, C., & Waldfogel, J. (2009). Income and child development. *Children and Youth Services Review*, 31(9), 978–989. https://doi.org/10.1016/j.childyouth.2009.04.013.

Bernier, A., Carlson, S. M., & Whipple, N. (2010). From external regulation to self-regulation: Early parenting precursors of young children's executive functioning. *Child Development*, 81(1), 326–339.

Bingham, G. E., Kwon, K. A., & Jeon, H. J. (2013). Examining relations among mothers', fathers', and children's language use in a dyadic and triadic context. *Early Child Development and Care*, 183(3–4), 394–414.

Black, M. M., Dubowitz, H., & Starr, R. H., Jr. (1999). African American fathers in low income, urban families: Development, behavior, and home environment of their three-year-old children. *Child Development*, 70(4), 967–978. https://doi.org/10.1111/1467-8624.00070.

Blair, C., Granger, D. A., Willoughby, M., Mills-Koonce, R., Cox, M., Greenberg, M. T., Kivlighan, K. T., Fortunato, C. K., & FLP Investigators. (2011). Salivary cortisol mediates effects of poverty and parenting on executive functions in early childhood. *Child Development*, 82(6), 1970–1984.

Blankenhorn, D. (1996). *Fatherless America: Confronting our most urgent social problems*. Perennial.

Bocknek, E. L., Dayton, C., Raveau, H. A., Richardson, P., Brophy-Herb, H. E., & Fitzgerald, H. E. (2017). Routine active playtime with fathers is associated with self-regulation in early childhood. *Merrill-Palmer Quarterly*, 63(1), 105–134. https://doi.org/10.13110/merrpalmquar1982.63.1.0105.

Bornstein, M. H. (2012). Cultural approaches to parenting. *Parenting, Science and Practice*, 12(2–3), 212–221. https://doi.org/10.1080/15295192.2012.683359.

Bornstein, M. H., & Cote, L. R. (2004). Mothers' parenting cognitions in cultures of origin, acculturating cultures, and cultures of destination. *Child Development*, 75(1), 221–235. https://doi.org/10.1111/j.1467-8624.2004.00665.x.

Bornstein, M. H., Hahn, C.-S., & Wolke, D. (2013). Systems and cascades in cognitive development and academic achievement. *Child Development*, 84(1), 154–162. https://doi.org/10.1111/j.1467-8624.2012.01849.x.

Bowlby, J. (1969). *Attachment and loss* (1st ed.). Hogarth Press and the Institute of Psycho-Analysis.

Bradley, R. H., Whiteside, L., Mundfrom, D. J., Casey, P. H., Caldwell, B. M., & Barrett, K. (1994). Impact of the Infant Health and Development Program (IHDP) on the home environments of infants born prematurely and with low birthweight. *Journal of Educational Psychology, 86*(4), 531–541. https://doi.org/10.1037/0022-0663.86.4.531.

Bradley, R. H., Casey, P. H., & Caldwell, B. M. (1997). Quality of the home environment. In R. T. Gross, D. Spiker, & C. W. Haynes (Eds.), *Helping low birth weight, premature babies: The Infant Health and Development Study* (pp. 242–256). Stanford University Press.

Braswell, K. (2025, January) What the child support rule change means for fathers and the work of fathers incorporated. https://dadspadblog.com/2024/12/13/child-support-rule-change-allows-employment-training-funding/

Brody, G. H., Yu, T., Nusslock, R, Barton, A. W., Miller, G. E., Chen, E., Holmes, C., McCormick, M., & Sweet, L. H. (2019). The protective effects of supportive parenting on the relationship between adolescent poverty and resting-state functional brain connectivity during adulthood. *Psychological Science, 30*(7), 1040–1049. https://doi.org/10.1177/0956797619847989.

Broidy, L. M., Tremblay, R. E., Brame, B., Fergusson, D., Horwood, J. L., Laird, R., Moffit, T. E., Nagin, D. S., Bates, J. E., Dodge, K. A., Loeber, R., Lynam, D. R., Pettit, G. S., & Vitaro, F. (2003). Developmental trajectories of childhood disruptive behaviors and adolescent delinquency: A six-site, cross-national study. *Developmental Psychology, 39*(2), 222–245.

Bronfenbrenner, U. (1979). *The ecology of human development: Experiments by nature and design.* Harvard University Press.

Bronfenbrenner, U., & Morris, P. A. (2006). The bioecological model of human development. In R. M. Lerner & W. Damon (Eds.). *Handbook of child psychology: Theoretical models of human development* (pp. 793–828). John Wiley & Sons, Inc.

Bronte-Tinkew, J., Carrano, J., Horowitz, A., & Kinukawa, A. (2008). Involvement among resident fathers and links to infant cognitive outcomes. *Journal of Family Issues, 29*(9), 1211–1244. https://doi.org/10.1177/0192513X08318145.

Brooks-Gunn, J., & Markman, L. B. (2005). The contribution of parenting to ethnic and racial gaps in school readiness. *The Future of Children, 15*(1), 139–168. www.eric.ed.gov/PDFS/EJ795847.pdf.

Brown, S. L., Manning, W. D., & Payne, K. K. (2017). Relationship quality among cohabiting versus married couples. *Journal of Family Issues, 38*(12), 1730–1753.

Brown, S. L., Manning, W. D., & Stykes, J. B. (2015). Family structure and child well-being: Integrating family complexity. *Journal of Marriage and the Family, 77*(1), 177–190. https://doi.org/10.1111/jomf.12145.

Brown, S. L. (2017). *Families in America* (1st ed). University of California Press.

Browne, M. W., & Cudeck, R. (1993). Alternative ways of assessing model fit. In K. A. Bollen and J. S. Long (Eds.), *Testing Structural Equation Models* (pp. 136–162). Sage.

Brustin, S., & Martin, L. (2015). Bridging the justice gap in family law: Repurposing federal IV-D funding to expand community-based legal and social services for parents. *Hastings Law Journal, 67*(5), 1265–1298.

Burbach, A. D., Fox, R. A., & Nicholson, B. C. (2004). Challenging behaviors in young children: The father's role. *The Journal of Genetic Psychology: Research and Theory on Human Development, 165*(2), 169–183. https://doi.org/10.3200/GNTP.165.2.169-189.

Bureau, J. F., Martin, J., Yurkowski, K., Schmiedel, S., Quan, J., Moss, E., Deneault, A. A., & Pallanca, D. (2017). Correlates of child–father and child–mother attachment in the preschool years. *Attachment & Human Development, 19*(2), 130–150.

Bzostek, S. H. and Berger, L. M., (2017). Family structure experiences and child socioemotional development during the first nine years of life: Examining heterogeneity by family structure at birth. *Demography, 54*(2), 513–540.

Cabrera, N., Brooks-Gunn, J., Moore, K., West, J., Boller, K., & Tamis-LeMonda, C. S. (2002). Bridging research and policy: Including fathers of young children in national studies. In C. S. Tamis-LeMonda & N. Cabrera (Eds.), *Handbook of father involvement: Multidisciplinary perspectives* (pp. 489–523). Erlbaum.

Cabrera, N. J., Fagan, J., Wight, V., & Schadler, C. (2011). Influence of mother, father, and child risk on parenting and children's cognitive and social behaviors. *Child Development, 82*(6), 1985–2005. https://doi.org/10.1111/j.1467-8624.2011.01667.x.

Cabrera, N. J., Fitzgerald, H. E., Bradley, R. H., & Roggman, L. (2014). The ecology of father-child relationships: An expanded model. *Journal of Family Theory & Review, 6*(4), 336–354.

Cabrera, N. J., Hennigar, A., Alonso, A., McDorman, S. A., & Reich, S. M. (2021). The protective effects of maternal and paternal factors on children's social development. *Adversity and Resilience Science, 2*, 85–98. https://doi.org/10.1007/s42844-021-00041-x.

Cabrera, N. J., Jeong Moon, U., Fagan, J., West, J., & Aldoney, D. (2020). Cognitive stimulation at home and in child care and children's preacademic skills in two-parent families. *Child Development, 91*(5), 1709–1717. https://doi.org/10.1111/cdev.13380.

Cabrera, N. J., Karberg, E., Malin, J. L., & Aldoney, D. (2017). The magic of play: Low-income mothers' and fathers' playfulness and children's emotion regulation and vocabulary skills. *Infant Mental Health Journal, 38*(6), 757–771. https://doi.org/10.1002/imhj.21682.

Cabrera, N. J., Ryan, R. M., Mitchell, S. J., Shannon, J. D., & Tamis-Lemonda, C. S. (2008). Low-income, nonresident father involvement with their toddlers: Variation by fathers' race and ethnicity. *Journal of Family Psychology, 22*(4), 643–647. https://doi.org/10.1037/0893-3200.22.3.643.

Cabrera, N. J., Shannon, J. F., & Tamis-LeMonda, C. (2007). Fathers' association on their children's cognitive and emotional development: From toddlers to pre-K. *Applied Development Science, 11*(4), 208–213. https://doi.org/10.1080/10888690701762100.

Cabrera, N. J., Shannon, J. D., West, J., & Brooks-Gunn, J. (2006). Parental interactions with Latino infants: Variation by country of origin and English proficiency. *Child Development, 77*(5), 1190–1207. https://doi.org/10.1111/j.1467-8624.2006.00928.x.

Cabrera, N. J., & Tamis-LeMonda, C. S. (Eds.). (2014). *Handbook of father involvement: Multidisciplinary perspectives* (2nd ed.). Routledge. https://doi.org/10.4324/9780203101414.

Cabrera, N. J., Tamis-LeMonda, C. S., Bradley, R. H., Hofferth, S., & Lamb, M. E. (2000). Fatherhood in the twenty-first century. *Child Development, 70*(1), 127–136. https://doi.org/10.1111/1467-8624.00126.

Cabrera, N. J., Volling, B. L., & Barr, R. (2018). Fathers are parents, too! Widening the lens on parenting for children's development. *Child Development Perspectives, 12*(3), 152–157. https://doi.org/10.1111/cdep.12275.

Calderon, R., & Low, S. (1998). Early social-emotional, language, and academic development in children with hearing loss: Families with and without fathers. *American Annals of the Deaf, 143*(3), 225–234. https://doi.org/10.1353/aad.2012.0115.

Cancian, M., Meyer, D. R., & Han, E. (2011). Child support: Responsible fatherhood and the quid pro quo. *The Annals of the American Academy of Political and Social Science, 635*(1), 140–162.

Cancian, M., Meyer, D. R., & Wood, R. G. (2022). Do carrots work better than sticks? Results from the national child support noncustodial parent employment demonstration. *Journal of Policy Analysis and Management, 41*(2), 552–578.

Casas, M., Daly, H., Lou, C., Maag, E., Hahn, H., & Steuerle, C. E. (2022). *Data appendix to Kids' Share 2022: Report on federal expenditures on children through 2021 and future projections*. Urban Institute.

Castillo, J. T., & Sarver, C.M. (2012). Nonresident fathers' social networks: The relationship between social support and father involvement. *Personal Relationships, 19*(4), 759–774.

Chacko, A., Fabiano, G. A., Doctoroff, G. L., & Fortson, B. (2018). Engaging fathers in effective parenting for preschool children using shared book reading: A randomized controlled trial. *Journal of Clinical Child and Adolescent Psychology, 47*(1), 79–93. https://doi.org/10.1080/15374416.2016.1266648.

Chang, M., Park, B., Singh, K., & Sung, Y. Y. (2009). Parental involvement, parenting behaviors, and children's cognitive development in low-income and minority families. *Journal of Research in Childhood Education, 23*(3), 309–324.

Cheadle, J. E., Amato, P. R., & King, V. (2010). Patterns of nonresident father contact. *Demography, 47*(1), 205–225.

Chetty, R., & Hendren, N. (2018). The impacts of neighborhoods on intergenerational mobility I: Childhood exposure effects. *The Quarterly Journal of Economics, 133*(3), 1107–1162.

Cheung, R. Y., Boise, C., Cummings, E. M., & Davies, P. T. (2018). Mothers' and fathers' roles in child adjustment: Parenting practices and mothers' emotion socialization as predictors. *Journal of Child and Family Studies, 27*, 4033–4043.

Choi, J. K., Palmer, R. J., & Pyun, H. S. (2014). Three measures of non-resident fathers' involvement, maternal parenting and child development in low-income single-mother families. *Child & Family Social Work, 19*(3), 282–291.

Choi, J. K., & Pyun, H. S. (2014). Nonresident fathers' financial support, informal instrumental support, mothers' parenting, and child development in single-mother families with low income. *Journal of Family Issues, 35*(4), 526–546.

Coleman-Jensen, A., Nord, M., & Singh, A. (2013). Household Food Security in the United States in 2012, ERR-155, U.S. Department of Agriculture, Economic Research Service, September 2013

Collins, L. M., Schafer, J. L., & Kam, C.-M. (2001). A comparison of restrictive strategies in modern missing data procedures. *Psychological Methods, 6*(4), 330–351.

Coltrane, S., & Hickman, N. (1992). The rhetoric of rights and needs: Moral discourse in the reform of child custody and child support laws. *Social Problems, 39*(4), 400–420.

Conger, R. D., & Donnellan, M. B. (2007). An interactionist perspective on the socioeconomic context of human development. *Annual Review of Psychology, 58*, 175–199. https://doi.org/10.1146/annurev.psych.58.110405.085551.

Conger, R. D., Ge, X., Elder, G. H., Lorenz, F. O., & Simons, R. L. (1994). Economic stress, coercive family process, and developmental problems of adolescents. *Child Development, 65*(2), 541–561. https://doi.org/10.2307/1131401.

Conger, R. D., Wallace, L. E., Sun, Y., Simons, R. L., McLoyd, V. C., & Brody, G. H. (2002). Economic pressure in African American families: A replication and extension of the family stress model. *Developmental Psychology, 38*(2), 179–193. https://doi.org/10.1037/0012-1649.38.2.179.

Conica, M., Kelly, L., Nixon, E. and Quigley, J. (2020). Fathers' but not mothers' repetition of children's utterances at age two is associated with child vocabulary at age four. *Journal of Experimental Child Psychology*, 191, 104738, https://doi.org/10.1016/j.jecp.2019.104738.

Conica, M., Kelly, L., Nixon, E. and Quigley, J. (2023). Father and toddler language during shared book reading with text-based and wordless picture books. *Reading Research Quarterly*. https://doi.org/10.1002/rrq.501.

Cooper, K., & Stewart, K. (2021). Does household income affect children's outcomes? A systematic review of the evidence. *Child Indicators Research*, 14(3), 981–1005.

Corcoran, M. E., & Chaudry, A. (1997). The dynamics of childhood poverty. *The Future of Children*, 7(2), 40–54. https://doi.org/10.2307/1602386.

Cowan, C. P. & Cowan, P.A. (2019). Changing families: A preventive intervention perspective. *Family Relations*, 68, 298–312. https://doi.org/10.1111/fare.12359

Cowan, P. A., Cowan, C. P., Pruett, M. K., Pruett, K., & Gillette, P. (2014), Evaluating a couples group to enhance father involvement in low-income families using a benchmark comparison. *Family Relations*, 63, 356–370. https://doi.org/10.1111/fare.12072.

Cowan, P. A., Cowan, C. P., Pruett, M. K., Pruett, K., & Wong, J. J. (2009). Promoting fathers' engagement with children: Preventive interventions for low-income families. *Journal of Marriage and Family*, 71, 663–679. https://doi.org/10.1111/j.1741-3737.2009.00625.x.

Craig, A. G., Thompson, J. M. D., Slykerman, R., Wall, C., Murphy, R., Mitchell, E. A., & Waldie, K. E. (2021). The father I knew: Early paternal engagement moderates the long-term relationship between paternal accessibility and childhood behavioral difficulties. *Journal of Family Issues*, 42(10), 2418–2437. https://doi.org/10.1177/0192513X20980128.

Crandall-Hollick, M. L. (2021). The child tax credit: Legislative history. Congressional Research Service Report, 45124.

Crosnoe, R., & Cooper, C. E. (2010). Economically disadvantaged children's transitions into elementary school: Linking family processes, school contexts, and educational policy. *American Education Research Journal*, 47(2), 258–291. https://doi.org/10.3102/000283120935156.

Culp, R. E., Schadle, S., Robinson, L., & Culp, A. M. (2000). Relationships among parental involvement and young children's perceived self-competence and behavioral problems. *Journal of Child and Family Studies*, 9(1), 27–38. https://doi.org/10.1023/A:1009455514587.

Cunha, F., & Heckman, J. (2007). The technology of skill formation. *American Economic Review*, 97(2), 31–47. https://doi.org/10.1257/aer.97.2.31.

Danziger, S. K., & Radin, N. (1990). Absent does not equal uninvolved: Predictors of fathering in teen mother families. *Journal of Marriage and the Family, 52*(3), 636–642.

Davis-Kean, P. (2005). The association of parent education and family income on child achievement: The indirect role of parental expectations and the home environment. *Journal of Family Psychology, 19*(2), 294–304.

Davis-Kean, P., & Sexton, H. R. (2009). Race differences in parental associations on child achievement: Multiple pathways to success. *Merrill-Palmer Quarterly, 55*(3), 285–318.

Davis-Kean, P. E., Tang, S., & Waters, N. E. (2019). Parent education attainment and parenting. In M. H. Bornstein (Ed.), *Handbook of parenting: Vol. 2. Biology and ecology of parenting* (3rd ed.) (pp. 400–420). Routledge. https://doi.org/10.4324/9780429401459-12.

Deneault, A., Cabrera, N., Ghosh, R. A., Tölle, A.-S., Seethaler, J., Majdandžić, M., & Reich, S. M. (2022). Challenging parenting behavior in ethnically diverse two-parent families in the United States: Association with infants' social competence and behavior problems. *Early Childhood Research Quarterly, 58*, 115–124. https://doi.org/10.1016/j.ecresq.2021.08.006.

Diener, M. L., Mangelsdorf, S. C., McHale, J. L., & Frosch, C. A. (2002). Infants' behavioral strategies for emotion regulation with fathers and mothers: Associations with emotional expressions and attachment quality. *Infancy: The Official Journal of the International Society on Infant Studies, 3*(2), 153–174. https://doi.org/10.1207/S15327078IN0302_3.

Diniz, E., Brandao, T., & Verissimo, M. (2023). Father involvement during early childhood: A systematic review of qualitative studies. *Family Relations, 72*(5), 2710–2730.

Dixon, W. (2002). *Twenty studies that revolutionized child psychology* (1st ed.). Prentice Hall.

Doolittle, F. C., & Lynn, S. (1998). *Working with low-income cases: Lessons for the child support enforcement system from Parents' Fair Share*. Manpower Demonstration Research Corporation.

Dowsett, C. J., Huston, A. C., Imes, A. E., & Gennetian, L. (2008). Structural and process features in three types of child care for children from high and low income families. *Early Childhood Research Quarterly, 23*(1), 69–93.

Dumont, C., & Paquette, D. (2013). What about the child's tie to the father? A new insight into fathering, father–child attachment, children's socio-emotional development and the activation relationship theory. *Early Child Development and Care, 183*(3–4), 430–446. https://doi.org/10.1080/03004430.2012.711592.

Duncan, G. J., & Brooks-Gunn, J. (Eds.). (1997). *Consequences of growing up poor*. Russell Sage Foundation.

Duncan, G. J., Gennetian, L. A., & Morris, P. (2007). Effects of welfare and antipoverty programs on participants' children. *Focus, 25*(2), 3–12.

Duncan, G. J., Gennetian, L. A., & Morris, P. (2009). Parental pathways to self-sufficiency and the well-being of younger children. In J. K. Scholz & C. Heinrich (Eds.), *Making the work-based safety net work better: Forward looking policies to help low income families* (pp. 117–148). Russell Sage Foundation Press.

Duncan, G., Magnuson, K., Murnane, R., & Votruba-Drzal, E. (2019). Income inequality and the well-being of American families. *Family Relations, 68*(3), 313–325.

Duncan, G. J., Morris, P. A., & Rodrigues, C. (2011). Does money really matter? Estimating associations of family income on young children's achievement with data from random-assignment experiments. *Developmental Psychology, 47*(5), 1263–1279. https://doi.org/10.1037/a0023875.

Duncan, G.J., Ziol-Guest, K.M., & Kalil, A. (2010). Early-childhood poverty and adult attainment, behavior, and health. *Child Development, 81*(1), 292–311. https://doi.org/10.1111/j.1467-8624.2009.01396.x.

Dunn, L. M., & Dunn, L. M. (1981). *Peabody Picture Vocabulary Test-Revised*. American Guidance Service,

Duursma, E. (2014). The effects of fathers' and mothers' reading to their children on language outcomes of children participating in early Head Start in the United States. *Fathering: A Journal of Theory, Research, and Practice about Men as Fathers, 12*(3), 283–302.

Duursma, E. (2016). Who does the reading, who the talking? Low-income fathers and mothers in the US interacting with their young children around a picture book. *First Language, 36*(5), 465–484. https://doi.org/10.1177/0142723716648849

Duursma, E., Pan, B. A., & Raikes, H. (2008). Predictors and outcomes of low-income fathers' reading with their toddlers. *Early Childhood Research Quarterly, 23*(3), 351–365. https://doi.org/10.1016/j.ecresq.2008.06.001.

Eissa, N., & Hoynes, H. W. (2004). Taxes and the labor market participation of married couples: The earned income tax credit. *Journal of Public Economics, 88* (9–10), 1931–1958.

Elam, L. H. W. A. W. (1985). The father and the law. *The American Behavioral Scientist (pre-1986), 29*(1), 78.

Ellerbe, C. Z., Jones, J. B., & Carlson, M. J. (2018). Race/ethnic differences in nonresident fathers' involvement after a nonmarital birth. *Social Science Quarterly, 99*(3), 1158–1182.

Englund, M. M., Luckner, A. E., Whaley, G. J., & Egeland, B. (2004). Children's achievement in early elementary school: Longitudinal effects of parental involvement, expectations, and quality of assistance. *Journal of Educational Psychology, 96*(4), 723.

Fagan J. (1996). A preliminary study of low-income African American fathers' play interactions with their preschool-age children. *Journal of Black Psychology, 22*(1), 7–19.

Fagan, J., & Iglesias, A. (1999). Father involvement program effects on fathers, father figures, and their Head Start children: A quasi-experimental study. *Early Childhood Research Quarterly, 14*(2), 243–269.

Fagan, J., & Iglesias, A. (2000). The relationship between fathers' and children's communication skills and children's behavior problems: A study of Head Start children. *Early Education and Development, 11*(3), 307–320. https://doi.org/10.1207/s15566935eed1103_5.

Fagan, J., Iglesias, A., & Kaufman, R. (2015). Associations among Head Start fathers' involvement with their preschoolers and child language skills. *Early Child Development and Care, 186*(8), 1342–1356. https://doi.org/10.1080/03004430.2015.1094654.

Fagan, J., & Lee, Y. (2012). Effects of fathers' and mothers' cognitive stimulation and household income on toddlers' cognition: Variations by family structure and child risk. *Fathering: A Journal of Theory, Research & Practice about Men as Fathers, 10*(2), 140–158.

Fagan, J., Wildfeuer, R., & Iglesias, A. (2022). Low-income mothers' and fathers' cognitive stimulation during early childhood and child vocabulary at age 9. *Journal of Child and Family Studies, 31*(2), 377–391.

Farver, J. A. M., Xu, Y., Eppe, S., & Lonigan, C. J. (2006). Home environments and young Latino children's school readiness. *Early Childhood Research Quarterly, 21*(2), 196–212. https://doi.org/10.1016/j.ecresq.2006.04.008.

Federal Interagency Forum on Child and Family Statistics. (2022). *America's Children: Key National Indicators of Well-Being, 2021.* US Government Printing Office. www.childstats.gov/pdf/ac2022/ac_22.pdf.

Ferjan Ramírez, N., Hippe, D. S., Correa, L., Andert, J., & Baralt, M. (2022). Habla conmigo, daddy! Fathers' language input in North American bilingual Latinx families. *Infancy, 27,* 301–323. https://doi.org/10.1111/infa.12450.

Ferjan Ramírez, N., Lytle, R. S., & Kuhl, P. (2020). Parent coaching increases conversational turns and advances infant language development. *PNAS, 177*(7), 3484–3491. https://doi.org/10.1073/pnas.1921653117.

Ferreira, T., Cadima, J., Matias, M., Vieira, J. M., Leal, T., & Matos, P. M. (2016). Preschool children's prosocial behavior: The role of mother–child, father–child and teacher–child relationships. *Journal of Child and Family Studies, 25*, 1829–1839.

Feugé, É. A., Cyr, C., Cossette, L., & Julien, D. (2018). Adoptive gay fathers' sensitivity and child attachment and behavior problems. *Attachment & Human Development, 22*(3), 247–268.

Finney, S. J., & DiStefano, C. (2006). Non-normal and categorical data in structural equation modeling. *Structural Equation Modeling: A Second Course, 10*(6), 269–314.

Finney, S. J., & DiStefano, C. (2013). Non-normal and categorical data in structural equation modeling. In G. R. Hancock, & R. O. Mueller (Eds.), *Structural equation modeling: a second course* (2nd ed., pp. 439–492). Information Age Publishing.

Flanders, J. L., Simard, M., Paquette, D., Parent, S., Vitaro, F., Pihl, R. O., & Séguin, J. R. (2010). Rough-and-tumble play and the development of physical aggression and emotion regulation: A five-year follow-up study. *Journal of Family Violence, 25*, 357–367.

Fletcher, R., St. George, J., & Freeman, E. (2013). Rough and tumble play quality: Theoretical foundations for a new measure of father–child interaction. *Early Child Development and Care, 183*(6), 746–759. https://doi.org/10.1080/03004430.2012.723439

Flippin, M., & Watson, L. R. (2015). Fathers' and mothers' verbal responsiveness and the language skills of young children with autism spectrum disorder. *American Journal of Speech-Language Pathology, 24*(3), 400–410. https://doi.org/10.1044/2015_AJSLP-13-0138.

Forget-Dubois, N., Dionne, G., Lemelin, J.-P., Pérusse, D., Tremblay, R. E., & Boivin, M. (2009). Early child language mediates the relation between home environment and school readiness. *Child Development, 80*(3), 736–749. https://doi.org/10.1111/j.1467-8624.2009.01294.x.

Foster T. D., Froyen L. C., Skibbe L. E., Bowles R. P., Decker K. B. (2016). Fathers' and mothers' home learning environments and children's early academic outcomes. *Reading and Writing, 29*, 1845–1863. https://doi.org/10.1007/s11145-016-9655-7.

Fox, S. F., Levitt, P., & Nelson, C. A. (2010). How the timing and quality of early experiences influence the development of brain architecture. *Child Development, 81*(1), 28–40. https://doi.org/10.1111/j.1467-8624.2009.01380.x.

Fraley, C. R., Roisman, G. I., & Haltigan, J. D. (2013). The legacy of early experiences in development: Formalizing alternative models of how early experiences are carried forward over time. *Developmental Psychology, 49*(1), 109–126.

Gard, A. M., McLoyd, V. C., Mitchell, C., & Hyde, L. W. (2020). Evaluation of a longitudinal family stress model in a population-based cohort. *Social Development, 29*(4), 1155–1175.

Gates, G. J. (2015). Marriage and family: LGBT individuals and same-sex couples. *The Future of Children, 25*(2), 67–87. https://doi.org/10.1353/foc.2015.0013.

Geller, A., Cooper, C. E., Garfinkel, I., Schwartz-Soicher, O., & Mincy, R. B. (2012). Beyond absenteeism: Father incarceration and child development. *Demography, 49*(1), 49–76. https://doi.org/10.1007/s13524-011-0081-9.

Gershoff, E. T. (2002). Corporal punishment by parents and associated child behaviors and experiences: A meta-analytic and theoretical review. *Psychological Bulletin, 128*(4), 539.

Gershoff, E. T., Aber, J. L., Raver, C. C., & Lennon, M. C. (2007). Income is not enough: Incorporating material hardship into models of income associations with parenting and child development. *Child Development, 78*(1), 70–95.

Gershoff, E. T., Sattler, K. M. P., & Holden, G.W. (2019). School corporal punishment and its associations with achievement and adjustment. *Journal of Applied Developmental Psychology, 63*, 1–8. https://doi.org/10.1016/j.appdev.2019.05.004.

Glasner, B., Jiménez-Solomon, O., Collyer, S. M., Garfinkel, I., & Wimer, C. T. (2022). No evidence the Child Tax Credit expansion had an effect on the well-being and mental health of parents: Study examines the effect of the Child Tax Credit expansion on the wellbeing and mental health of parents. *Health Affairs, 41*(11), 1607–1615.

Golombok, S. (2015). *Modern families: Parents and children in new family forms*. Cambridge University Press. https://doi.org/10.1017/CBO9781107295377.

Graham, J. W. (2003). Adding missing-data-relevant variables to FIML-based structural equation models. *Structural Equation Modeling, 10*(1), 80–100.

Graham, M. H. (2003). Confronting multicollinearity in ecological multiple regression. *Ecology, 84*(11), 189–220.

Grant, M., Meissel, K., & Exeter, D. (2023). Promoting temporal investigations of development in context: A systematic review of longitudinal research linking childhood circumstances and learning-related outcomes. *Educational Psychology Review, 35*(1), 19.

Guo, G., & Harris, M. K. (2000). The mechanisms mediating the effects of poverty on children's intellectual development. *Demography, 37*(4), 431–447. https://doi.org/10.1353/dem.2000.0005.

Ha, Y., Cancian, M., & Meyer, D. R. (2010). Unchanging child support orders in the face of unstable earnings. *Journal of Policy Analysis and Management, 29*(4), 799–820.

Han, W.-J., Leventhal, T., & Linver, M. R. (2004). The Home Observation for Measurement of the Environment (HOME) in middle childhood: A study of three large-scale data sets. *Parenting: Science and Practice*, 4(2–3), 189–210.

Haney, L. (2018). Incarcerated fatherhood: The entanglements of child support debt and mass imprisonment. *American Journal of Sociology*, 124(1), 1–48.

Hart, B., & Risley, T. R. (1995). *Meaningful differences in the everyday experience of young American children*. Paul H. Brookes Publishing Company.

Haveman, R., & Wolfe, B. (1994). *Succeeding generations: On the effects of investments in children*. Russell Sage Foundation.

Hawkins, A. J. (2019). *Are federally supported relationship education programs for lower-income individuals and couples working?* American Enterprise Institute. http://bit.ly/4nzAZuC.

Hawkins, A. J., Hokanson, S., Loveridge, E., Milius, E., Duncan, M., Booth, M., & Pollard, B. (2022). How effective are ACF-funded couple relationship education programs? A meta-analytic study. *Family Process*, 61(3), 970–985. https://doi.org/10.1111/famp.12739.

He, M., Cabrera, N., Renteria, J., Chen, Y., Alonso, A., McDorman, S. A., Kerlow, M. A., & Reich, S. M. (2021). Family functioning in the time of COVID-19 among economically vulnerable families: Risks and protective factors. *Frontiers in Psychology*, 12, 730447. https://doi.org/10.3389/fpsyg.2021.730447.

Hernandez, D. J. (2011). Double jeopardy: How third-grade reading skills and poverty influence high school graduation. *Annie E. Casey Foundation*. ERIC Number: ED518818, 15 pgs.

Higgs, E., Gomez-Vidal, C., & Austin, M. J. (2018). Low-income nonresident fatherhood: A literature review with implications for practice and research. *Families in Society*, 99(2), 110–120.

Hill, R. (1949). *Families under stress: Adjustment to the crises of war separation and return*. Harper.

Hodel, A. S. (2018). Rapid infant prefrontal cortex development and sensitivity to early environmental experience. *Developmental Review*, 48, 113–144

Hodges, L., & Vogel, L. K. (2021). Too much, too little, or just right? Recent changes to state child support guidelines for low-income noncustodial parents. *Journal of Policy Practice and Research*, 2(3), 146–177.

Hofferth, S. L. (2006). Residential father family type and child well-being: Investment versus selection. *Demography*, 43(1), 53–77. https://doi.org/10.1353/dem.2006.0006.

Holmes, E. K., Egginton, B. R., Hawkins, A. J., Robbins, N. L., & Shafer, K. (2020). Do responsible fatherhood programs work? A comprehensive meta-analytic study. *Family Relations, 69*(5), 967–982. https://doi.org/10.1111/fare.12435.

Hook, J. L., & Wolfe, C. M. (2012). New fathers? Residential fathers' time with children in four countries. *Journal of Family Issues, 33*(4), 415–450. https://doi.org/10.1177/0192513X11425779.

Hu, L. T., & Bentler, P. M. (1999). Cutoff criteria for fit indexes in covariance structure analysis: Conventional criteria versus new alternatives. *Structural Equation Modeling: A Multidisciplinary Journal, 6*(1), 1–55.

Huang, C. C., & Pouncy, H. (2005). Why doesn't she have a child support order?: Personal choice or objective constraint. *Family Relations, 54*(4), 547–557.

Huerta, M. C., Adema, W., Baxter, J., Han, W. J., Lausten, M., Lee, R., & Waldfogel, J. (2013). *Fathers' leave, fathers' involvement, and child development: Are they related? Evidence from four OECD countries* (No. 140). OECD Publishing.

Islamiah, N., Breinholst, S., Walczak, M. A., & Esbjørn, B. H. (2023). The role of fathers in children's emotion regulation development: A systematic review. *Infant and Child Development, 32*(2), e2397.

Jackson, A. P., Choi, J. K., & Preston, K. S. (2015). Nonresident fathers' involvement with young black children: A replication and extension of a mediational model. *Social Work Research, 39*(4), 245–254.

Jacobvitz, D., Aviles, A. I., Aquino, G. A., Tian, Z., Zhang, S., & Hazen, N. (2022). Fathers' sensitivity in infancy and externalizing problems in middle childhood: The role of coparenting. *Frontiers in Psychology, 13*, Article 805188. https://doi.org/10.3389/fpsyg.2022.805188.

Jerome, E. M., Hamre, B. K., & Pianta, R. C. (2008). Teacher-child relationships from kindergarten to sixth grade: Early childhood predictors of teacher-perceived conflict and closeness. *Social Development, 18*(4), 915–945.

Jeynes, W. H. (2016). Meta-analysis on the roles of fathers in parenting: Are they unique? *Marriage & Family Review, 52*(7), 665–688. https://doi.org/10.1080/01494929.2016.1157121.

Jia, R., Kotila, L. E., & Schoppe-Sullivan, S. J. (2012). Transactional relations between father involvement and preschoolers' socioemotional adjustment. *Journal of Family Psychology, 26*(6), 848–857. https://doi.org/10.1037/a0030245.

Jones, J., & Mosher, W. D. (2013). Fathers' involvement with their children: United States, 2006–2010. National health statistics reports, 71. National Center for Health Statistics.

Kalil, A., & Ryan, R. (2020). Parenting practices and socioeconomic gaps in childhood outcomes. *The Future of Children, 30*(1), 29–54.

Kalil, A., Ryan, R., & Chor, E. (2014). Time investments in children across family structures. *Annals of American Academy of Political and Social Science, 654*(1), 150–168. https://doi.org/10.1177/0002716214528276.

Karberg, E., Aldoney, D., & Cabrera, N. (2017). Fatherhood in America: The context, practice, and gaps in responsible fatherhood programs. In C. Mazza (Ed.), *Fatherhood in America: Social work perspectives on a changing society* (pp. 302–352). Charles C. Thomas Publisher.

Karberg, E., Cabrera, N., Malin, J., & Kuhns, C. (2019). Chapter VI: Longitudinal contributions of maternal and paternal intrusive behaviors to children's sociability and sustained attention at prekindergarten. *Monographs of the Society for Research in Child Development, 84*(1), 79.

Karney, B. R., Bradbury, T. N., & Lavner, J. A. (2018). Supporting healthy relationships in low-income couples: Lessons learned and policy implications. *Policy Insights from the Behavioral and Brain Sciences, 5*(1), 33–39. https://doi.org/10.1177/2372732217747890.

Karpman, M., Maag, E., Kenney, G.M., & Wissoker, D.A. (2021). *Who has received advance child tax credit payments, and how were the payments used?* Urban Institute. http://bit.ly/44w4PHt.

Kelly, J. B. (1994). The determination of child custody. *The Future of Children*, 121–142.

Kelley, M. L., Smith, T. S., Green, A. P., Berndt, A. E., & Rogers, M. C. (1998). Importance of fathers' parenting to African-American toddler's social and cognitive development. *Infant Behavior & Development, 21*(4), 733–744. https://doi.org/10.1016/S0163-6383(98)90041-8.

Kenny, D. A., & West, T. V. (2008). Zero acquaintance: Definitions, statistical model, findings, and process. In N. Ambady, & J. Skowronski (Eds.), *First Impressions* (pp. 129–146). Guilford Press.

Kessler, R. C., Andrews, G., Mroczek, D., Ustun, B., & Wittchen, H.-U. (2006). The World Health Organization Composite International Diagnostic Interview Short-Form (CIDI-SF). *International Journal of Methods in Psychiatric Research, 7*(4), 34–59.

King, S. M., Iacono, W. G., & McGue, M. (2004). Childhood externalizing and internalizing psychopathology in the prediction of early substance use. *Addiction, 99*(12), 1548–1559.

King, V. (2006). The antecedents and consequences of adolescents' relationships with stepfathers and nonresident fathers. *Journal of Marriage and Family, 68*(4), 910–928.

King, V., & Sobolewski, J. M. (2006). Nonresident fathers' contributions to adolescent well-being. Journal of Marriage and Family, *68*(3), 537–557.

Kline, R. B. (2011). *Principles and practice of structural equation modeling* (3rd ed.). The Guilford Press.

Knox, V. W. (1996). The effects of child support payments on developmental outcomes for elementary school-age children. *Journal of Human Resources, 31*(34), 816–840.

Kolak, A. M., & Dean, C. H. (2022). Fathers' stimulation of toddlers' cognitive development contributes to children's executive function skills at five years of age. *Early Child Development and Care, 193*(4), 519–530. https://doi.org/10.1080/03004430.2022.2110086.

Kreider, R. M., & Ellis, R. (2011). Living Arrangements of Children: 2009. *Current Population Reports*, 70–126. US Department of Commerce, Economics and Statistics Administration, US Census Bureau.

Krugman, P. & Wells, R., (2021). *Economics* (6th ed.). Worth Publishers.

Kwon, K.-A., Han, S., Jeon, H.-J., & Bingham, G. E. (2013). Mothers' and fathers' parenting challenges, strategies, and resources in toddlerhood. *Early Child Development and Care, 183*(3–4), 415–429. https://doi.org/10.1080/03004430.2012.711591.

Lamb, M. E. (1975). Fathers: Forgotten contributors to child development. *Human Development, 18*(4), 245–266. https://doi.org/10.1159/000271493.

Lamb, M. E. (Ed.). (2010). *The role of the father in child development* (5th ed.). John Wiley & Sons.

Lamb, M., Pleck, J., Charnov, E., & Levine, J. (1985). Paternal behavior in humans. *Integrative and Comparative Biology, 25*(3), 883–894. https://doi.org/10.1093/icb/25.3.883.

Landers, P. A. (2021). *Demographic and socioeconomic characteristics of nonresident parents* (R46942). Congressional Research Service. www.congress.gov/crs-product/R46942.

Landry, S. H., Smith, K. E., & Swank, P. R. (2006). Responsive parenting: Establishing early foundations for social, communication, and independent problem-solving skills. *Developmental Psychology, 42*(4), 627.

Lang, S. N., Schoppe-Sullivan, S. J., Kotila, L. E., Feng, X., Kamp Dush, C. M., & Johnson, S. C. (2014). Relations between fathers' and mothers' infant engagement patterns in dual-earner families and toddler competence. *Journal of Family Issues, 35*(8), 1107–1127.

Lankinen, V., Lähteenmäki, M., Kaljonen, A., & Korpilahti, P. (2020). Father–child activities and paternal attitudes in early child language development: The STEPS study. *Early Child Development and Care, 190*(13), 2078–2092. https://doi.org/10.1080/03004430.2018.1557160.

Lee, J.-K., & Schoppe-Sullivan, S. J. (2017). Resident fathers' positive engagement, family poverty, and change in child behavior problems. *Family Relations*, *66*(4), 484–496. https://doi.org/10.1111/fare.12283.

Lee, S. J., Kim, J., Taylor, C. A., & Perron, B. E. (2011). Profiles of disciplinary behaviors among biological fathers. *Child Maltreatment*, *16*(1), 51–62. https://doi.org/10.1177/1077559510385841.

Leech, K. A., Salo, V. C., Rowe, M. L., & Cabrera, N. J. (2013). Father input and child vocabulary development: The importance of wh questions and clarification requests. *Seminars in Speech and Language*, *34*(4), 249–259. https://doi.org/10.1055/s-0033-1353445.

Lerman, R. I. (1996). The impact of the changing family structure on child poverty and income inequality. *Economica*, *63*(250), S119–S139. https://doi.org/10.2307/2554812.

Lerman, R. I. (2010). Capabilities and contributions of unwed fathers. *The Future of Children*, 63–85.

Levant, R. F., Richmond, K., Cruickshank, B., Rankin, T. J., & Rummell, C. M. (2014). Exploring the role of father involvement in the relationship between day care and children's behavior problems. *American Journal of Family Therapy*, *42*(3), 193–204. https://doi.org/10.1080/01926187.2013.814390.

Little, T. D. (2013). *Longitudinal structural equation modeling*. Guilford Press.

Liu, C., & Chung, K.K.H. (2022). Effects of fathers' and mothers' expectations and home literacy involvement on their children's cognitive–linguistic skills, vocabulary, and word reading. *Early Childhood Research Quarterly*, *60*, 1–12. https://doi.org/10.1016/j.ecresq.2021.12.009.

Liu, Y., Zhang, X., Song, Z., Yang, W. (2019). The unique role of father–child numeracy activities in number competence of very young Chinese children. *Infant and Child Development*, *28*, e2135. https://doi.org/10.1002/icd.2135.

MacCallum, R. C., Browne, M. W., & Sugawara, H. M. (1996). Power analysis and determination of sample size for covariance structure modeling. *Psychological Methods*, *1*(2), 130.

Majdandžić, M., de Vente, W., Colonnesi, C., & SBögels, S. M. (2018). Fathers' challenging parenting behavior predicts less subsequent anxiety symptoms in early childhood. *Behaviour Research and Therapy*, *109*, 18–28. https://doi.org/10.1016/j.brat.2018.07.007.

Malin, J. L., Cabrera, N. J., Karberg, E., Aldoney, D., & Rowe, M. (2014a). Low-income minority fathers' control strategies and children's regulatory skills. *Infant Mental Health Journal*, *35*(5), 462–472

Malin, J. L., Cabrera, N. J., & Rowe, M. L. (2014b). Low-income minority mothers' and fathers' reading and children's interest: Longitudinal contributions to children's receptive vocabulary skills. *Early Childhood Research Quarterly, 29* (4), 425–432. https://doi.org/10.1016/j.ecresq.2014.04.010.

Malmberg, L. E., Lewis, S., West, A., Murray, E., Sylva, K., & Stein, A. (2016). The influence of mothers' and fathers' sensitivity in the first year of life on children's cognitive outcomes at 18 and 36 months. *Child Care, Health and Development, 42*(1), 1–7. https://doi.org/10.1111/cch.12294.

Mare, R. D., & Winship, C. (1990). *Socioeconomic change and the decline of marriage for Blacks and Whites*. Center for Urban Affairs and Policy Research, Northwestern University.

Martin, A., Ryan, R. M., & Brooks-Gunn, J. (2007). The joint influence of mother and father parenting on child cognitive outcomes at age 5. *Early Childhood Research Quarterly, 22*(4), 423–439. https://doi.org/10.1016/j.ecresq.2007.07.001.

Masarik, A. S, & Conger, R. D. (2017). Stress and child development: A review of the Family Stress Model. *Current Opinion in Psychology, 13*, 85–90. https://doi.org/10.1016/j.copsyc.2016.05.008.

Masten, A. S., Roisman, G. I., Long, J. D., Burt, K. B., Obradovic, J., Riley, J. R., Boelcke-Stennes, K., & Tellegen, A. (2005). Developmental cascades: Linking academic achievement and externalizing and internalizing symptoms over 20 years. *Developmental Psychology, 41*(5), 733–746.

Masten, A. S., & Cicchetti, D. (2010). Developmental cascades. *Development and Psychopathology, 22*(3), 491–495. https://doi.org/10.1017/S0954579410000222.

Masten, A. S., Desjardins, C. D., McCormick, C. M., Kuo, S. I., & Long, J. D. (2010). The significance of childhood competence and problems for adult success in work: A developmental cascade analysis. *Development and Psychopathology, 22*(3), 679–694. https://doi.org/10.1017/S0954579410000362.

Masten, A. S., Roisman, G. I., Long, J. D., Burt, K. B., Obradovic, J., Riley, J. R., Boelcke-Stennes, K., & Tellegen, A. (2005). Developmental cascades: Linking academic achievement and externalizing and internalizing symptoms over 20 years. *Developmental Psychology, 41*(5), 733–746. https://doi.org/10.1037/0012-1649.41.5.733.

Matas, L., Arend, R. A., & Sroufe, L. A. (1978). Continuity of adaptation in the second year: The relationship between quality of attachment and later competence. *Child Development, 49*(3), 547–556.

Maurin, E. (2002). The impact of parental income on early schooling transitions: A re-examination using data over three generations. *Journal of Public Economics, 85*(3), 301–332. https://doi.org/10.1016/S0047-2727(01)00131-1.

Mayer, J. D., & Salovey, P. (1997). What is emotional intelligence? In P. Salovey & D. J. Sluyter (Eds.), *Emotional development and emotional intelligence* (pp. 3–34). Harper Collins,.

McArdle, J. J. (2009). Latent variable modeling of differences and changes with longitudinal data. *Annual Review of Psychology, 60,* 577–605.

McCabe, J., & Berman, E.P. (2016). American exceptionalism revisited: Tax relief, poverty reduction, and the politics of child tax credits. *Sociological Science, 3,* 540–567. https://doi.org/10.15195/v3.a24.

McHale, J., Waller, M. R., & Pearson, J. (2012), Coparenting interventions for fragile families: What do we know and where do we need to go next? *Family Process, 51,* 284–306. https://doi.org/10.1111/j.1545-5300.2012.01402.x.

McLanahan, S. (2004). Diverging destinies: How children are faring under the second demographic transition. *Demography, 41*(4), 607–627. https://doi.org/10.1353/dem.2004.0033.

McLanahan, S., & Beck, A. N. (2010). Parental relationships in fragile families. *The Future of children/Center for the Future of Children, the David and Lucile Packard Foundation, 20*(2), 17.

McLanahan, S., & Sawhill, I. (2015). Marriage and child wellbeing revisited: Introducing the issue. *The Future of Children, 25*(2), 3–9.

McLanahan, S., Seltzer, J. A., Hanson, T. L., & Thomson, E. (1994). Child Support Enforcement and Child Well-Being: Greater Security or Greater Conflict." In I. Garfinkel, S. McLanahan, & P. K. Robins (Eds.), *Child Support and Child Well-Being.* Urban Institute Press.

McLanahan, S., Tach, L., & Schneider, D. (2013). The causal effects of father absence. *Annual Review of Sociology, 39,* 399–427. https://doi.org/10.1146/annurev-soc-071312-145704.

McMunn, A., Martin, P., Kelly, Y., & Sacker, A. (2017). Fathers' involvement: Correlates and consequences for child socioemotional behavior in the United Kingdom. *Journal of Family Issues, 38*(8), 1109–1131. https://doi.org/10.1177/0192513X15622415.

Meaney, M. J., & Szyf, M. (2005). Environmental programming of stress responses through DNA methylation: Life at the interface between a dynamic environment and a fixed genome. *Dialogues in Clinical Neuroscience, 7*(2): 103–123.

Meece, D., & Robinson, C. M. (2014). Father–child interaction: Associations with self-control and aggression among 4.5-year-olds. *Early Child Development and Care, 184*(5), 783–794. https://doi.org/10.1080/03004430.2013.818990.

Mellgren, L. M. (1992). The significance of SIPP for child support research and policy formulation. *Journal of Economic and Social Measurement, 18*(1–4), 253–270.

Meuwissen, A. S., & Carlson, S. M. (2015). Fathers matter: The role of father parenting in preschoolers' executive function development. *Journal of Experimental Child Psychology, 140*, 1–15. https://doi.org/10.1016/j.jecp.2015.06.010.

Miller, C., & Knox, V. (2001). *The challenge of helping low-income fathers support their children: Final lessons from parents' fair share*. Manpower Development Research Corporation. http://bit.ly/44yhMRc.

Miller, D. P., & Mincy, R. B. (2012). Falling further behind? Child support arrears and fathers' labor force participation. *Social Service Review, 86*(4), 604–635.

Miller, D. P., Thomas, M. M., Waller, M. R., Nepomnyaschy, L., & Emory, A. D. (2020). Father involvement and socioeconomic disparities in child academic outcomes. *Journal of Marriage and Family, 82*(2), 515–533.

Mincy, R. B. (2001). Marriage, child poverty, and public policy. *American Experiment Quarterly, 4*(2), 68–71.

Mincy, R. B., Jethwani, M., & Klempin, S. (2014). *Failing our fathers: Confronting the crisis of economically vulnerable nonresident fathers*. Oxford University Press.

Mincy, R. B., & Pouncy, H. (2003). The marriage mystery: Marriage, assets, and the expectations of African American families. In O. Clayton, R. B. Mincy, & D. Blankenhorn (Eds.), *Black fathers in contemporary society: Strengths, weaknesses, and strategies for change* (pp. 45–70). Russell Sage Foundation.

Mincy, R. B., Pouncy, H., & Zilanawala, A. (2016). "Race, Romance and Nonresident Father Involvement Resilience: Differences by Types of Involvement." Fragile Families Working Paper No. WP 15-06-FF. Available at https://fragilefamilies.princeton.edu/sites/fragilefamilies/files/wp16-05-ff.pdf.

Mincy, R. B., & Sorensen, E. J. (1998). Deadbeats and turnips in child support reform. *Journal of Policy Analysis and Management: The Journal of the Association for Public Policy Analysis and Management, 17*(1), 44–51.

Mincy, R. B., & Um, H. (2019). Growth and change in the composition of vulnerable nonresident fatherhood. *US 2050 Research Projects*. Peter G. Peterson Foundation. http://bit.ly/4ezDKbf.

Mistry, R. S., Benner, A. D., Biesanz, J. C., Clark, S. L., & Howes, C. (2010). Family and social risk, and parental investments during the early childhood years as predictors of low-income children's school readiness outcomes. *Early Childhood Research Quarterly, 25*(4), 432–449. https://doi.org/10.1016/j.ecresq.2010.01.002.

Mostofi, L. (2004). Legitimizing the bastard: The supreme court's treatment of the illegitimate child. *Journal of Contemporary Legal Issues, 14*, 453.

Mott, F. L. (1990). When is a father really gone? Paternal–child contact in father-absent homes. *Demography, 27*(4), 499–517.

Mullins, D. F. (2011). Linkages between children's behavior and nonresident father involvement: A comparison of African American, Anglo, and Latino families. *Journal of African American Studies, 15*, 1–21.

Muthén, L. K., & Muthén, B. O. (1998–2010). *Mplus statistical analysis with latent variables: User's guide*. Muthén & Muthén.

Muthén, L. K., & Muthén, B. (2011). Multilevel modeling with latent variables using Mplus: Longitudinal analysis. http://www.statmodel.com/download/Topic%208.pdf.

Nagin, D., & Tremblay, R. E. (1999). Trajectories of boys' physical aggression, opposition, and hyperactivity on the path to physically violent and nonviolent juvenile delinquency. *Child Development, 70*(5), 1181–1196.

Nam, H., & Beyer, M. (2016). Infant mother and father attachment predict child behavior at 24 months. *Modern Psychological Studies, 22*(1), 5.

National Academies of Sciences, Engineering, and Medicine. (2016). Parenting Matters: Supporting Parents of Children Ages 0–8. The National Academies Press. https://doi.org/10.17226/21868.

Nepomnyaschy, L., Emory, A. D., Eickmeyer, K. J., Waller, M. R., & Miller, D. P. (2021). Parental debt and child well-being: What type of debt matters for child outcomes? *RSF: The Russell Sage Foundation Journal of the Social Sciences, 7*(3), 122–151. https://doi.org/10.7758/RSF.2021.7.3.06.

Nepomnyaschy, L., & Garfinkel, I. (2010). Child support enforcement and fathers' contributions to their nonmarital children. *Social Service Review, 84*(3): 341–380.

Nepomnyaschy, L., Magnuson, K. A., & Berger, L. M. (2012). Child support and young children's development. *Social Service Review, 86*(1): 3–35.

Nepomnyaschy, L., Miller, D. P., & Garfinkel, I. (2014). Nonresident fathers and the economic well-being of children. *Social Service Review, 88*(3), 386–427. https://doi.org/10.1086/677761

Nepomnyaschy, L., & Waldfogel, J. (2007). Paternity leave and fathers' involvement with their young children: Evidence from the American Ecls-B. *Community, Work, and Family, 10*(4), 427–53. https://doi.org/10.1080/13668800701575077.

Noyes, J., Vogel, L. K., & Howard, L. (2018). Final implementation findings from the child support noncustodial parent employment demonstration (CSPED) evaluation. *Institute for Research on Poverty*, University of Wisconsin–Madison.

Nurilla, A.E., Hendrawan, D., Arbiyah, N. (2017). Optimising executive function in early childhood: The role of maternal depressive symptoms and father involvement in parenting. In *Diversity in Unity: Perspectives from Psychology and Behavioral Sciences*, 141–149. https://doi.org/10.1201/9781315225302-18.

Oh, W., Kim, H. K., Park, S. J., Mastergeorge, A. M., & Roggman, L. (2022). Maternal and paternal insensitivity, adaptive engagement, and school readiness skills among economically disadvantaged children: A dynamic approach. *Early Childhood Research Quarterly, 58*, 220–230. https://doi.org/10.1016/j.ecresq.2021.09.003.

Okano, L., Jeon, L., Crandall, A., Powell, T., & Riley, A. (2020). The cascading effects of externalizing behaviors and academic achievement across developmental transitions: Implications for prevention and intervention. *Prevention Science, 21*(2), 211–221.

Owen, M. T., Caughy, M. O. B., Hurst, J. R., Amos, M., Hasanizadeh, N., & Mata-Otero, A.-M. (2013). Unique contributions of fathering to emerging self-regulation in low-income ethnic minority preschoolers. *Early Child Development and Care, 183*, 464–482. https://doi.org/10.1080/03004430.2012.711594.

Palkovitz, R. (1997). Reconstructing "involvement": Expanding conceptualizations of men's caring in contemporary families. In A. J. Hawkins & D. C. Dollahite (Eds.), *Generative fathering: Beyond deficit perspectives* (pp. 200–216). Sage Publications, Inc.

Pancsofar, N., & Vernon-Feagans, L. (2006). Mother and father language input to young children: Contributions to later language development. *Journal of Applied Developmental Psychology, 27*(6), 571–587. https://doi.org/10.1016/j.appdev.2006.08.003.

Pancsofar, N., Vernon-Feagans, L., & The Family Life Project Investigators. (2010). Fathers' early contributions to children's language development in families from low-income rural communities. *Early Childhood Research Quarterly, 25*(4), 450–463. https://doi.org/10.1016/j.ecresq.2010.02.001.

Panter-Brick, C., Burgess, A., Eggerman, M., McAllister, F., Pruett, K., & Leckman, J. F. (2014). Practitioner review: Engaging fathers–recommendations for a game change in parenting interventions based on a systematic review of the global evidence. *Journal of Child Psychology and Psychiatry, 55*(11), 1187–1212.

Paquette, D., Carbonneau, R., Dubeau, D., Bigras, M., & Tremblay, R. E. (2003). Prevalence of father-child rough-and-tumble play and physical aggression in preschool children. *European Journal of Psychology of Education, 18*, 171–189. https://doi.org/10.1007/BF03173483.

Park, S., & Dotterer, A. M. (2018). Longitudinal associations of family stressors, fathers' warmth, and Korean children's externalizing behaviors. *Journal of Family Psychology, 32*(8), 1036–1045. https://doi.org/10.1037/fam0000486.

Parolin, Z., Ananat, E., Collyer, S. M., Curran, M., & Wimer, C. (2021). The initial effects of the expanded Child Tax Credit on material hardship (NBER Working Paper No. w29285). National Bureau of Economic Research. https://doi.org/10.3386/w29285.

Parolin, Z., Ananat, E., Collyer, S., Curran, M., & Wimer, C. (2023, May). The effects of the monthly and lump-sum Child Tax Credit payments on food and housing hardship. In *AEA Papers and Proceedings, 113*, 406–412. American Economic Association.

Pearson, J. (2015). Establishing parenting time in child support cases: New opportunities and challenges. *Family Court Review, 53*(2), 246–257. https://doi.org/10.1111/fcre.12147.

Pearson, J. (2018). *State approaches to including fathers in programs and policies dealing with children and families*. Father Research & Practice Network. http://bit.ly/4ezWyXS.

Pearson, J., & Wildfeuer, R. (2022). *Policies and programs affecting fathers: A State-by-State Report*. Center for Policy Research and Father Would Research & Practice Network. http://bit.ly/4lcI6HE.

Pearson, J., Henson, A., & Fagan, J. (2020). What nonresident mothers and fathers have to say about a mother-only coparenting intervention: A qualitative assessment of understanding Dads™. *Families in Society, 101*(2), 167–179. https://doi.org/10.1177/1044389419899601.

Piaget, J. (1978). *Behavior and Evolution* (D. Nicholson-Smith, Trans.) Random House.

Pleck, J. (1983). *Myth of Masculinity*. MIT Press.

Pleck, J. H. (2010). Paternal involvement: Revised conceptualization and theoretical linkages with child outcomes. In M. E. Lamb (Ed.), *The role of the father in child development*, 58–93. John Wiley & Sons, Inc.

Poehlmann-Tynan, J., & Turney, K. (2021). A developmental perspective on children with incarcerated parents. *Child Development Perspectives, 15*(1), 3–11.

Princeton University. (2023). *FFCWS changes name to The Future of Families and Child Wellbeing Study*. Future of Families & Child Wellbeing Study, Princeton University.

Psychogiou, L., Nath, S., Kallitsoglou, A., Dimatis, K., Parry, E., Russell, A. E., Yilmaz, M., Kuyken, W., & Moberly, N. J. (2018). Children's emotion understanding in relation to attachment to mother and father. *The British*

Journal of Developmental Psychology, 36(4), 557–572. https://doi.org/10.1111/bjdp.12239.

Puff, J., & Renk, K. (2014). Relationships among parents' economic stress, parenting, and young children's behavior problems. *Child Psychiatry & Human Development, 45,* 712–727.

Raley, R. K., Sweeney, M. M., & Wondra, D. (2015). The growing racial and ethnic divide in US marriage patterns. *The Future of Children, 25*(2), 89–109. https://doi.org/10.1353/foc.2015.0014.

Reichman, N. E., Teitler, J. O., Garfinkel, I., & McLanahan, S. S. (2001). Fragile families: Sample and design. *Children and Youth Services Review, 23*(4/5), 303–326. https://doi.org/10.1016/S0190-7409(01)00141-4.

Rescorla, L., Achenbach, T., Ivanova, M. T., Dumenci, L., Almqvist, F., ... & Verhulst, F. (2007). Behavioral and emotional problems reported by parents of children ages 6 to 16 in 31 societies. *Journal of Emotional and Behavioral Disorders, 15*(3), 130–142.

Reynolds, E., Vernon-Feagans, L., Bratsch-Hines, M., Baker, C. E., & Family Life Project Key Investigators. (2019). Mothers' and fathers' language input from 6 to 36 months in rural two-parent-families: Relations to children's kindergarten achievement. *Early Childhood Research Quarterly, 47,* 385–395. https://doi.org/10.1016/j.ecresq.2018.09.002.

Richman, E. R., & Rescorla, L. (1995). Academic orientation and warmth in mothers and fathers of preschoolers: Effects on academic skills and self-perceptions of competence. *Early Education and Development, 6*(3), 197–213. https://doi.org/10.1207/s15566935eed0603_1.

Robbins, N. L., Waller, M. R., Nepomnyaschy, L., & Miller, D. P. (2022). Child support debt and the well-being of disadvantaged fathers of color. *Journal of Marriage and Family, 84*(5), 1366–1386.

Rodriguez, E. T., & Tamis-LeMonda, C. S. (2011). Trajectories of the home learning environment across the first 5 years: Associations with children's vocabulary and literacy skills at prekindergarten. *Child Development, 82*(4), 1058–1075.

Rollè, L., Gullotta, G., Trombetta, T., Curti, L., Gerino, E., Brustia, P., & Caldarera, A. M. (2019). Father involvement and cognitive development in early and middle childhood: A systematic review. *Frontiers in Psychology, 10.* https://doi.org/10.3389/fpsyg.2019.02405.

Rosman, E. A., & Yoshikawa, H. (2001). Effects of welfare reform on children of adolescent mothers: moderation by maternal depression, father involvement, and grandmother involvement. *Women & Health, 32*(3), 253–290. https://doi.org/10.1300/J013v32n03_04.

Rowe, M. L., David, C., & Pan, B.A. (2004). A comparison of fathers' and mothers' talk to toddlers in low-income families. *Social Development, 13*(2), 278–291. https://doi.org/10.1111/j.1467-9507.2004.000267.x.

Rowe, M. L., Leech, K. A., & Cabrera, N. (2016). Going beyond input quantity: Wh-questions matter for toddlers' language and cognitive development. *Cognitive Science, 41*, 162–179. https://doi.org/10.1111/cogs.12349.

Rubin, D. B. (1976). Inference and missing data. *Biometrika, 63*(3), 581–592.

Ryan, R. M., Kalil, A., & Ziol-Guest, K. M. (2008). Longitudinal patterns of nonresident fathers' involvement: The role of resources and relations. *Journal of Marriage and Family, 70*(4), 962–977.

Salo, V. C., Rowe, M. L., Leech, K. A., & Cabrera, N. J. (2016). Low-income fathers' speech to toddlers during book reading versus toy play. *Journal of Child Language, 43*(6), 1385–1399

Salovey, P., & Sluyter, D. J. (1997). *Emotional development and emotional intelligence : educational implications* (1st ed.). Basic Books.

Sameroff, A. (Ed.). (2009). *The transactional model of development: How children and contexts shape each other*. American Psychological Association. https://doi.org/10.1037/11877-000.

Sameroff, A. J., & Chandler, M. J. (1975). Reproductive risk and the continuum of caretaker casualty. In F. D. Horowitz, E. M., Hetherington, S., Scarr-Salapatek, & G. M. Siegel (Eds.), *Review of child development research* (pp. 112–135). University of Chicago Press.

Sariscsany, L., Garfinkel, I., & Nepomnyaschy, L. (2019). Describing and understanding child support trajectories. *Social Service Review, 93*(2), 143–182.

Sawhill, I. V., & Chadwick, L. (1999). *Children in cities: Uncertain futures*. Brookings Institution, Center on Urban and Metropolitan Policy.

Sayer, L. (2015). The complexities of interpreting changing household patterns. *Council on Contemporary Families, 7*.

Sayer, L., Bianchi, S. M., & Robinson, J. P. (2004). Are parents investing less in children? Trends in mothers' and fathers' time with children. *American Journal of Sociology, 110*(1), 1–43. https://doi.org/10.1086/386270.

Schafer, J. L., & Graham, J. W. (2002). Missing data: Our view of the state of the art. *Psychological Methods, 7*(2), 147.

Schoppe-Sullivan, S. J., & Fagan, J. (2020). The evolution of fathering research in the 21st century: Persistent challenges, new directions. *Journal of Marriage and Family, 82*(1), 175–197.

Schwab, J. F., Rowe, M. L., Cabrera, N., & Lew-Williams, C. (2018). Fathers' repetition of words is coupled with children's vocabularies. *Journal of*

Experimental Child Psychology, 166, 437–450. https://doi.org/10.1016/j.jecp.2017.09.012.

Scrimin, S., Mastromatteo, L. Y., Hovnanyan, A., Zagni, B., Rubaltelli, E., & Pozzoli, T. (2022). Effects of socioeconomic status, parental stress, and family support on children's physical and emotional health during the COVID-19 pandemic. *Journal of Child and Family Studies, 31*(8), 2215–2228.

Sénéchal, M., & LeFevre, J. A. (2002). Parental involvement in the development of children's reading skill: A five-year longitudinal study. *Child Development, 73*(2), 445–460.

Sethna, V., Perry, E., Domoney, J., Iles, J., Psychogiou, L., Rowbotham, N. E., Stein, A., Murray, L., & Ramchandani, P. G. (2017). Father–child interactions at 3 months and 24 months: Contributions to children's cognitive development at 24 months. *Infant Mental Health Journal, 38*(3), 378–390.

Shafer, P. R., Gutiérrez, K. M., Ettinger de Cuba, S., Bovell-Ammon, A., & Raifman, J. (2022). Association of the implementation of child tax credit advance payments with food insufficiency in us households. *JAMA Network Open, 5*(1), e2143296. https://doi.org/10.1001/jamanetworkopen.2021.43296.

Shay, D., Shavit, Y., & Sasson, I. (2024). Poverty in early childhood and future educational achievements. *Early Child Development and Care, 194*(5–6): 655–668.

Shea, John. 2000. Does Parents' Money Matter? *Journal of Public Economics, 77*(2): 155–184.

Shrider, E. A., & Creamer, J. (2023). Poverty in the United States: 2022. *US Census Bureau*. September 2023. Report Number: P60-280. www.census.gov/library/visualizations/2023/demo/p60-280.html.

Shrout, P. E., & Bolger, N. (2002). Mediation in experimental and nonexperimental studies: new procedures and recommendations. *Psychological Methods, 7*(4), 422–438. https://doi.org/10.1037/1082-989X.7.4.422.

Sillence, K. (2020). Don't be a deadbeat dad: Non-custodial fathers, stereotypes, and family. *Canadian Journal of Family and Youth/Le Journal Canadien de Famille et de la Jeunesse, 12*(2), 84–94.

Silver, A. M., Chen, Y., Smith, D. K., Tamis-LeMonda, C. S., Cabrera, N., & Libertus, M. E. (2023). Mothers' and fathers' engagement in math activities with their toddler sons and daughters: The moderating role of parental math beliefs. *Frontiers in Psychology, 14*, [1124056]. https://doi.org/10.3389/fpsyg.2023.1124056.

Silver, R. B., Measelle, J. R., Armstrong, J. M., & Essex, M. J. (2005). Trajectories of classroom externalizing behavior: Contributions of child characteristics, family characteristics, and teacher-child relationship during the school transition. *Journal of School Psychology, 43*(1), 39–60.

Sims, J., & Coley, R. L. (2016) Independent contributions of mothers' and fathers' language and literacy practices: Associations with children's kindergarten skills across linguistically diverse households. *Early Education and Development, 27* (4), 495–512. https://doi.org/10.1080/10409289.2016.1091973.

Sinkewicz, M., & Garfinkel, I. (2009). Unwed fathers' ability to pay child support: New estimates accounting for multiple-partner fertility. *Demography, 46*(2), 247–263.

Smith-Donald, R., Raver, C. C., Hayes, T., & Richardson, B. (2007). Preliminary construct and concurrent validity of the Preschool Self-Regulation Assessment (PSRA) for field-based research. *Early Childhood Research Quarterly, 22*(3), 173–187.

Solomon-Fears, C., & Tollestrup, J. (2016). *Fatherhood Initiatives: Connecting Fathers to Their Children.* Congressional Research Service.

Sorensen, E. (1997). A national profile of nonresident fathers and their ability to pay child support. *Journal of Marriage and the Family,* 785–797.

Sorensen, E. (2010). Rethinking public policy toward low-income fathers in the child support program. *Journal of Policy Analysis and Management, 29*(3), 604–610.

Sorensen, E. (2021a, May). Certified child support arrears shows a sharp decline. http://bit.ly/3IbZUUU.

Sorensen, E. (2021b, September). Most arrears more than five years ago. http://bit.ly/4ezOxlx.

Sorensen, E., Sousa, L., & Schaner, S. (2007). Assessing child support arrears in nine large states and the nation [report]. The Urban Institute.

Sorensen, E., & Zibman, C. (2001). Getting to know poor fathers who do not pay child support. *Social Service Review, 75*(3), 420–434.

Sparks, R. L., Patton, J., & Murdoch, A. (2014). Early reading success and its relationship to reading achievement and reading volume: Replication of "10 years later." *Reading and Writing, 27*(1), 189–211.

Sroufe, L. A. (2005). Attachment and development: A prospective, longitudinal study from birth to adulthood. *Attachment & Human Development, 7*(4), 349–367.

St. George, J., Fletcher, R., & Palazzi, K. (2017). Comparing fathers' physical and toy play and links to child behaviour: An exploratory study. *Infant and Child Development, 26*(1), e1958. https://doi.org/10.1002/icd.1958.

Steinmetz, K. (2015, February 21). The Dad 2.0 Summit: Making the Case for a New Kind of Manhood. *TIME.* https://time.com/3717511/dad-summit-manhood/.

Stevenson, M., & Crnic, K. (2013). Intrusive fathering, children's self-regulation and social skills: A mediation analysis. *Journal of Intellectual Disability Research, 57*(6), 500–512. https://doi.org/10.1111/j.1365-2788.2012.01549.x.

Straus, M. A., Hamby, S. L., Finkelhor, D., Moore, D. W., & Runyan, D. (1998). Identification of child maltreatment with the Parent-Child Conflict Tactics Scales: Development and psychometric data for a national sample of American parents. *Child Abuse & Neglect, 22*(4), 249–270.

Tach, L., Mincy, R., & Edin, K. (2010). Parenting as a "package deal": Relationships, fertility, and nonresident father involvement among unmarried parents. *Demography, 47*(1), 181–204. https://doi.org/10.1353/dem.0.0096.

Tamis-LeMonda C. S., & Cabrera N. 2002. *Handbook of father involvement: Multidisciplinary perspectives.* Erlbaum.

Tamis-LeMonda, C. S., Shannon, J. D., Cabrera, N. J., & Lamb, M. E. (2004). Fathers and mothers at play with their 2- and 3-year-olds: Contributions to language and cognitive development. *Child Development, 75*(6), 1806–1820. https://doi.org/10.1111/j.1467-8624.2004.00818.x.

Taylor, B. A., Dearing, E., & McCartney, K. (2004). Incomes and Outcomes in Early Childhood. *Journal of Human Resources, 39*(4), 980–1007. https://doi.org/10.2307/3559035.

Teti, D. M., & Candelaria, M. A. (2002). Parenting competence. In M. H. Bornstein (Ed.), *Handbook of parenting volume 4: Social conditions and applied parenting* (pp. 149–180). Lawrence Erlbaum Associates.

Teti, D. M., Cole, P., Cabrera, N., Goodman, S., & McLoyd, V. (2017). Supporting parents: How six decades of parenting research can inform policy and best practice. *Social Policy Report, 30*(5), 1–34. https://doi.org/10.1002/j.2379-3988.2017.tb00090.x.

Teufl, L., Deichmann, F., Supper, B., & Ahnert, L. (2020). How fathers' attachment security and education contribute to early child language skills above and beyond mothers: Parent-child conversation under scrutiny. *Attachment & Human Development, 22*(1), 71–84. https://doi.org/10.1080/14616734.2019.1589063.

Thomas, A., & Sawhill, I. (2002). For richer or for poorer: Marriage as an antipoverty strategy. *Journal of Policy Analysis and Management: The Journal of the Association for Public Policy Analysis and Management, 21*(4), 587–599.

Thompson, R. A. (2014). Stress and child development. *The Future of Children, 24*(1), 41–59. https://doi.org/10.1353/foc.2014.0004.

Thomson, D., Casey, B. M., Lombardi, C. M., Nguyen, H. N. (2020). Quality of fathers' spatial concept support during block building predicts their daughters' early math skills – but not their sons'. *Early Childhood Research Quarterly, 50* (3), 51–64. https://doi.org/10.1016/j.ecresq.2018.07.008

Tollestrup, J. (2019). Child Support Enforcement: Program Basics. Congressional Research Survey Report, 22380.

Tollestrup, J & Landers, P. (2024) Employment and Training Services for Noncustodial Parents in the Child Support Program: Background and Summary of Proposed Rule. Congressional Research Service.

Towe-Goodman, N. R., Willoughby, M., Blair, C., Gustafsson, H. C., Mills-Koonce, W. R., Cox, M. J., & The Family Life Project Key Investigators. (2014). Fathers' sensitive parenting and the development of early executive functioning. *Journal of Family Psychology, 28*(6), 867–876. https://doi.org/10.1037/a0038128.

Troller-Renfree, S. V., Costanzo, M. A., Duncan, G. J., Magnusun, K., Gennetian, L. A., Yoshikawa, H., Halpern-Meekin, S., Fox, N. A., & Noble, K. G. (2022). The impact of a poverty reduction intervention on infant brain activity. PNAS, *119*(5), e2115649119. https://doi.org/10.1073/pnas.2115649119.

Turetsky, V., & Waller, M. R. (2020). Piling on debt: The intersections between child support arrears and legal financial obligations. *UCLA Criminal Justice Law Review, 4*(1). https://escholarship.org/uc/item/7vd043jw.

Turner, K. J. and Waller, M. R. (2017). Indebted relationships: Child support arrears and nonresident fathers' involvement with children. *Journal of Marriage and Family, 79*(1), 24–43.

Urban Institute, and Child Trends. National Survey of America's Families (NSAF) (1997). Inter-university Consortium for Political and Social Research [distributor], 2007-10-04. https://doi.org/10.3886/ICPSR04581.v1.

US Census Bureau. (2020). America's Families and Living Arrangements: 2020. *Current Population Survey, Annual Social and Economic Supplement.* www.census.gov/data/tables/2020/demo/families/cps-2020.html.

US Department of Health and Human Services, Administration for Children and Families. (2011). *Child Support Fact Sheet Series No. 4: Promoting Child Well-Being & Family Self-Sufficiency, Economic Stability.*

Um, H. (2019). *Factors and outcomes associated with patterns of child support arrears.* Columbia University. https://doi.org/10.7916/d8-xbkr-8h79.

Varghese, C., & Wachen, J. (2015). The determinants of father involvement and connections to children's literacy and language outcomes: Review of the literature. *Marriage & Family Review, 52*(4), 331–359. https://doi.org/10.1080/01494929.2015.1099587

Violato, M., Petrou, S., Gray, R., & Redshaw, M. (2011). Family income and child cognitive and behavioural development in the United Kingdom: does money matter? *Health Economics, 20*(10), 1201–1225.

Vogel, L. K. (2020a). Help me help you: Identifying and addressing barriers to child support compliance. *Children and Youth Services Review, 110,* 104763. https://doi.org/10.1016/j.childyouth.2020.104763.

Vogel, L. K. (2020b). Barriers to meeting formal child support obligations: Noncustodial father perspectives. *Children and Youth Services Review, 110,* 104764. https://doi.org/10.1016/j.childyouth.2020.104764

Volling, B. L., & Cabrera, N. J. (2019). Advancing research and measurement on fathering and child development. *Monographs of the Society for Research in Child Development, 84*(1), 7–17. https://doi.org/10.1111/mono.12404.

Volling, B. L., & Palkovitz, R. (2021). Fathering: New perspectives, paradigms, and possibilities. *Psychology of Men & Masculinities, 22*(3), 427.

Volling, B. L., Blandon, A. Y., & Kolak, A. (2006). Marriage, parenting, and the emergence of early self-regulation in the family system. *Journal of Child and Family Studies, 15,* 489–502. https://doi.org/10.1007/s10826-006-9027-z.

Votruba-Drzal, E. (2006). Economic disparities in middle childhood development: Does income matter? *Developmental Psychology, 42*(6), 1154–1167. https://doi.org/10.1037/0012-1649.42.6.1154.

Waller, M.R., & Emory, A.D. (2018). Visitation orders, family courts, and fragile families. *Journal of Marriage and Family, 80*(3), 653–670. https://doi.org/10.1111/jomf.12480.

Wang, L., Li, H., Dill, S. E., Zhang, S., & Rozelle, S. (2022). Does paternal involvement matter for early childhood development in rural China? *Applied Developmental Science, 26*(4), 741–765.

Wang, L., Yang, C., Jiang, D., Zhang, S., Jiang, Q., Rozelle, S. (2022) Impact of parental beliefs on child developmental outcomes: A quasi-experiment in rural China. *International Journal of Environmental Research and Public Health, 19*(12), 741–765. https://doi.org/10.1080/10888691.2021.1990061.

Ward, K. P., & Lee, S. J. (2020). Mothers' and fathers' parenting stress, responsiveness, and child wellbeing among low-income families. *Children and Youth Services Review, 116,* 10521

Webster, L. L., Low, J., Siller, C., & Hackett, R. K. (2013). Understanding the contribution of a father's warmth on his child's social skills. *Fathering: A Journal of Theory, Research, and Practice About Men As Fathers, 11*(1), 90–113. https://doi.org/10.3149/fth.1101.90.

Wechsler, D. (1981). *Manual for the Wechsler Adult Intelligence Scale-Revised.* The Psychological Corp.

Weiss, Y., & Willis, R. J. (1985). Children as collective goods and divorce settlements. *Journal of Labor Economics, 3*(3), 268–292.

Whitehurst, G. J., & Lonigan, C. J. (1998). Child development and emergent literacy. *Child Development, 69*(3), 848–872.

Wimer, C., & Wolf, S. (2020). Family income and young children's development. *The Future of Children, 30*(2), 191–211.

Woodcock, R. W., & Johnson, M. B. (1989). *Woodcock-Johnson tests of cognitive ability*. DLM Teaching Resources.

Yeung, W. J., Linver, M. R., & Brooks-Gunn, J. (2002). How money matters for young children's development: Parental investment and family processes. *Child Development, 73*(6), 1861–1879. https://doi.org/10.1111/1467-8624.t01-1-00511.

Yoo, P. Y., Duncan, G. J., Magnuson, K., Fox, N. A., Yoshikawa, H., Halpern-Meekin, S., & Noble, K. G. (2022). Unconditional cash transfers and maternal substance use: Findings from a randomized control trial of low-income mothers with infants in the US. *BMC Public Health, 22*(1), 897.

Yoshikawa, H., Atlman Rosman, E., & Hsueh, J. (2001). Variation in teenage mothers' experiences of child care and other components of welfare reform: Selection processes and developmental consequences. *Child Development, 72* (1), 299–317. https://doi.org/10.1111/1467-8624.00280.

Ziliak, J. P. (2019). Restoring economic opportunity for "the people left behind": Employment strategies for rural America. *Aspen Institute*, 100–126. http://bit.ly/3GkgaTd.

Ziliak, J. P., Figlio, D. N., Davis, E. E., & Connolly, L. S. (2000). Accounting for the decline in AFDC caseloads: Welfare reform or the economy? *Journal of Human Resources*, 570–586.

Index

academic achievement
    income, effect of, 74, 111, 146–147
    learning activities, effect of, 92
    maternal involvement, effect of, 40
    measurement of, 150, 163
    nonresident families, in, 91, 147
    paternal involvement and, 58, 69–70
    stimulating learning environment and, 38
    transfer payments, effect of, 111
ACF. see Administration for Children and Families (ACF)
activation relationship theory (ART), 22
Additional Child Tax Credit (ACTC), 112
Administration for Children and Families (ACF), 122, 124, 126, 127, 142
aggression
    changes over time
        empirical results, 100–101
        father's education, effect of, 106
        gender, effect of, 106
        income, effect of, 106
        maternal involvement, effect of, 102–103, 106
        nonresident families. in, 99, 103, 106, 107
        race/ethnicity, effect of, 106
        resident families, in, 99, 101, 102, 106, 107
    coefficients, 177
    data, 172
    data analysis, 174–177
    demographic characteristics, measurement of, 174
    ecological model of father–child relationships and, xiii
    explaining development of, 101
    FFCWS data, 172
    household income, measurement of, 173–174
    maternal reports of, 96
    means and variances of latent factors, 177
    measurement of, 97, 98, 150, 163, 172
    nonresident families, in
        changes over time, 99, 103, 106, 107
        income, effect of, 106, 108–109
        maternal involvement, effect of, 103, 106, 108–109
        paternal involvement, effect of, 102
        resident families compared, 99, 101, 107, 108, 146
        temperament of child, effect of, 102
    other characteristics, measurement of, 174
    overview, xiii, 96
    parent involvement, measurement of, 173
    research limitations, 109–110
    resident families, in
        changes over time, 99, 101, 102, 106, 107
        father's education, effect of, 106
        gender, effect of, 101–102, 106
        income, effect of, 106, 108–109
        maternal involvement, effect of, 101–102, 106, 108–109
        nonresident families compared, 99, 101, 107, 108, 146
        race/ethnicity, effect of, 102, 106
        temperament of child, effect of, 101–102
Aid to Families with Dependent Children (AFDC), 115, 117, 118–119, 120
Altenburger, L. E., 63
American Rescue Plan Act (ARPA), 112–113
analysis of contribution to child development
    aggression (see aggression)
    changes over time, 96–98, 100
    cognitive skills (see cognitive skills)
    early parenting, effect on later development, 95–96
    ecological model of father–child relationships and, 94–95

analysis of contribution (cont.)
    FFCWS data, 98
    overview, 17–18, 94–98
Anderson, S., 71
anecdotes, xx
attachment theory, 9–10

Baby's First Years (BFY), 39–40
Baker, C. E., 64
"bastard laws," 116–117
Bayley Scales of Infant Development, 66
Berger, L. M., 38–39, 40–41, 163
best interest of child standard, 115–116
Biden, Joe, 112, 131
Black–White marriage gap, 122, 124
Blankenhorn, David, 44
Bocknek, E. L., 60
breadwinner role of fathers, 114
Bronfenbrenner, U., 28–29
Brooks-Gunn, Jeanne, 12
Build Back Better, 131
Building Strong Families (BFI), 123
Bureau of Labor Statistics (BLS), 48

Cabrera, Natasha J., xi, xii–xiii, 23, 58, 61, 66, 165
Charnov, E., 20–21
Cheung, R. Y., 62–63
Child Behavior Checklist (CBCL), 150, 163, 172
child custody
    best interest of child standard, 115–116
    female presumption in, 47, 114–115
child labor, 114
child-rearing
    divorce, female presumption upon, 47
    historical decline of male presumption in, 46–47, 114
    mothers and, 7–8
children's problem behavior (CPB), 22–23
child support
    arrears
        compromise programs, 141
        nonresident fathers and, 46, 68–69, 137–138
    Child Support Noncustodial Parent Employment Demonstration (CSPED), 139–140
    discretion to provide relief from, 141–142
    Early Head Start and, 142

employment pilot programs, 137, 142
enforcement, 117–121
Flexibility, Efficiency, and Modernization in Child Support Enforcement Programs, 140–141
Head Start and, 142
historical evolution of, 113–114
inappropriate amount set by magistrates, 138–139
intimate partner violence and, 144
low-income adjustments, 141
low-income fathers and, 118, 121
nonresident fathers and
    arrears, 46, 68–69, 137–138
    emotional contribution of fathers in, 68–69
    financial contribution of fathers in, 46, 53
    formal versus informal financial support, 49–50, 52–53, 83, 89, 91, 92
    low-income fathers, 118, 121
    Parents Fair Share (PFS), 121
    penalties, 119–120
Office of Child Support Enforcement (OCSE), 118, 139, 143
overview, xiv, 113
Parents Fair Share (PFS), 121
race/ethnicity and, 120
recommendations
    federal subsidies, 147
    informal financial support, 142
    parental education programs, 144–145
    parenting time, 143–144, 148–149
    supplementing income, 142–143
    visitation, increasing, 143–144
refusal versus inability to pay, 121, 136
Responsible Fatherhood (RF) programs and
    increasing payments, goal of, 124–125
    relief from, 142
rule changes, 140–141
self-support reserves, 141
unpaid, 120–121
wraparound services, 137, 142
Child Support Noncustodial Parent Employment Demonstration (CSPED), 139–140

Child Tax Credit (CTC), 112–113, 130–131, 142–143
Choi, Jeong-Kyun, 90
Cichetti, D., 32
cognitive skills
  changes over time
    father's education, effect of, 105, 106
    gender, effect of, 105, 106
    lack of significant effect by factors of interest, 105
    nonresident families, in, 99–100, 105–106, 107
    overview, 103
    race/ethnicity, effect of, 105, 106
    resident families, in, 99–100, 106, 107
  coefficients, 177–185
  data, 172
  data analysis, 174–177
  demographic characteristics, measurement of, 174
  ecological model of father–child relationships and, xiii
  executive function, measurement of, 173
  explaining development of, 103–104
  father effects, 66
  FFCWS data, 172
  income
    effect of, 39–40, 74, 111, 146–147
    measurement of, 173–174
  intrusiveness, effect of, 61
  language skills
    empirical research, 103
    empirical results, 82–83
    income, effect of, 74
    literacy activities and, 57–58, 96
    nonresident families, in, 105–107
    play, effect of, 58–59
    presence versus absence, 55–56
    resident families, in, 105
  means and variances of latent factors, 177
  measurement of, 97, 98–99, 150, 163
  nonresident families, in
    changes over time, 99–100, 105–106
    child temperament, effect of, 105
    father's education, effect of, 105
    gender, effect of, 105–107
    income, effect of, 105, 108–109
    lack of significant effect by factors of interest, 105

    maternal involvement, effect of, 108–109
    race/ethnicity, effect of, 105, 106–107
    resident families compared, 99–100, 104, 107, 108, 146–147
  other characteristics, measurement of, 174
  overview, xiii, 96
  parent involvement, measurement of, 173
  play, effect of, 58–59
  receptive vocabulary
    empirical research, 99–100, 103
    learning activities, effect of, 92
    maternal reports of, 96
    measurement of, 97–99, 173
    transfer payments, effect of, 111
  research limitations, 109–110
  resident families, in
    changes over time, 99–100, 106, 107
    emotional contribution of fathers, 57–59
    father's education, effect of, 104, 106
    financial contribution of fathers, 80
    gender, effect of, 106
    income, effect of, 104, 106, 108–109
    maternal involvement, effect of, 106, 108–109
    nonresident families compared, 99–100, 104, 107, 108, 146–147
    race/ethnicity, effect of, 104, 106
  risk, effect of, 66
Composition International Diagnostic Interview-Short Form (CIDI-SF), 174
Conflicts Tactics Scale, 77
Congressional Research Service, 5
Cooper, K., 24–25
couples and relationship education (CRE) services, 122, 132
Crnic, K., 62
cross-disciplinary approach, current lack of, xii–xiii
Current Population Survey (CPS), 48

DAD 2.0, 37
Dads' Parenting Interactions with Children: Checklist of Observations Linked to Outcomes (PICCOLO-D), 71, 72
"deadbeat dad" stereotype, 44

Department of Labor, 141–142, 147
dependent exemption, 111–112
developmental cascade model
    emotional contribution of fathers
        generally, 32
    nonresident families, financial
        contribution of fathers in
            constructs, 164
            overview, 83, 89–90
    overview, 32
    resident families, financial contribution
        of fathers in
            constructs, 152
            overview, 74
            receptive vocabulary, 152
developmental theories, 29–30
discipline
    resident families, in
        emotional contribution of fathers
            and, 62–63
        maternal harsh discipline, family
            stress model (FSM) and, 151
    spanking
        fathers, by, 79
        mothers, by, 77–78
DiStefano, C., 153, 165
division of labor, 7–8, 114–115
divorce
    Black–White marriage gap, 122, 124
    female presumption in child custody
        upon, 47, 114–115
    parental education courses, 116
    race/ethnicity and, 122, 124
    rising divorce rates, 115
    visitation upon, 47
dual role of fatherhood, xvii, xix, 17
Duckworth, Angela, 12
Duncan, Greg, 12

early childhood, focus on, 3, 15
Early Childhood Longitudinal Study-Birth
    Cohort (ECLS-B), 57–58, 69–70
Early Head Start
    child support and, 142
    Healthy Marriage Initiative (HMI)
        compared, 132
    increasing father participation in, 145
    recommendations, 145
    Research and Evaluation Project
        (EHSREP), 60, 62, 71–72

Responsible Fatherhood (RF) programs
    compared, 134–135
Earned Income Tax Credit (EITC), 112, 113
ecological model of father–child
    relationships, xiii, 23, 94–95
ecological model of human development,
    28–29
economists
    basic principles of agreement with
        psychologists, 13
    psychologists, collaboration with, 12–13
emotional contribution of fathers
    attachment theory and, 9–10
    combination with financial contribution,
        xvii, xix, 17
    developmental cascade model and, 32
    developmental theories, 29–30
    disconnect from financial
        contribution, 6
    ecological model of human development,
        28–29
    financial contribution of fathers
        compared, 55
    integration of theoretical frameworks,
        34–35
    knowledge, attitudes, and practices
        (KAPS), 30
    lack of empirical evidence, 10, 11–12
    mothers compared, xviii–xix, 16, 54–55,
        63–64
    nonresident families, in (see nonresident
        families – emotional contribution of
        fathers)
    overview, xviii–xix, 5–6, 17, 54–55
    predominant focus of existing research on
        mothers, effect of, 11
    race/ethnicity and, 10–12
    resident families, in (see resident families – emotional contribution of
        fathers)
    theoretical perspectives, 28–30
    time, importance of, 9, 13
    transactional development model,
        30–31
emotional depth, xix
empirical models
    overview, 17
    research limitations
        aggression, 109–110
        cognitive skills, 109–110

INDEX 225

empirical research
  exclusion of fathers from, 33
  financial contribution of fathers
    nonresident families, in (see nonresident families – financial contribution of fathers)
    resident families, in (see resident families – financial contribution of fathers)
  predominant focus of existing research on mothers, effect of, 11
  race/ethnicity and, 32–33
  research limitations
    overview, 32–33
    resident families, emotional contribution of fathers in (see resident families – emotional contribution of fathers)
    resident families, financial contribution of fathers in (see resident families – financial contribution of fathers)
ethnicity. see race/ethnicity
evolving nature of fatherhood, xx
Expanded Child Tax Credit (ECTC), 112–113, 131, 142–143

Fagan, J., 71
families
  modern family, 1–2
  nonresident families (see nonresident families – generally)
  resident families (see resident families – generally)
  transformation of, 1
  two-parent, heterosexual, biological families, focus on, 2
family investment model (FIM)
  empirical evidence, lack of, 41–42
  family stress model (FSM), relation to, 52–53
  financial contribution of fathers
    generally
      overview, 25
      purchases and investments, 25–26
      testing, 34–35
      timeliness of investments, 27
    learning activities and, 25–27
    nonresident families, financial contribution of fathers in
      generally, 26–27, 52–53
      constructs, 164
      empirical research, 83, 89–90
      food insecurity, 164
      learning materials, 164
    overview, xiii
    resident families, financial contribution of fathers in, 74
      constructs, 151
      learning activities, 151
      learning materials, 151
      maternal responsiveness, 151
      timeliness of investments, 27
Family Life Project, 64
family stress model (FSM)
  empirical evidence, lack of, 41–42
  family investment model (FIM), relation to, 52–53
  nonresident families, financial contribution of fathers in
    generally, 45–46, 49, 52–53
    constructs, 164
    empirical research, 83, 90, 91–92
  overview, 27–28
  resident families, financial contribution of fathers in, 74
    constructs, 151
    maternal harsh discipline, 151
    maternal stress, 151
  testing, 34–35
family systems theory, 133
Fatherhood Academy, 135
Fatherhood Initiative, 13–14
Fatherless America (Blankenhorn), 44
FFCWS. see Future of Families and Child Well-being Survey (FFCWS)
FIM. see family investment model (FIM)
financial contribution of fathers
  child development
    income, contribution of, 7, 19–20
    time, contribution of, 7, 13
  combination with emotional contribution, xvii, xix, 17
  disconnect from emotional contribution, 6
  division of labor and, 7–8
  emotional contribution of fathers compared, 55
  existing focus on to exclusion of emotional contribution, 16

financial contribution of fathers (cont.)
    family investment model (FIM)
        overview, 25
        purchases and investments, 25–26
        testing, 34–35
        timeliness of investments, 27
    FFCWS data, 37–39
    importance of, 8–9
    integration of theoretical frameworks, 34–35
    measurement of, 8
    nonresident families, in (*see* nonresident families – financial contribution of fathers)
    overview, xviii, 5–6, 17, 36
    poverty, overcoming, 20
    productivity, effect of changes in, 8
    randomized controlled trials (RCT), 24–25
    resident families, in (*see* resident families – financial contribution of fathers)
    theoretical perspectives, 24–25
    time
        child development, contribution to, 7
        consumption good, as, 19
        mothers' labor force participation, effect on, 19
Finney, S. J., 153, 165
Flanders, J. L., 60
Fletcher, R., 72
Flexibility, Efficiency, and Modernization in Child Support Enforcement Programs, 140–141
Foster, Tricia D., 64
Fragile Families and Child Well-being Survey (FFCWS). *see* Future of Families and Child Well-being Survey (FFCWS)
FSM. *see* family stress model (FSM)
Future of Families and Child Well-being Survey (FFCWS)
    aggression, 172
    analysis of contribution to child development and, 98
    cognitive skills, effect of positive fathering on, 58
    financial contribution of fathers generally, 37–39
    integration of theoretical frameworks and, 17, 35
    maternal engagement and, 40–41
    nonresident families, financial contribution of fathers in, 163
    resident families, financial contribution of fathers in, 150

Gadsden, Vivian, xi–xii
Garfinkel, I., 163–164
gender
    aggression, effect on
        changes over time, 106
        resident families, in, 101–102, 106
    cognitive skills, effect on
        changes over time, 105, 106
        nonresident families, in, 105–107

Handbook of Father Involvement: Multidisciplinary Perspectives, First and Second Editions (Cabrera and Tamis-LeMonda), 24
Haveman, Robert, 25
Hawkins, Alan, xi
Head Start
    child support and, 142
    effect size and, 39
    emotional contribution of fathers in nonresident families, empirical evidence, 70–71
    Healthy Marriage Initiative (HMI) compared, 132
    Responsible Fatherhood (RF) programs compared, 134–135
Healthy Marriage Initiative (HMI)
    Black–White marriage gap and, 122, 124
    Building Strong Families (BFI), 123
    core components, 122
    couples and relationship education (CRE) services, 122, 132
    criticism of, 124, 131
    Early Head Start compared, 132
    evaluations of, 123–124
    Head Start compared, 132
    interventions, 123–124
    Parents and Children Together (PACT), 123
    proponents of, 131
    recommendations
        child well-being and, 131–132
        couples and relationship education (CRE) services and, 132

direct support for fathers, 132
Responsible Fatherhood (RF) programs versus, 127–128, 132–133
Supporting Healthy Marriage (SHI), 123
Healthy Start, 135
historical role of fatherhood, 19
HMI. *see* Healthy Marriage Initiative (HMI)

Iglesias, Aquiles, xi, 71
illegitimate children, 116–117
Industrial Revolution, 46–47, 114
integration of theoretical frameworks, 17, 34–35
intimate partner violence, 144

Jackson, Aurora P., 49, 69–70
Jacobvitz, D., 66–67
Jay-Z, 1
Journal of Child Development, 12

Karberg, E., 61
knowledge, attitudes, and practices (KAPS), 30

Lamb, M. E., 20–21, 23
language skills
   empirical research, 103
   empirical results, 82–83
   income, effect of, 74
   literacy activities and, 57–58, 96
   nonresident families, in, 105–107
   play, effect of, 58–59
   presence versus absence, 55–56
   resident families, in, 105
learning activities
   academic achievement, effect on, 92
   changes over time, 78–79, 80
   family investment model (FIM) and, 25–27
   fathers versus mothers, 63–64
   income, effect of, 40–41, 74
   nonresident families, financial contribution of fathers in, 26–27, 92
   nonresident families, in, 87–89, 92, 147
   receptive vocabulary, effect on, 92
   resident families, financial contribution of fathers in, 25–26, 151
   time, importance of, 9
   two-parent families, in, 77
Lee, S. J., 62

Leiter International Performance Scale-Revised, 173
Levitt, Steven, 12
literacy activities
   language skills and, 57–58, 96
   mothers and, 78–79
   resident families
      emotional contribution of fathers in, 57–58
      financial contribution of fathers in, 80
"love story." *see* emotional contribution of fathers

Majdandžić, Mirjana, 22–23
Malin, J. L., 56
Masten, A. S., 32
Mincy, Ronald, xii–xiii
modern family, 1–2
"money story." *see* financial contribution of fathers
mothers
   academic achievement, effect of maternal involvement, 40
   aggression, effect of maternal involvement
      changes over time, 102–103, 106
      nonresident families, in, 103, 106, 108–109
      resident families, in, 101–102, 106, 108–109
   child-rearing and, 7–8
   cognitive skills, effect of maternal involvement on
      nonresident families, in, 108–109
      resident families, in, 106, 108–109
   emotional contribution generally
      fathers compared, xviii–xix, 16, 54–55
      predominant focus of existing research on mothers, 11
   family investment model (FIM), maternal responsiveness and, 151
   family stress model (FSM) and
      maternal harsh discipline, 151
      maternal stress, 151
   labor force participation
      effect of time invested by fathers on, 19
      increase in, 114–115
   literacy activities and, 78–79

mothers (cont.)
    maternal harsh discipline, family stress model (FSM) and, 151
    nonresident families, emotional contribution of fathers in
        relationship with mother, effect of, 68, 69
        repartnering of mother, effect of, 69
    nonresident families, financial contribution of fathers in, purchases by mothers and, 44–45, 147
    resident families, emotional contribution of fathers in, mothers compared, 63–64
    resident families, financial contribution of fathers in
        lack of control for mother effects, 66
        mechanisms, 40–41
        research limitations, 42
    responsible fatherhood (RF) programs, mother-only programs, 135
Mullins, David F., 50

National Academies of Sciences, Engineering, and Medicine, 30
National Center for Fathers and Families (NCOFF), xi–xii
national datasets, 14
National Fatherhood Research Network Initiative, 13–14
National Head Start Association, 135
National Longitudinal Survey of Youth (NLSY), 40
National Survey of America's Families (NSAF), 50
neighborhood quality, 45
Nepomnyaschy, L., 91, 163–164
nonresident families – generally
    aggression in (see aggression)
    child support and
        arrears, 46, 68–69, 137–138
        emotional contribution of fathers in, 68–69
        financial contribution of fathers in, 46, 53
        formal versus informal financial support, 49–50, 52–53, 83, 89, 91, 92
        low-income fathers, 118, 121
        Parents Fair Share (PFS), 121
        penalties, 119–120
    cognitive skills in (see cognitive skills)
    demographics of, 5
    family investment model (FIM) generally, 26–27, 52–53
    Responsible Fatherhood (RF) programs and, 127–128, 133–136
nonresident families – emotional contribution of fathers
    child support and, 68–69
    data, 69–70
    empirical evidence, 70–72
        Early Head Start Research and Evaluation Project (EHSREP), 71–72
        Head Start, 70–71
        PICCOLO-D, 71, 72
        rough-and-tumble play quality scale (RTPQ), 72
    methodological considerations, 69–70
    race/ethnicity and, 67–68
    relationship with mother, effect of, 68, 69
    repartnering of mother, effect of, 69
nonresident families – financial contribution of fathers
    ambiguous findings, 52
    child support, 46, 53
    data, 47–48
    "deadbeat dad" stereotype, 44
    empirical evidence, 49–51
        child cognitive development and, 49
        formal versus informal financial support, 49–50, 52–53
        level of financial support, 49
        race/ethnicity and, 50–51
    empirical research
        age five, results at, 87–88
        age nine, results at, 88
        aggression, 163
        analytic plan, 165
        analytic sample, 86–87
        cognitive skills, 163
        data, 84–86, 163
        data analysis, 73
        demographic controls, 164–165
        developmental cascade model and, 83, 89–90, 164
        family investment model (FIM) and, 83, 89–90, 164

family stress model (FSM) and, 83, 90,
    91–92, 164
father's financial support,
    163–164, 165
FFCWS data, 163
financial support reports of
    mothers, 84
formal versus informal financial
    support, 83, 89, 91, 92
income level, effect of, 87
indirect effects, 87–89
learning activities and, 92
measures, 163–164
moderated mediation of indirect
    effects, 165
overview, 83–84
parental investment, mediation
    by, 83
race/ethnicity and, 87
receptive vocabulary, 92
research limitations, 91
resident families compared,
    91–92, 93
results, 87–89
scope of, 84
summary of indirect effects, 165–170
unstandardized descriptive statistic,
    165–167
family investment model (FIM) and,
    26–27, 52–53
family stress model (FSM) and, 45–46, 49,
    52–53
learning activities and, 87–89, 92, 147
methodological considerations, 47–48
neighborhood quality and, 45
overview, 44–47, 52–53
purchases by mothers and, 44–45, 147
resident families compared, 2–3, 44–45,
    146, 147
statistics, 5
surveys, 47–48
visitation and, 47
nurturing model of fathering, 21

observational data, 14–15
Office of Child Support Enforcement (OCSE),
    118, 139, 143
one-dimensional view of fatherhood,
    16–17
other factors, impact of, 15

Palkovitz, Rob, xi, 21
Palm, Glen, xi
Panel Study of Income Dynamics (PSID), 40
Paquette, D., 22
parental education courses, 116
parental education programs, 144–145
parent–child relationship, complexity of, 16
*Parenting Matters: Supporting Parents of
    Children Ages 0-8* (National
    Academies of Sciences, Engineering,
    and Medicine), 30
parenting time, 148–149
Parents and Children Together (PACT), 123
Parents Fair Share (PFS), 121, 128
Paxson, C., 163
Peabody Picture Vocabulary Test (PPVT), 80,
    96, 97–98, 99–100, 103, 164, 173,
    174–176, 177
Pearson, Jessica, xi, xiv
Personal Responsibility and Work
    Opportunity Reconciliation Act
    (PROWRA), 121–122
PICCOLO-D (Dads' Parenting Interactions
    with Children: Checklist of
    Observations Linked to Outcomes),
    71, 72
Pleck, J., 20–22
policies and programs
    Aid to Families with Dependent Children
        (AFDC), 115, 117, 118–119, 120
    child support (*see* child support)
    Healthy Marriage Initiative (HMI) (*see*
        Healthy Marriage Initiative (HMI))
    overview, 18, 111, 128–129
    Parents Fair Share (PFS), 121, 128
    Responsible Fatherhood (RF) programs
        (*see* responsible fatherhood (RF)
        programs)
    transfer payments (*see* transfer payments)
poverty, overcoming, 20
PPVT. *see* Peabody Picture Vocabulary Test
    (PPVT)
psychologists
    basic principles of agreement with
        economists, 13
    economists, collaboration with, 12–13
race/ethnicity
    aggression and
        changes over time, 106

race/ethnicity (cont.)
    resident families, in, 102, 106
    Black–White marriage gap, 122
    child support and, 120
    cognitive skills
        changes over time, 105, 106
        nonresident families, in, 105, 106–107
        resident families, in, 104, 106
    divorce and, 122, 124
    emotional contribution of fathers and, 10–12
    empirical research, 32–33
    nonresident families, financial contribution of fathers in
        empirical evidence, 50–51
        empirical research, 87
randomized controlled trials (RCT), 24–25
receptive vocabulary
    empirical research, 99–100, 103
    learning activities, effect of, 92
    maternal reports of, 96
    measurement of, 97–99, 173
    transfer payments, effect of, 111
recommendations
    child support
        federal subsidies, 147
        informal financial support, 142
        parental education programs, 144–145
        parenting time, 143–144, 148–149
        supplementing income, 142–143
        visitation, increasing, 143–144
    Early Head Start, 145
    Healthy Marriage Initiative (HMI)
        child well-being and, 131–132
        couples and relationship education (CRE) services and, 132
        direct support for fathers, 132
    overview, 18, 129, 130
    Responsible Fatherhood (RF) programs, 133–136
    transfer payments, 130–131
    Young Child Tax Credit, 147–148
research. *see* empirical research
resident families – generally
    aggression in (*see* aggression)
    cognitive skills in (*see* cognitive skills)
    demographics of, 3–5
    nonresident families compared, 2–3
    statistics, 3–5
resident families – emotional contribution of fathers
    cognitive skills, effect on, 57–59
        language and speech and, 59
        literacy activities and, 57–58
        play and, 58–59
        school activities and, 58
    discipline and, 62–63
    empirical evidence, 56–57
    individual differences, 64–65
    insensitivity and, 61–62
    intrusiveness and, 61–62
    measurement of, 56
    mothers compared, 63–64
    negative parenting, effect of, 61
    positive fathering, effect of, 57
    presence versus absence, 55–56
    quantity versus quality, 55–57
    research limitations, 65–67
        low father participation, 65
        mechanisms, 66–67
        mother effects, lack of control for, 66
        small-scale studies, 65
    social skills of child, effect on, 59–60
    videotaped parent–child interactions, 56
resident families – financial contribution of fathers
    behavior problems and, 38
    deeply held beliefs regarding role of fathers, 37
    early childhood, 44
    effect size and, 38–40, 43
    empirical research
        age five, results at, 82
        age nine, results at, 82–83
        analytic plan, 153
        analytic sample, 75–77
        cognitive skills, 80
        comparison sample, 75–76
        data, 75–77
        data analysis, 73, 80–81
        demographic controls, 152
        developmental cascade model and, 74, 152
        early years, 83
        empirical research, 81–83
        family investment model (FIM) and, 74, 151
        family stress model (FSM) and, 74, 151

father parenting, 74, 79–80
father's earnings, measurement of, 150–151
FFCWS data, 150
household income, measurement of, 150
how income affects child development, 74
learning materials, 74
literacy activities, 80
measures, 150–151
mediating processes, 74
missing data analysis, 152–153
mother parenting, 74, 77–79
nonresident families compared, 91–92, 93
overall model fit, 154
receptive vocabulary, 80, 82–83
selection bias, 75
spanking, 77–78, 79
summary of indices, 154–162
two-parent families, 77
unstandardized descriptive statistic, 154–160
whether income is associated with child development, 73–74
evolution of role of fathers, 36–37
importance of, 40–41
low-income versus high-income families, 44
mechanisms, 40–41
maternal engagement, 40–41
parental stress and, 41
nonexperimental studies, 43
nonresident families compared, 44–45, 146, 147
overview, 36–40, 43–44
research limitations, 41–43
empirical evidence, lack of, 41–42
maternal engagement and, 42
quality of time spent, 43
self-perspective of fathers, 42–43
type of experience and, 43–44
responsible fatherhood (RF) programs
child support and
increasing payments, goal of, 124–125
relief from, 142
co-parenting programs, 134
criticism of, 125–126

Early Head Start compared, 134–135
evaluations of, 125
father-only programs, 135
Head Start compared, 134–135
Healthy Marriage Initiative (HMI) versus, 127–128, 132–133
Healthy Start compared, 135
meta-analysis of, 125
mother-only programs, 135
nonresident families and, 127–128, 133–136
recommendations, 133–136
Supporting Father Involvement (SFI), 126–127
True Dads, 126–128, 135
revised tripartite model of father involvement, 21–22
Reynolds, E., 64
RF programs. *see* responsible fatherhood (RF) programs
The Role of the Father in Child Development (Lamb), 23
rough-and-tumble play quality scale (RTPQ), 72
Rowe, M. L., 56

small-scale studies, 14–15, 65
Social Security Act Section IV-D, 118–119
spanking
fathers, by, 79
mothers, by, 77–78
Stevenson, M., 62
Stewart, K., 24–25
Succeeding Generations: On the Effects of Investments on Children (Haveman and Wolfe), 25
Supporting Father Involvement (SFI), 126–127
Supporting Healthy Marriage (SHI), 123
Survey of Program Participation (SIPP), 48

temperament of child
aggression, effect on, 101–102
cognitive skills, effect on, 105
nonresident families, in, 102, 105
resident families, in, 101–102
Temporary Assistance to Needy Families (TANF), 137–138
theoretical perspectives
activation relationship theory (ART), 22

theoretical perspectives (cont.)
  children's problem behavior (CPB), 22–23
  developmental cascade model (*see* developmental cascade model)
  developmental theories, 29–30
  ecological model of father–child relationships, xiii, 23, 94–95
  ecological model of human development, 28–29
  emotional contribution of fathers, 28–30
  evolution of scholarship, 23–24
  family investment model (FIM) (*see* family investment model (FIM))
  family stress model (FSM) (*see* family stress model (FSM))
  financial contribution of fathers, 24–25
  integration of theoretical frameworks, 17, 34–35
  knowledge, attitudes, and practices (KAPS), 30
  nurturing model of fathering, 21
  overview, 17, 35
  randomized controlled trials (RCT), 24–25
  revised tripartite model of father involvement, 21–22
  transactional development model, 30–31
  tripartite model of father involvement, 20–21
Thomson, D., 56
Three-City Study, 63
transactional development model, 30–31
transfer payments
  academic achievement, effect on, 111
  Additional Child Tax Credit (ACTC), 112
  Child Tax Credit (CTC), 112–113, 131, 142–143
  dependent exemption, 111–112
  Earned Income Tax Credit (EITC), 112, 113
  Expanded Child Tax Credit (ECTC), 112–113, 131, 142–143
  receptive vocabulary, effect on, 111
  recommendations, 130–131
transformation of family, 1
tripartite model of father involvement, 20–21
True Dads, 126–128, 135
two-parent, heterosexual, biological families, focus on, 2

Uniform Marriage and Divorce Act of 1970, 115–116

Vernun-Feagans, L., 64
visitation, 47, 143–144
vocabulary skills. *see* receptive vocabulary

Waldfogel, J., 163
Walk-A-Line, 173
Wildfeuer, R., xiv
Wolfe, Barbara, 25
Woodcock-Johnson Achievement Test-Revised, 150

Yeung, W. J., 38, 40, 165
Young Child Tax Credit (proposed), 147–148

For EU product safety concerns, contact us at Calle de José Abascal, 56–1°, 28003 Madrid, Spain or eugpsr@cambridge.org.

www.ingramcontent.com/pod-product-compliance
Lightning Source LLC
LaVergne TN
LVHW011813060526
838200LV00053B/3758